CUBA AND THE FUTURE

Cuba and the Future

Edited by
DONALD E. SCHULZ

Contributions in Latin American Studies,
Number 4

GREENWOOD PRESS
Westport, Connecticut • London

Library of Congress Cataloging-in-Publication Data

Schulz, Donald E.
    Cuba and the future / edited by Donald E. Schulz.
       p.   cm. — (Contributions in Latin American studies, ISSN
1054–6790 ; no. 4)
    Includes bibliographical references and index.
    ISBN 0–313–28784–8
    1. Cuba—Politics and government—1959- 2. Cuba—Economic
conditions—1959- 3. Cuba—Social conditions—1959- 4. Cuba—
Relations—Foreign countries. 5. United States—Foreign
relations—1993- I. Title. II. Series.
    F1788.S393   1994
    972.9106'4—dc20   93–21140

British Library Cataloguing in Publication Data is available.

Library of Congress Catalog Card Number: 93–21140
ISBN: 0–313–28784–8
ISSN: 1054–6790

First published in 1994

Greenwood Press, 88 Post Road West, Westport, CT 06881
An imprint of Greenwood Publishing Group, Inc.

Printed in the United States of America

The paper used in this book complies with the
Permanent Paper Standard issued by the National
Information Standards Organization (Z39.48–1984).

10 9 8 7 6 5 4 3 2 1

Copyright Acknowledgment
An earlier version of Andrew Zimbalist's "Treading Water: Cuba's Economic
and Political Crisis" was published under the title "Teetering on the Brink" in
the *Journal of Latin American Studies*. The article has been updated and
expanded and is reprinted here with permission of the *Journal*.

To Deborah

Contents

Preface

The crisis of the Cuban revolution has once again raised a number of security issues for the United States, along with important questions about the effectiveness and wisdom of the three-decade-old U.S. policy of containment and punishment. Many observers believe that the Castro regime is in its final hour and that its passing may be accompanied by massive bloodshed and a new wave of refugees to southern Florida.

Given the potential explosiveness of the Cuban crisis and the possibility that it might lead to U.S. military involvement, it would seem appropriate to take a closer look at the Cuban situation. In particular, we need a better understanding of both those forces promoting political stability and instability and the impact of U.S. policy. If, as some of the authors suggest, American policy may actually be strengthening the regime in the short run, while building up tension that may lead to a violent explosion in the longer run, then a strong case can be made that it is time for a change to a strategy better suited to fostering a peaceful transition.

Special thanks must be given to Colonel John Auger, director of the Strategic Outreach Program at the U.S. Army War College, for financing the Strategic Studies Institute's January 1992 roundtable on "Cuba and the Future." This conference was vital in providing the initial impetus out of which this book subsequently developed. Needless to say, the views expressed are those of the authors and do not necessarily reflect the position of the U.S. Army or the U.S. government.

CUBA AND THE FUTURE

1

Introduction: The Crises of the Castro Regime

Donald E. Schulz

On January 16, 1992, a distinguished group of civilian and military intellectuals met, under the auspices of the Strategic Studies Institute at the U.S. Army War College, for a roundtable on "Cuba and the Future." Not long thereafter, the editor of this volume received a phone call from a *Newsweek* correspondent, who was working on a story on Cuba. The reporter, it seemed, had gotten wind of the meeting from the magazine's Miami office. According to his sources, the Army's top strategists had recently gathered in Carlisle Barracks for a top-secret session that included Joseph Fernandez, Felix Rodriguez, and other covert types of Iran-contra and similar fame. Reportedly, by the end of the day the participants had come to the unanimous conclusion that the United States ought to invade Cuba.

This information took me somewhat aback, since I had organized and attended the roundtable and had witnessed nothing of the kind. Accordingly, I killed the report as quickly and definitively as possible: The Iran-contra folk had not been at the meeting. This was a brainstorming, rather than a planning, session. It was unclassified and open to selected members of the public. The views expressed were entirely those of the participants and did not necessarily reflect the position of the U.S. Army. (So far as I know, the Army has no position on Cuba.) There had been no talk of an invasion. Indeed, to the extent that a consensus had been reached at all, it was rather "dovish" in character.

In contrast to the conventional wisdom, most of the participants felt that Castro would probably survive in the short run and, quite possibly, for much longer. They were unanimous in the view that socioeconomic hardship alone would not be enough to create a revolutionary situation. In recent years, the security apparatus had been purged and strengthened, and the regime showed little reluctance in aggressively using it to suppress dissent and prevent the formation of an organized opposition. This absence of any autonomous agent of change, it was felt, was likely to be the crucial missing variable in any revolutionary scenario. As long as the security apparatus could effectively penetrate and neutralize civil society and the political-military institutions of the state, the likelihood of a coup or popular uprising seemed fairly remote.

Still, revolutions are hard to predict. There was a general feeling that, should a serious threat to the regime emerge, the resulting conflict could get very bloody. In spite of the current crisis, Castro still seemed to retain a substantial base of popular support among the Cuban public. And many of those who did not actually support him saw no viable alternative. Some 60 percent of the populace was now non-white. Many would almost certainly be willing to fight to prevent a return to power of the predominantly white Cuban exile leaders in Miami, whose colonial attitudes were widely resented. By the same token, the Cuban elite (especially the Communist Party and the Revolutionary Armed Forces) had a strong vested interest in the status quo. A change of regime would seriously jeopardize its power and privileges. It seemed likely to react to any challenge to those interests with armed violence.

In sum, a bureaucratic, racial, and class infrastructure still existed to support the regime. Any attempt to overthrow it could very well lead to massive bloodshed, if not civil war.

Beyond this, most of the panelists felt that U.S. policy was one of the factors that enabled Castro to remain in power. As one of them put it, Castro plays the "confrontation game" very well. Over the years, he had been highly successful in manipulating the specter of the "Yankee threat" to mobilize the Cuban people behind his leadership and policies. In effect, successive U.S. administrations, both Republican and Democratic, had repeatedly played into his hands by enabling him to wrap himself in the cloak of besieged nationalism. In contrast, Castro played the "peace game" much less skillfully. Thus, the sooner the United States could change the nature of the relationship in a way that opened up the island to U.S. influence, the better. Such a change would undermine the rationale for the garrison state (continuing sacrifice and vigilance) and make the regime's task of political and social control much more difficult.

Several of the participants also made telling individual points. Radio Martí's J. Richard Planas asked: "Why does Castro survive?" and answered: "Because of the man, the system, and its enemies." He described Castro as a self-centered, violent personality who "uses people as a survivalist does—to survive." He survives by fostering political passivity among the masses and by solidifying his support among those who have supported him in the past. He does this by "recreating reality" through disinformation and other means. Within this context, Planas noted that predictions of Castro's imminent fall by U.S. and Cuban exile leaders present a problem: They send the wrong message to the Cuban people. When Cubans hear about the exiles' plans and when it is hinted that the solution to the Cuban problem will come from abroad, it suggests that there will be little role for those Cubans still in Cuba. If Castro is going to be toppled by external forces, there is no incentive for "Cuban Cubans" to take the initiative and risk their lives. Moreover, these predictions mislead the masses about events in Cuba and relieve them from the responsibility of dealing with their own problems. The message promotes passivity among the masses and helps energize and mobilize Castro's supporters, thus enabling the regime to further entrench itself. Castro's supporters fear that if they don't stick with Fidel, it will be their heads that will roll. They fear being replaced by the "Miamians."

In short, "by pushing rather than pulling," the United States was helping to prop up the regime.

Gillian Gunn commented that, while the Bush administration had not increased the pressure on the Cuban government all that much, for domestic political reasons it was not likely to lessen it either. There was no political payoff for changing our Cuba policy, and there were some substantial costs (in terms of lost support among Cuban-Americans and the Republican right). What you ended up with was drift, masked by ineffectual policies and contradictory and confusing rhetoric. At the same time that the administration claimed to have no aggressive intentions, it wooed the Cuban-American community with predictions that Castro will fall and a tightening of the U.S. embargo. The result was counterproductive. Gunn advocated a "communications strategy" that would get rid of the siege mentality that justified the regime's repression. She had little hope, however, that such measures would be adopted. More likely would be a "dithering, reactive" policy that would be easily swept off course.

In the year following the roundtable, little changed, except that the socioeconomic crisis in Cuba grew worse. The analyses and forecasts of the participants had stood the test of at least the immediate future. During these months, the original contributors strengthened and updated their manuscripts. New collaborators were approached to provide additional views that dealt with facets of the problem that had previously been ignored or slighted. The result is a book that covers the social, economic, domestic political and foreign policy dimensions of the crisis in a reasonably comprehensive fashion.

While no work of this kind can be entirely without ideological influences, I have attempted to counter any tendencies toward a single, monolithic perspective by including scholars representing a wide range of political views. The assumption is that by approaching the problem from different directions, we may be able to see elements of reality that would otherwise be screened out by the intellectual straitjacket of ideology.

Not all of the contributors will concur with everything that follows. Yet I am struck by the degree to which—in spite of the political diversity of the authors—the chapters hang together as a coherent analysis. Even many of the policy prescription elements can be embraced by liberals as well as conservatives. Similarly, both enemies and sympathizers of the revolution will find much of use here.

The account begins with Andrew Zimbalist's definitive analysis of the Cuban economic crisis. Appropriately titled "Treading Water," the piece describes in detail the causes and nature of the current crisis—the worst in Cuban history—and suggests that the country is unlikely to pull out of it for the foreseeable future. Barring a major oil discovery or the reinsertion of the economy into the world capitalist system (which would probably require the demise of the Castro regime) the best that can be expected is a bottoming out of the economy and the resumption of modest growth. Put simply, Cuba is caught in a trap. Under current circumstances, what has been lost will not be regained for a long time. In consequence, the country is likely to be a miserable place to live for as long as Castro remains in power.

The chapters by Enrique A. Baloyra, J. Richard Planas, and Phyllis Greene Walker go on to examine the political dimensions of the crisis. What are the prospects for political stability and change? Though recognizing that a revolutionary uprising or a coup is a possibility, none is willing to predict such developments. Baloyra believes that the repression of the opposition is the only issue that might lead to an explosion, but he thinks it unlikely. Dissident leaders have been cautious, and without a leadership willing to lead there may not be a mass willing to follow. Neither does he see the military playing a major role. The Ochoa affair was an object lesson. The message was that if *he* could be killed, anyone can be killed. This has deterred other dissidents from trying to organize. At the elite level, this key strategic actor—the military—is not there.

Neither are these analysts optimistic about the prospects for a democratic transition. Castro is still Castro. He continues to view Cuba and the world through the prism of his own ego needs, and that probably means that no fundamental political changes are in the offing. The most likely scenario is more of the same, with growing tensions continuing to be contained by repression and atomization and the prospect of violence and turmoil increasing as time goes on.

Within this context, how do Cubans manage to survive? Damian J. Fernandez and J. Richard Planas explore the social dimensions of the crisis, looking at the attitudes and behavior patterns of ordinary Cubans and the strategies that enable them to cope on a daily basis. Both stress the importance of informal kinds of political and social participation—that is, the tendency of people to go outside official channels in seeking the means of survival. They also discuss all of the psychological mechanisms—resignation, adaptation, dissimulation, and escapism—that help people to survive, but also, by fostering passivity, enable the regime to survive. As long as these patterns are dominant, they suggest, the prospects for both revolution and a democratic transition are not good.

The latter part of the book deals with the foreign policy dimensions of the crisis. Steve Blank traces the decline of Cuban-Soviet relations during the 1980s, culminating in the "end of the affair." Mark Falcoff and Gillian Gunn look at U.S. policy from contending conservative and liberal perspectives. In the original concluding chapter, Donald E. Schulz attempts to synthesize the analyses of the volume's contributors, while offering some of his own thoughts. Among other things, he sets forth a detailed set of policy recommendations that, he argues, might be more effective in fostering a peaceful transition to the post-Castro era than the "strategy of conflict" to which the United States has been wed for so long.

Since these chapters were completed in spring 1993, a number of developments have occurred which have implications for the book's conclusions and recommendations. Socioeconomic deterioration in Cuba has accelerated, and so has popular unrest. In response, Castro has introduced a series of daring new reforms: Cubans are now permitted to hold and spend U.S. dollars. More exiles will be allowed to visit the island. Over one hundred categories of workers—from plumbers and electricians to cooks and computer programmers—will be permitted to engage in private business. Cooperative farms have been granted greater autonomy; private citizens will be allowed to farm unused state land. The question is whether this combination of worsening socioeconomic conditions and the regime's efforts to deal with them have fundamentally changed the nature of the Cuban political equation. Put simply, is Cuba now, partially as a result of Castro's own policies, in the process of becoming destabilized? And, if so, what implications does this have for the United States? A short postscript by the editor has been added to address these issues.

2

Treading Water: Cuba's Economic and Political Crisis

Andrew Zimbalist

The historical conditions that allowed for the survival of a socialist state just ninety miles from the world's largest and most powerful capitalist state have changed. There is no longer a protective socialist community to buffer Cuba from the ravages of the U.S. embargo. The institutions of Cuba's socialist state already have been transformed and the economy is moving toward a mixed system.

The proximate cause of Cuba's present predicament is not hard to identify. Cuba has a small and heavily trade-dependent economy. In the presence of the U.S. embargo, Cuba came to depend on the former Soviet trade bloc (CMEA) for over four-fifths of its imports. Without access to the U.S. market, with access to other markets restricted, and with imports from the former CMEA countries reduced by over three-fourths, Cuba's economy and its people are struggling to survive.

The government's response to the crisis has been deliberate but inadequate. A number of reforms initiated prior to 1989 are being continued,[1] while others are being accelerated and some new programs are being put in place. The new emphasis on foreign investment and tourism, structural reforms in the operation of foreign trade, and the impossibility of central planning in the presence of ubiquitous supply uncertainties have combined to transform the nature of Cuba's economic mechanism. Despite the promise of some extension of private enterprise and the market in the service sector, however, the needed and more concerted introduction of a broader market mechanism has not been forthcoming.

CUBA'S TRADE DEPENDENCY

Similar to other small economies, Cuba has always been very trade dependent. Indeed, during 1987–89, Cuba's imports as a share of its *Ingreso*

Nacional Creado (roughly, net domestic product minus "non-productive" services) averaged 61.5 percent, and as a share of its estimated gross domestic product (GDP) averaged approximately 35 percent. The more typical ratio of imports to GDP for small, medium-income countries in Latin America is around 25 percent.

Cuba's overall import dependency was aggravated by an excessive vulnerability to CMEA trade. During 1987–89 an average 84.2 percent of Cuban imports came from Eastern Europe and the Soviet Union. Cuban imports from Eastern Europe, which accounted for approximately 15 percent of Cuban imports, fell by roughly one-half in 1990 and practically disappeared in 1991. Imports from the Soviet Union, which accounted for over 70 percent of Cuba's imports, fell by over 30 percent in 1990 (measured in current prices), then dropped precipitously in 1991 and again in 1992.[2]

A sense of the magnitude and importance of the reduction in Soviet exports to Cuba is conveyed by the following figures. In 1989, Cuba imported $5.52 billion worth of goods from the Soviet Union, including 13.11 million tons of petroleum (8.5 million tons of which was crude oil).[3] The revised trade agreement for 1991 called for Soviet exports of $3.36 billion to Cuba, including 10 million tons of petroleum. As of October 1, 1991, however, the Soviets had only exported $1.31 billion worth of goods, or 38.8 percent of the planned yearly total. At this pace, by year's end Soviet exports would have reached $1.74 billion. Even this level, however, appears optimistic because the pace of shipments slowed in September following the aborted Soviet coup in August, and both political events and economic disorder in the former Soviet republics conspired to further reduce deliveries during the last trimester. Some reports out of Cuba indicate that there were no petroleum shipments the entire month of December 1991.[4] But even assuming the trade pace of the first nine months was maintained and the full $1.74 billion of goods arrived in Cuba during 1991,[5] this would represent only 31.5 percent of the value of Soviet imports two years earlier![6]

The collapse of the CMEA and the economies of Eastern Europe and the Soviet Union have led to a reduction of Cuba's overall imports of over 60 percent. Since imports represented 38 percent of estimated GDP, this implies an import decrease above 22.5 percent of GDP. Further, since most of the would-be imports are raw materials and intermediate goods, their absence can have a multiplicatively downward effect on production.[7]

Consider the following examples. In 1991, Cuba was to receive from the Soviet Union 35,000 tons of caustic soda, which is used in the production of livestock feed, paper, cardboard, soap, and detergents, but received nothing at all through May 31. Cuba was to receive 17,000 tons of sodium carbonate, used in the production of glass for construction and containers, but received nothing at all through September 30. Fifteen thousand tons of pulpwood, used for paper and cardboard production, was to be delivered, but as of September 30, nothing arrived.

As of September 30, 1991, the share of annual contracted deliveries actually fulfilled by the Soviet Union for the following commodities was: rice, 0 percent; peas, 50 percent; raw vegetable oil, 16 percent; cooking lard, 7 percent; condensed milk, 11 percent; butter, 47 percent; canned meat 18 percent; powdered milk, 22 percent; fresh and canned fish, 6 percent; fertilizers, 16 percent; sulfite, 0 percent; cut lumber, 24 percent; paper and cardboard, 2 percent; rolled steel, 1.9 percent; tin-plate, 15 percent; detergents, 0 percent; tires, 1.6 percent; synthetic rubber, 11 percent; cotton, 0 percent; spare parts for consumer goods, 1.1 percent; nonferrous metals and laminates, 26 percent; and, glazed bricks, 10 percent.[8] Fulfillment of machinery and equipment contracts was at a similar level, although the initial plans for imports in this area were substantially reduced from previous years because of Cuba's economic crisis.

The shortage of these materials not only disrupts the productive apparatus of Cuba's economy, but it engenders widespread demoralization. Workers question why they should go to work if the production line will limp along or be shut down due to lack of inputs, particularly when public transportation has been curtailed, when extra hours are needed each day to acquire basic food supplies for the home, when lunch ceases to be provided at the workplace, and when there are no consumer goods to buy with one's peso income anyway. Some absent workers, of course, lead to more absent workers, and the economic mechanism begins to flirt with breakdown.

To compound the shortfall in Soviet supplies, the price of raw sugar on the world spot market fell from an average of 13.6 cents per pound from November 1989 to September 1990 to 9.1 cents per pound during November 1990 to September 1991. By the end of 1992, the price had fallen further to just above 8 cents per pound. Further, and partly due to imported input shortages, Cuba's sugar harvest decreased from 8.1 million tons in 1989–90 to 7.6 million tons in 1990–91. The lower price and smaller output cost the Cuban economy at least an additional $100 million in lost hard-currency earnings in 1991. The 1992 harvest fell to 7 million tons, and the world market price fell below 9 cents.

Making matters still worse, the Bush administration took significant measures to tighten its embargo. The U.S. Treasury Department progressively has denied licenses to companies in Third World countries that are subsidiaries of U.S. corporations or are trading products containing U.S. components. In his speech to the UN General Assembly on November 13, 1991, Cuban Ambassador Ricardo Alarcon listed over 25 products that were formally granted licenses for trade with Cuba and were now prohibited, affecting the following companies: Siemens AG, Germany; LKB and Alfa-Laval, Sweden; Toshiba and Nihon Kohden, Japan; CGR, France; and Medix, Argentina. In other cases, pressure and threats of exclusion from the U.S. market by the U.S. Treasury or Department of Commerce rather than license denial damaged Cuban trade: for example, an aborted joint venture between Sao Paolo's VASP and Cubana de Aviacion, a frustrated large-scale tourist project on Cayo Coco between Cubanacan and Tabacalera of Spain, terminated Pepsi Cola sales from a Canadian subsidiary, and terminated medical book exports from Editorial Interamericana of Spain after it was acquired by McGraw-Hill. In September 1991, the U.S. Treasury Department also announced new restrictions on remittances to Cuba and travel-related expenditures in Cuba.[9]

In October 1992, in response to political pressures from the right-wing Cuban American National Foundation and the electoral campaign, President Bush signed the so-called Cuba Democracy Act, which threatens a further tightening of the embargo. Among other things, it attempts to prohibit trade between subsidiaries of U.S. corporations based in third countries and Cuba, and it prevents ships from docking at U.S. ports that have been to Cuba in the previous six months. In 1991, somewhere between 9 and 13 percent of Cuba's imports came from U.S. subsidiaries.[10] The Act violates the trade sovereignty of third countries and has been sharply criticized by the United States' major trading partners. It is unclear to what extent the Clinton administration will attempt to enforce its provisions. [Editor's note: The administration has announced its intention to fully comply with the law.] In the meantime, the Act serves to raise the political risk of commerce with Cuba, and some companies reportedly have charged a risk premium in their trade with the island.

Although Soviet aid to Cuba per se ceased in 1990, the 1991 trade agreement called for Cuba to receive 22 cents per pound of raw sugar and for Cuba to pay the world market oil price.[11] Whether the 13 cents differential between the spot market and Soviet prices is termed aid or not is subject to interpretation. Less than 20 percent of world sugar sells on the spot market; the rest is sold on the basis of preferential medium-term contracts, most with prices considerably above those on the spot market. The United States, for instance, buys raw sugar from Caribbean Basin countries at nearly 22 cents per pound, and the price paid in the European Common Market is similar. In any event, the exchange of Soviet oil for Cuban sugar took place at very close to world (spot) market prices in 1992 and is scheduled to do so again in 1993, according to the new agreement signed on November 3, 1992. Thus, it is likely that instead of receiving 8 million to 8.3 million tons of oil for the 4 million-plus tons of sugar sold to the Soviet Union in 1992, Cuba can look forward to receiving in the neighborhood of 6 million tons of oil (from Russia, Kazahkstan, South American and Middle East producers) for the same 4 million tons of sugar in 1993. Meanwhile, current petroleum and other input shortages can be expected to lower the 1992–93 *zafra* (sugar harvest) well below the already reduced 1991–92 level of 7 million tons.[12] [Editor's note: The 1992–93 harvest was only 4.28 million tons.]

If there is a force still holding the economy together, it is centrally planned economies' two traditional strengths: to distribute scarce resources equitably and to mobilize resources for the support of prioritized projects. The former has prevented mass unemployment and generalized malnutrition to date[13]; the latter has enabled Cuba to slow down the bleeding by developing sources for earning hard currency. Together they form the backbone of the Castro government's strategy to cope with its crisis.

RESPONSE TO THE CRISIS

As implemented since the fall of 1990, the strategy of the "special period in time of peace" has had four prongs: first, to reduce consumption of oil and other products through the introduction of universal rationing and increasingly stringent restrictions; second, to increase the production of staple foods through the colonization of new land, shifting surplus labor to the countryside, extending microjet irrigation and parcel draining techniques and introducing new seed varieties; third, to pursue aggressively foreign investment through joint ventures and production-sharing arrangements in order to promote hard-currency earnings and loosen the domestic production bottlenecks; and, fourth, to facilitate the economy's re-entry into world markets by undertaking management and selective structural reforms.

The first two aspects of this strategy have been written about rather extensively. For our purposes, it suffices to note that the shortage of consumer goods has reached dramatic proportions, especially in Havana and Santiago. Inconvenience is being transformed into hardship. It is not uncommon for shoppers to spend hours each day attempting to purchase basic supplies. Frequently, rationed goods are not available for days or weeks after their scheduled distribution. Scheduled blackouts of up to eight hours a day were being experienced in Havana during December 1992, and the regular, legal distribution of gasoline to private automobiles had virtually ceased.

Despite a political crackdown, the black market is used in one form or another by virtually everyone. Pilfering of supplies from factories and delivery centers has become widespread, and common theft and prostitution are increasingly practiced. Malnutrition is undoubtedly suffered by some. Promised benefits from the new food program are difficult to perceive, although the planting program for most crops is still young and increased output may be forestalling even greater catastrophe from the plummeting of food imports.

We do know that fertilizer imports fell from 1.3 million tons in 1989 to an expected 0.25 million tons in 1992 and that the quantity of diesel fuel used in agriculture fell by over one-third. Although the production of most crops has fallen, root crop and vegetable output increased by 16 percent and 68 percent, respectively, between 1990 and 1992. The largest drop has occurred in milk production, which fell from 740 million liters in 1989 to 335 million in 1992.[14]

The third aspect of the Cuban crisis strategy is to enlist foreign capital to provide the know-how and the resources in order to promote hard-currency earnings and to facilitate Cuba's reintegration into the world marketplace. Cuba's 1982 foreign investment code has been made more liberal in practice, permitting *inter alia* minority or majority foreign-ownership, tax holidays, and free profit repatriation.[15] Production-sharing arrangements, whereby foreign companies provide lacking inputs, technology, finance, marketing, or packaging for an operation and receive a percentage of its revenues, have also been introduced. As of January 1992, there were some 60 joint venture or production-sharing deals functioning, with another 40 signed deals poised for introduction. Most of the initial deals were in tourism, but during 1991 their scope broadened considerably to involve biotechnology, pharmaceuticals, nickel, oil, textiles, construction, sugar derivatives, transportation, cosmetics, and food processing. Some of the deals entail substantial investments; for instance, Canada's Sherritt Gordon company is reported to have investment plans for $1.2 billion in the Cuban nickel industry.[16] In another deal, industrialists from Monterrey, Mexico, will invest $611 million in a joint textile venture, with Cuba investing $500 million.[17] Cuba is in negotiations with over 100 foreign companies on future deals.

Cuba has released few details on these mixed enterprises, in large part to protect their foreign partners from the retaliation of the U.S. Treasury. It is thus difficult to gauge the potential significance of these projects for the Cuban economy. It is possible, however, to deduce the broad outlines of their short- and medium-run impact by evaluating the principal sectors affected.

Tourism has been the primary locus of the new joint ventures. The number of tourists visiting Cuba has grown steadily from 243,056 in 1985, to 340,329 in 1990 and to 424,000 in 1991. The number of tourists visiting Cuba during the first seven months of 1992 increased by a further 24.4 percent in relation to the same period in 1991.[18] The gross revenue from the tourist trade in 1990 was approximately $250 million. Because foreign inputs needed to be purchased to service this sector and since profits were shared with Cuba's foreign partners, the net foreign exchange earned from this activity probably did not exceed $80 million or $90 million. Even if Cuba's most optimistic predictions are realized, gross tourist income will reach $400 million in 1991 and $600 million in 1992. This would imply net foreign exchange earnings from tourism of roughly $135 million in 1991 and $200 million in 1992. Every little bit helps, but Cuba lost approximately $4 billion in imports from the CMEA between 1989 and 1991.

Nickel is likely to be a more significant contributor to replacing Cuba's lost trade. In 1990, nickel exports produced around $450 million in foreign exchange. The 1991 figure will be lower, but if the joint ventures are successful in modernizing the Punta Gorda, Moa, and Nicaro plants and in opening the new Camariocas smelter in 1993, Cuba's nickel exports could nearly double by 1994. If the world nickel price returned to its level of 1990 at $8,000 per ton, this could yield an additional $400 million in earnings. Unfortunately for Cuba, the price at the end of 1992 had fallen below $6,000 per ton.

Biotechnology and medical exports are much more uncertain. Cuba has advanced impressively in this area and produces over 150 products, with a few at the technological cutting edge. Being at the cutting edge, however, does not necessarily help, particularly if one lacks the testing, marketing, packaging, and financing skills and contacts to break into the world market of this dynamic sector, which is dominated by large multinational corporations.[19] The pressure of the U.S. blockade further complicates Cuban prospects. Until now, Cuba has relied upon niche marketing in the CMEA and Latin America (primarily Brazil) for these products. Plans for 1991 included biotechnology and medical product exports to the Soviet Union of some $700 million, with an additional $100 million to Latin America. Three years earlier, exports from this sector were zero. As long as the CMEA niche remained open, the future for this sector of Cuba's economy looked bright. Now Cuba must develop new niches in the former Soviet republics and elsewhere in the Third World. New deals for the export of interferon and other medical products have been signed with former Soviet republics, as well as with Mexico and India.[20] Cuba's meningitis B vaccine will continue to be sold to Brazil and other Latin American countries, yielding a reported $100 million to $200 million annually.[21] It is also possible that in the case of a few products, such as streptokinase (which can interrupt and limit damage from a heart attack), the epidermal growth factor, monoclonal antibodies, and various reagents, with the assistance of a foreign partner, Cuba will be able to penetrate the world market. According to a 1992 report of the scientists at the University of Geneva, Cuba's anti-cholesterol drug, PPG, is the most effective available. Cuba's potential income from PPG is suggested by the experience of the U.S. pharmaceutical giant Merck, which earned $1.6 billion for revenue during 1992 from the sale of its anti-cholesterol drug, Mevacor.[22] Here again, the trick for Cuba seems to lie in marketing. In short, there is some promise in this sector, but the road to progress is fraught with obstacles and uncertainty.

Virtually all of Cuba's remaining important export products (sugar derivatives, citrus, fish, tobacco, steel products, copper) do not realistically have the potential to grow by more than $10 million or $20 million per year each. The one possible exception, and Cuba's one ace in the whole, is oil. Cuba is involved in a joint venture with France's Total and Compagnie de Petrole in offshore development. Initial seismographic testing has been completed and drilling has begun. A basin as rich as Mexico's offshore deposits is possible, though not probable.[23] Cuba has also signed prospecting contracts with Swedish, Brazilian, and Canadian concerns, but a prospective contract with British Petroleum never materialized. According to some sources, Brit-

Table 2.1
Estimates of Macroeconomic Indicators

	1987	1988	Est. 1989	Est. 1990	Est. 1991	Forecast 1992	1993
Real GDP (bn $)	31.4	32.5	32.5	31.5	23.6	20.3	20.4
Real GDP Growth	-5.2	3.5	0.1	-3.1	-25.0	-14.0	0.4
Total Exports (bn pesos)	5.4	5.5	5.4	5.9	3.3	2.8	3.0
Total Imports (bn pesos)	7.6	7.6	8.1	7.1	4.0	3.1	3.4
Hard Currency (bn $)							
exports fob	1.0	1.1	1.3	1.4	3.3	2.8	3.0
imports fob	1.0	1.0	1.3	1.4	4.0	3.1	3.4
external debt	5.7	6.7	6.2	7.0	7.2	7.2	7.3

Source: Estimates by the author based on Andrew Zimbalist and Claes Brundenius, *The Cuban Economy: Measurement and Analysis of Socialist Performance* (Baltimore: Johns Hopkins University Press, 1989), chapter 4, and official Cuban government data.

ish Petroleum was told by the United States to stay away from Cuba and obliged.[24] As of December 1992, no new offshore oil has been found and no revenue produced.

Last, in a variety of areas foreign resources will facilitate import substitution. In the best of cases, several tens of millions of additional foreign exchange earnings can be saved here. (See Table 2.1.)

All told, it seemed that without new oil, Cuba's various projects do not promise to bring in much more than a billion dollars in new revenue annually in the coming year. The loss of CMEA trade is far in excess of this, and the 1992 reduction of Soviet oil deliveries, along with the expected smaller sugar harvest, lower sugar and nickel prices, and the tightening U.S. blockade, make it unlikely that the Cuban economy can look forward to any significant growth in 1993. Nonetheless, Cuba has already taken its biggest "hit," with its GDP in 1992 approximately 40 percent below what is was in 1989, and 1993 may be the first year since 1989 that national output does not fall.

The fourth prong of Cuba's strategy entails an interesting effort at economic reform. Most aspects of the present reform have their roots in policies from the early and mid–1980s, but two efforts in particular have been given strong emphasis during the current crisis. The first is enterprise management reform. The initiative for serious changes in Cuba's enterprise management system came, oddly enough, from the Ministry of the Armed Forces. In July 1987 the decision was taken to begin sweeping experiments in the management of a number of military enterprises. The experiments involved a variety of modern Western management techniques, such as management by consensus, group work, quality-control circles, job rotation, and participatory decision-making. The experimentation began in the machine shop of the Che Guevara military products factory during September and October of 1987. Over the next production period, quality indicators rose by 20 to 60 percent despite a reduction in quality control personnel of 33 percent.[25]

The success of these experiments led to the decision to generalize the techniques throughout the economy. A national management training system (SUTCER) was set up in 1988 to help introduce and disseminate these methods. Western experts have been called upon to help design course modules, give specialized seminars to enterprise directors and union leaders, build a curriculum for a new master's program in management, and engage directly in enterprise consulting. Over 1,000 administrators have taken short courses, and several industrial sectors have successfully introduced management reforms.

More than a dozen enterprises under the Ministry of Basic Industry have introduced Japanese-style quality-control circles. Initial reports suggest impressive quality and productivity gains. It appears that one of the important reasons for these gains is the absence of a rigid quantity plan. That is, the uncertain planning environment liberates ministries and enterprises from the quantity fetishism of conventional central planning. The more rational and democratic methods are being applied because of the space created by aberrant conditions in the macroeconomy. One interesting result of these reforms is that a larger constituency is being built at the base for greater decentralization in the economic mechanism.

In addition to its efforts to promote democratic management practices, SUTCER worked with the United Nations Development Programme to develop instruction in market-oriented management. Seminars have been conducted in negotiation marketing, intellectual property, business strategy, accounting, and finance, and Cuban managers have been sent for internships in multinational companies and foreign business schools. Although SUTCER was dissolved in mid–1992, the program continues under the auspices of the State Committee on Economic Cooperation (CECE).

The second reform being stressed at the moment is the decentralization of Cuba's foreign trade structures. Several corporations have been established, such as Cubanacan, Gaviota, Cimex, Uneca, Consa, Banco Financiero Internacional, and Cubalse, which for most purposes are allowed to operate independently of the central state apparatus. They behave as profit-maximizing entities and engage in joint ventures inside and outside Cuba. Foreign trade increasingly is conducted by decentralized trading companies, not the Ministry of Foreign Trade. At the beginning of 1991, there were thirty such trade companies functioning; at the end of 1991, there were seventy-two.[26] In the case of an increasing number of several large undertakings, such as Antillana de Acero, the enterprises are largely handling their own foreign trade and they are allowed to retain up to 70 percent of their foreign exchange earnings to purchase needed foreign inputs. That is, bureaucratic procedures for allocations via the Ministry of Foreign Trade have been reduced or, in many cases, obviated. As of October 1992, 500 Cuban enterprises were self-financing in foreign exchange.

Concomitant to the reorganization of the state sector of the economy, a vibrant informal market has blossomed. The average Cuban in 1992 spends more than half of his or her income on informal or black market purchases, including food, clothing, household appliances and services. The $300 million-odd sent by Miami relatives plus the additional tens of millions of dollars circulating from expenditures by foreign travelers have spawned a widespread underground economy with prices paralleling those at dollar shops, converted at the going black market exchange rate (roughly 40 pesos to the dollar in November 1992). Except in the most egregious cases, the Cuban government seems to have accepted these new marketing networks as a necessary component of the population's efforts to survive. Although a black market always existed in Cuba and has been growing over the last ten years, its present dimensions are unique and contribute to a thoroughly overhauled economic landscape on the island.

These management reforms and informal markets are, of course, congruent with the endeavor to attract foreign investment and reincorporate into the world market. They are welcome developments, but they will not extricate Cuba from its economic stranglehold. A broader commitment to an internal market mechanism along with privatization of small and some medium-size activities is necessary,[27] both to bring greater efficiency to Cuba's internal economic mechanism and to convey the positive vision of a new economic model adapted to the realities of the post-CMEA world. The extensive demoralization of the Cuban people can be shaken by nothing less.

THE POLITICAL CONTEXT AND THE FUTURE

Political reforms in Cuba have been even more modest than economic reforms. The decision at the Fourth Party Congress to allow secret, direct elections for all seats to the National Assembly and to remove the Communist Party from the nominating process appears conducive to creating a more democratic environment. Similarly, the permission for believers to become party members and, hence, enterprise managers and administrative leaders, is also a positive development.

The reforms, however, do not make a decisive break from party control. No opposition party is allowed, and candidates for the Provincial and National Assemblies will be nominated from above. No opposition media is allowed. To the extent that election outcomes challenge party control, it is nearly a sure bet that they will be reversed. Indeed, Castro and the party justifiably perceive Cuba to be more under siege from external forces today than at

any time in the revolution's past. This perception has always brought increased repression at home. The incarceration of political dissidents, the
operation of the *brigadas de respuesta rapida*, the enhanced control over
the media, the cancellation of the satiric film *Alicia en el pueblo de maravillas*
("Alice in Wonderland"),[28] the death penalty for two of the three exiles who
returned to Cuba to promote insurrection, and other signs all points to
increased repression, concurrent with the suggested liberalization reforms
of the Fourth Party Congress. The regime sees the repression as requisite
for its survival. It is probably right.

Castro is still viewed as the legitimate defender of Cuban sovereignty by
large numbers of Cubans. It is improbable in the extreme that the roughly
40 to 50 percent of the Cuban population that is black or mulatto will accept
supinely the visions of Cuba's future offered by right-wing, white Cuban
exiles in Miami.[29] Large numbers of white Cubans, of course, are also pre-
pared to defend the Castro government. As long as the perceived alternative
is violence along with the highly publicized visions of the Cuban American
National Foundation (CANF), even strong critics of the Castro government
will defend it.

To be sure, as Cuba's economic hardship continues and deepens, the
number of Cubans willing to accept a radical political change increases, but
the size of the force ready to defend Castro, Cuban nationalism, and the
social gains of the revolution will always remain substantial and formidable.
Most Cuban adults have received training in the use of firearms and can be
supplied with weapons in short order.

The tightening of the U.S. embargo is clearly aimed, as the thirty-two-
year policy has always been aimed, at overthrowing Castro. Now more than
ever before, it is a counterproductive and perilous policy. The stated reasons
for not ending the embargo—Cuba's foreign aggression, advancing human
rights and democracy—are either anachronistic or misguided. As Cuba's
leading dissident Elizardo Sanchez has said repeatedly, the best way to serve
the cause of human rights in Cuba is by ending the embargo and entering
a dialogue.

The optimistic scenario for U.S. policy presumably would be that the
blockade succeeds in aggravating human suffering in Cuba to the point of
sparking a spontaneous riot that escalates into a rebellion. The Cuban army
would then refuse to quell the uprising.

The problem here is twofold. First, it is not likely to happen. One way
or the other, Castro has defied repeated predictions of his imminent demise
in the past. His appreciable legitimacy, only bolstered by the U.S. hard
line, and his tight political control make his survival more likely than his
removal. The apparent absence of any significant oppositional group in Cuba
reinforces the perception of Castro's durability.[30] Second, if events did unfurl
as suggested by the above scenario, Cuba would be plunged into a civil war.
Tens of thousands would die, and the political outcome will be a far cry from

stable or democratic government. The United States will have a mess and a liability on its hands many times greater than what Reagan/Bush policy created in Panama. Neither the interests of human rights, democracy, economic development nor U.S. business will have been served.

It is interesting, however, that the growing expectations of Castro's collapse have created a new lever for changing U.S. policy. These expectations have encouraged U.S. companies to begin serious study of investment and trade opportunities in Cuba. At the same time that these business opportunities are becoming appreciated by hundreds of U.S. firms, the Castro government has been aggressively courting foreign investment. Dozens of European, Canadian and Latin American companies are taking advantage of Cuba's lucrative market and its resources. The U.S. companies have been forced by the embargo to sit on the sidelines, as attractive oil, nickel, biotechnology, tourism, and telecommunications investments have been made by their competitors from other countries.

Lifting the blockade is good political policy as well. Without the specter of U.S. aggression, Castro not only loses much of his indispensability as a nationalist leader but also most of his justification for retaining tight political control. The flooding of U.S. tourists and investments into Cuba would have a powerful effect of further opening the country's political and economic mechanisms. The process of reform, already begun in Cuba, would be given a strong and irreversible impulse. From the standpoint of the economic and political welfare of the Cuban people, this outcome is infinitely more desirable than that engendered by the policy of the Bush administration. The irony is that, from the perspective of the United States' perceived geopolitical and economic interests, it is also more desirable.

NOTES

1. For a full discussion of these reforms, see A. Zimbalist, "Industrial Reform and the Cuban Economy," in I. Jeffries, ed. *Industrial Reform in Socialist Countries* (London: Edward Elgar, 1992), and A. Zimbalist and W. Smith, "Reform in Cuba," in Illpyong Kim and Jane Zacek, eds., *Reform in Communist Systems: Comparative Perspectives* (Washington, D.C.: Washington Institute, 1991).

2. The 1990 figure for Soviet trade is from *Cuba Business*, October 1991, p. 2. The figure for trade with Eastern Europe is based on proportions in import reduction reported in Elena C. Alvarez, "Algunos efectos en la economia cubana de los cambios en la coyuntura internacional," Instituto de Investigaciones Economicas, Havana, Cuba, June 1991, reprinted in FBIS, *Daily Report Supplement: Latin America*, October 14, 1991. According to one source, Cuba's total imports from the countries of the former Soviet Union and Eastern Europe in 1992 came to $830 million; Inter Press Service Corresponsalia, *Informacion Quincenal sobre Cuba*, Vol. 5, No. 21, p. 6.

3. These figures and others, unless otherwise noted, are from the *Anuario Estadistico de Cuba, 1989* published by the Comite Estatal de Estadisticas, and the

Resumen Estadistico del Comercio Exterior, 1986–88, published by the Ministerio de Comercio Exterior.

4. Reconstructing estimates from Castro's speeches during December 1991 and other sources suggests that Cuba received somewhere between 8 million and 8.3 million tons of petroleum from the former Soviet Union in 1991. Of course, the bulk of this arrived to Cuba via triangular trade wherein the former Soviet Union sent oil (contracted with South American oil exporters) to Western Europe and Japan; and Venezuela, Colombia, and Ecuador (contracted with the former Soviet Union) sent oil to Cuba.

For 1992 Cuba signed a pact with Russia to exchange 2.5 tons of raw sugar for 4.5 tons of petroleum. Although Cuba received less than 2 million tons of oil from Russia during 1992, this exchange ratio implies a price about 10 percent above the spot market sugar prices (with benchmark crude at around $18 a barrel and spot sugar at around 9 cents a pound). Cuba signed additional agreements with Kazahkstan and St. Petersburg to exchange sugar, citrus, and medical products for oil. Cuba is scheduled to receive 3.3 million tons of oil from Russia during 1993. Although this exchange will be at world market prices, the trade protocol allows Cuba to renew its exports of biotechnology products, citrus fruits, and other goods that have had limited success in international markets.

5. In his speech to the National Assembly of People's Power on December 27, 1991, Castro stated that as of December 21, 1991, only $1.67 billion worth of goods had arrived from the former Soviet Union (*Granma International*, January 12, 1992, p. 4). There is, however, some ambiguity as to whether Castro's figures refer only to goods that were scheduled for delivery in 1991 or whether they also include goods scheduled for delivery in 1990 but delivered with a delay in 1991.

6. These numbers are in current prices. It is likely that in constant prices the fall-off would be a bit less sharp, because the price Cuba paid for Soviet oil fell approximately $7 a barrel between 1989 and 1991.

7. For some imports, however, the reduction in domestic output is minimal. For instance, some of the reduced oil imports resulted in more careful use of electricity in the household. Here all that is lost is the value added from domestic electricity generation—considerably less than the value of lost imports. Overall, we can estimate that an import fall of between 50 and 60 percent would result in a GDP drop on the order of 25 to 35 percent between 1989 and 1991. A further reduction in imports of 20 to 30 percent is possible for 1992, leading to an additional drop of 9 to 16 percent of GDP. At such a level, however, the Cuban economy would appear to have hit bottom. See Table 2.1.

8. Figures are from Castro's opening speech to the Fourth Party Congress.

9. Under the new regulations, a U.S. citizen may send no more than $500 for travel expenses, including airfare, to a Cuban national intending to visit the United States, and the funds may not be sent until a visa has been issued to the traveler by the U.S. Interests Section in Havana. A limit of $500 has also been placed on the amount a U.S. citizen can spend in Cuba for those categories of citizens exempt from the travel blockade (Cuban exiles, journalists, politicians, and professionals). Allowable family remittances were reduced from a maximum of $500 to $300. The author did not independently confirm the accuracy of Alarcon's allegations.

10. Total Cuban imports in 1991 came to approximately $4 billion. Licensed imports from U.S. subsidiaries in 1991 were authorized up to $533 million (13.3

percent of total imports). Of this authorization level, however, it is not known how much was actually imported. Cargill, the grain trading company, for instance, seemed to have traded only one-sixth of its authorized level in 1991.

11. There was also a year-end credit clearing accord, but it is unclear how this worked out.

12. Cuba has also shifted some sugar cane land to the production of root crops and vegetables. Prior to 1990, Cuba could sell virtually all the sugar it desired to the Soviet Union at a stable, preferential price. Now that is no longer the case, and the Cubans seem to have reformulated their traditional goal of maximizing yearly cane production.

13. More generally, Cuba's greatest asset, human capital in the form of a highly educated and healthy labor force, is being preserved through a commitment to maintain expenditures in education and health.

14. Inter Press Service Corresponsalia, *Informacion Quincenal sobre Cuba*, Vol. 5, No. 21, p. 6.

15. An ongoing problem with the code, however, is that it provides inadequate guarantees to foreign investors; most notably, the government retains the right to reallocate labor to and from joint ventures. In at least one instance that was called to this author's attention, workers who had been trained by a foreign company were transferred to another enterprise by the Cuban government. The Cuban government also retains the right to select the pool of domestic workers from which the foreign enterprise may hire. See recommendations for further liberalization of the Cuban joint venture law in Stuart Diamond, *Cuba: The Biotechnology Industry, Key Issues in Marketing and Strategy* (Report to the Cuban government. United Nations Center on Transnational Corporations, New York, December 1991), pp. 12–14.

16. *Cuba Business*, October 1991, p. 5. The former president of Cuba's Chamber of Commerce, Julio Garcia Oliveras, estimated the value of foreign investment in Cuba during 1991 to be around $500 million. Oliveras also estimated that only between 30 and 35 percent of the joint ventures and production sharing projects were in tourism. (Interview with the author, January 9, 1992.)

17. See *Cuba Business*, Vol. 6, No. 5, October 1992, p. 3.

18. FBIS-LAT–92–198, 13 October 1992, p. 6.

19. An excellent analysis of Cuba's deficiencies in this regard is provided by Diamond, *Cuba*, 1991.

20. *Cuba Business*, December 1991, p. 6.

21. There were early quality-control problems in production with the Cuban vaccine. Its present effectiveness is around 85 percent, which is considerably above the competing products (with a reported effectiveness closer to 65 percent).

22. Inter Press Service Corresponsalia, *Informacion Quincenal sobre Cuba*, Vol. 5, No. 21, p. 1.

23. According to the British magazine *Cuba Business* (Vol. 6, No. 5, p. 2), Cuba's top economic spokesman, Carlos Lage, stated that Total's seismic tests were very promising. Earlier reports in the United States, however, suggested the opposite.

24. *Cuba Business*, Vol. 6, No. 5, p. 1.

25. Grupo de Perfeccionamiento de las Organizaciones Empresariales e Instituciones del MINFAR, *Bases Generales del Perfeccionamiento en el MINFAR* (Havana, September 1989), p. 198.

26. In 1989, there were 300 Cuban enterprises and economic entities involved in foreign trade. At the end of 1991, there were some 500.

27. The Fourth Party Congress of October 1991 did affirm the party's intention to expand the very limited private service sector (including mechanical and electrical repair, carpentry, plumbing, artesanry, among others), but the implementation of this new policy seems have gotten off to a slow start.

28. One post-cancellation showing was allowed, however, at the Havana Film Festival in December 1991.

29. The 1981 Cuban Census reports that blacks and mulattos together constitute around 33 percent of the population (*Censo de Poblacion y Viviendas*, 1981, pp. 10–12), but this is according to the self-definition of the Cuban people. In the 1950s it was common for mulattos with lighter skin to be referred to as *mas adelantados* (more advanced), and this prejudice has not been completely erased. The Census count thus is likely to understate the true proportion of black and mulatto Cubans. It is also true that the birth rate among black and mulatto Cubans has been somewhat higher, so that the 1981 figures would tend to understate the 1992 realities in this regard as well. Of course, the precise number cannot be scientifically established because of centuries of intermarriage and the consequent existence of a continuing color spectrum.

30. We exclude here, perhaps naively, the possibility that U.S. forces would invade the island. Should a second invasion take place, the prospects would be little different from those described in the text that follows.

3

Where Does Cuba Stand?

Enrique A. Baloyra

A RIDDLE

Is Cuba different? Ever since the fall of the Berlin wall in November 1989, and particularly since the disintegration of the Soviet Union in summer 1991, predictions about the imminent collapse of the Castro regime have been more frequent.[1]

Scholars and analysts agree that the regime confronts its worst crisis ever and that it can not possibly escape it unscathed.[2] By this they do not mean that the regime will inevitably fall, only that in order to avoid more catastrophic alternatives, including widespread violence or outright civil war, the historic revolutionary leadership must innovate considerably more than it has ever been willing to. Indeed, it appeared that in order to prevent a complete national collapse that would destroy the regime, the leadership had already introduced changes that it would normally have refused to consider.

If the Cuban leadership is acting under duress, why have we not witnessed more dramatic developments? If social and economic conditions are so harsh and growing worse, why have people not gone into the street to march and protest? Why are we yet to witness domestic political opposition effectively challenging the regime? Why have the leaders in the so-called left wing of the Cuban Communist Party refrained from expressing their criticisms and disagreements in public? Why have the armed forces apparently remained loyal? Is Cuba unique?[3]

Some could argue that the Cuban system of domination is so perfect, so omnipresent, and so omnipotent that, as many of the characters in the plays of Vaclav Havel claimed, "There is no alternative but to submit." Others would claim that the regime still enjoys a fair amount of foundational legitimacy and that the government is firmly in control of the situation and capable of experimenting with ad hoc strategies of re-equilibration. Which is actually the case?

ON CUBAN UNIQUENESS

For a long time, specialists have dealt with Cuba as a deviant, almost unique, case. We need to review the factors making Cuba different, not to drive home the point that it will remain so—that is, invulnerable to the changes that broke down other socialist regimes—but to understand how these factors are retarding the process of change. In very schematic fashion, here is how five of those factors seem to be operating in the early 1990s.

1. Cuba's insularity and proximity to the United States have always militated against regime change for a number of historical and political reasons. These are well-known and do not require additional elaboration except to point out that they have allowed the Castro regime to play politics in terms of north-south (small versus large, independent versus neocolonial) oppositions and to isolate the Cuban public from external stimuli. In the Cuban case, the north-south contradictions have very profound historical roots and become specific as a test of strength between nationalism and imperialism. The result has been that the more relevant contradiction of Cuban politics in the last four decades—pitting of an oppressive regime against a dominated society—has been overlooked and neglected.

Far too frequently, political actors in the United States address Cuba as a domestic U.S. issue, seek to project power and influence through American institutions, advance proposals that ignore the historical antecedents of U.S.-Cuban relations, or fail to incorporate the nuances of contemporary Cuban politics. Regardless of the intent, the result is the perception in Cuba that outside actors want to dictate solutions that, in many cases, run contrary to the explicit wishes or public positions of their would-be Cuban allies.

2. None of the peaceful processes of regime transition has been determined by external factors. In the 1970s, military defeat abroad contributed to the deterioration of the Salazarist regime in Portugal and to the collapse of the colonels' regime in Greece. Similarly, the defeat in the Falklands unravelled the Argentine military regime, but only after General Galtieri committed his government to a gamble of his and his colleagues own choosing, rather than one that was imposed on them. In Central Europe, where the Soviet Union instigated the removal of Erich Honecker in East Germany, helped plot the overthrow of Nicolae Ceaucescu in Romania, and orchestrated the ouster of Todor Zhikov in Bulgaria, the Soviets had to act through local intermediaries who had their own interests and priorities. The outcome of these interventions was far from uniform. Such intermediaries have not been available in the Cuban case, and potential local allies have been unwilling and/or unable to assist in this project. The United States lacks an effective domestic presence in Cuba and, for the reasons adduced before, an American

connection would likely be a delegitimizing factor in the eyes of the majority of the Cuban population, rather than a factor that would increase the prestige and legitimacy of the opposition. In too many cases, opponents of the regime, particularly those operating in the United States, have chosen to highlight their closeness and support for the Cuba policies of the incumbent administration.

3. Cuba was a model of national Communism that, despite heavy reliance on the Soviet Union, maintained a degree of independence and autonomy that could not have been predicted from a cursory inspection of the country's strategic assets and resource potential. Cuban willingness to experiment in the delivery of collective goods at home and aggressive pursuit of proletarian internationalism abroad—including programs of fraternal economic assistance—preserved the freshness of the revolutionary experience for a long time. The boredom and despair of the disaffected coexisted side by side with the optimism and heightened sense of personal efficacy of the committed. That sense of efficacy was probably much more widespread in Cuba than in other socialist countries.

To be sure, the Cuban revolutionaries failed the test of creating wealth. Nevertheless, they have evolved a winning competitive ethos yet to be contradicted by military defeat or catastrophic political setbacks. This ethos stands behind the arrogance and self-sufficiency of the leading figures of the regime. In the final analysis, they have a point: They are yet to be defeated in the political arena. Castro and his closest associates publicly reacted to the collapse of the socialist regimes as something that Eastern European leaders had brought upon themselves.[4] They find no fault in their own policies and insist that they are not to be blamed for the mistakes of their former comrades.[5]

In a way, the worst foreign policy defeat—the collapse of the Soviet Union and its world system of political economy, which had major domestic political consequences for the Cuban regime—was not a complete political catastrophe for Castro. This defeat came precisely at a time of heightening tensions between a Soviet reformist cohort, younger than the Cuban historic leadership, who had mounted a major offensive along the lines of transparency in government (*glasnost*) and economic restructuring (*perestroika*). On their own, each of these objectives had profoundly destabilizing consequences for the Cuban regime, which not only resisted these changes but presented its own alternative policies of rectification.[6] Precisely at a time when he was in the uncomfortable situation of defending Stalinist positions against what Mikhail Gorbachev had presented as another effort at Leninist restoration, a worldwide crisis of Leninism ended this threat against Castro.[7]

4. Another element comes as a direct result of the effectiveness of the Cuban formula of political domination. Given the drawbacks of the "totalitarian model" and its shortcomings in describing the dynamics of life under Communist Party domination, using what appear to be the more accurate

labels to describe this system is problematic. In a structural sense, the contemporary Cuban regime has resembled the Stalinist much more than any other variety of Leninist regimes. Unfortunately, Stalinism is a term laden with very strong ideological implications, linked to a particular world-view (Sovietology) that was neither a discipline nor scientific, and was at best a remnant of the Cold War. Nevertheless, the absence of civil society in Cuba cannot be understood except in reference to this form of Communist domination, at least in an institutional way.

As a result, there are no practically autonomous intermediary institutions in Cuban Society. In Cuba, there is no Christian Church that can mobilize the masses as was the case in Poland or in East Germany. Despite one of the richest traditions of unionism anywhere, an independent labor movement such as Solidarnosc is nowhere in sight in Cuba. In the same vein, in spite of a few well-publicized rows with the government, Cuban dissidents and intellectuals have been unable to come together into anything comparable to Charter 77, the Petofi Circle or the *samizdat* movement.[8]

Absent institutional sanctuaries and social spaces in which to evolve and camouflage political activity, the atomization that characterizes Stalinist forms of political control has been singularly effective in preventing the development of horizontal solidarities that normally precede the crystallization of organized forms of public protest. Without continued protest, the government has not been forced to engage in major exercises of public repression. The water cannon, the baton, the cattle prods, the gas canisters, and the gas masks are all ready to be utilized but they have been unnecessary. Thus far, the government has found it sufficient to deploy the "rapid reaction brigades" against actual and suspected dissidents to prevent the massification of public protests.

This dominance can also be seen at the level of the political elite. Only three organizations have sufficient institutional strength to pose serious challenges to the leadership: the Communist Party of Cuba (PCC), the Revolutionary Armed Forces (FAR), and the Interior Ministry (MININT). In June 1989, the regime demonstrated its strength as it moved to publicly try and convict one of Cuba's most revered and decorated military heroes, Division General Arnaldo Ochoa Sanchez. Ochoa was found guilty and summarily executed along with three other officers, including Colonel Antonio de la Guardia, a MININT insider. This would have been inconceivable in most Latin American countries. Subsequently, a thorough purge gutted the MININT, sending the interior minister, Division General Jose Abrantes, to jail for twenty years and meting stiff sentences to a large number of his colleagues.[9] For all practical purposes, MININT was put under the receivership of the FAR, which, as was the case in other socialist countries, seemed obedient to the party.[10]

As for the party itself, some of the worst and most sensational purges conducted in Cuba—in 1962, 1964, and 1968—were against those who allegedly were trying to use the party organization to establish their own political base. More recently, during the 1980s, party leaders and professional cadre were under relentless pressure to make government policy work: Turnover rates in the Central Committee, provincial and municipal secretariats, and the party bureaucracy reached historic highs. In 1985, Humberto Perez, chief of the Central Planning Board (JUCEPLAN) and one of the prime defenders of economic reform, was demoted from his job and ultimately expelled from the Central Committee. In early 1992, a similar fate befell ideologist Carlos Aldana, whose position on change remained ambiguous and whose rising fortunes quickly faded as he was accused of corruption and demoted to a menial job.

5. One final element of paradigmatic nature is uncertainty, both at the level of the elite and of the attentive public. In all previous cases of peaceful transition, elite agreements have paved the way for elections or for agreed *rupturas* (ruptures) offering at least minimal guarantees to those departing. In a way, a process of transition is a process of managing uncertainty and, in the Cuban case, the last few years have been a period of increasing uncertainty. This has gone beyond the fear of and intimidation by official mechanisms of political control. Party elites that could have pronounced themselves against the current political course have yet to receive clear, unmistakable pledges of non-retribution. They are concerned that U.S. policies of economic denial through embargo and political ostracism are geared to bring down the entire apparatus, not just the diehard Stalinists. They read those policies as intending to destroy everyone ever associated with the regime. This, to say the least, has not been helpful. At the level of ordinary citizens, many are certainly fed up with Castro, with his foolhardy experiments, and with having to live in permanent dissimulation. But they were not looking forward to ending thirty-odd years of revolution—bearing little personal freedom but accompanied by a number of tangible social benefits—only to fall prey to a group of extremists and *arrivistes* from the other end of the spectrum.

In short, Cubans are preoccupied about the alternatives to their present predicament. Elites and mass are deeply worried about the future. In the past, many had experienced considerable social mobility and/or had seen their children reach positions and distinctions that they could not have dreamed of. The rampant neoliberal rhetoric, the costs of changing economic models in Central Europe, and the continuing dire economic conditions of millions of Latin Americans are constantly being highlighted by official propaganda. In short, the public is not entirely convinced that life would be better under capitalism.

Why is this important? A generic argument, advanced by Adam Przeworski, among others, is that a crisis of legitimacy does not change or make a regime.[11] There have to be alternative leadership, policies, and strategies available to mobilize people in favor of change.[12] And change can only come from two directions: from "above," that is, from dissident factions of the leadership, or from "below," from within the ranks of ordinary Cubans. Once there are leaders willing to lead and masses available to be mobilized, there can be an alternative.

THE PARADOX RESTATED

To be sure, in the spring of 1993 the Cuban regime was being bruised by dire conditions. Judging by historical and comparative standards, those conditions should at the very least have produced a deterioration, if not a near breakdown, of the regime. But Cuban leaders continued formulating and implementing policy as if they were not confronting a terminal crisis.[13]

There are three ways of evaluating this paradox. The first is to consider chaos without breakdown as the normal order of things in revolutionary Cuba. This proposition rests on three assumptions: First, the historical continuity of the ruling group suggests that the Cuban regime has never changed.[14] Second, it has been argued that, except for 1975 through 1984, turmoil, crises, and experimentation have characterized the operational style of the Cuban regime. This has been variously described as *socialismo con pachanga* (socialism without a blueprint, or informal socialism) and wartime Communism (for the 1960s), and *sociolismo* (cronyism), provisional institutions in perpetuity, or simply, the "anti-model."[15] Third, as has been the case in the past, despite all the avatars, Fidel Castro and his closest associates may somehow find the means and opportunity to remain in power without changing the regime. Each of these statements clearly exaggerates what may have actually been or will be the case. The bottom line of this first option asks: Where, except in its depth, is the novelty of this crisis? Are Cubans not accustomed to living in crisis?

The second option would be to reject the paradox altogether on grounds that the regime really is deteriorating and that it cannot possibly continue relying on traditional mechanisms for reproducing its legitimacy and control. This assumes that the vectors of change are already in place and that it is simply a matter of time before we witness regime breakdown. No matter how astute a leadership, how willing to rule, and how much support it may still have, it is hard to imagine that it can survive a complete economic collapse. In early summer 1993, the news from Cuba consisted of a steady staple of power outages, a generalized breakdown of transportation, increased scarcity and hunger, and the threat of epidemics of different sorts. Was a collapse anywhere near?

The third option anticipates change, but in more gradual fashion. It rejects unescapable economic determinism and suggests that continued selective application of pragmatic macroeconomic policies and political repression (the linchpin of the strategy of re-equilibration used by the leadership in the early 1990s), combined with the strategies used by ordinary Cubans to survive the crisis, may change the regime in a gradual and largely unanticipated way. It is conceivable that the same or a very similar ruling group could preserve the ethos of the revolutionary regime in a new structural configuration.[16]

Despite the official rhetoric and the supposedly diehard attitude of the historic leadership, which has vowed to uphold principle and resist until the end, re-equilibration is no revival of "Guevarism" but an attempt by the historic leaders to subordinate the scope and nature of change to their own political and physical survival. Stated in the language of transition analysis, this is a "re-equilibration without liberalization." Therefore, the early 1990s are not simply a repetition of the late 1960s. Creeping capitalism, the loss of ideological referents, and deeper and more widespread popular resentment against the regime are pushing Cuba into uncharted territory. Cubans may not be ready to immolate themselves to improve matters, but this does not mean that they will respond enthusiastically to narrowly defined policies of elite survival and regime continuity. In short, elite-guided re-equilibration and mass-based avoidance and disengagement are the stuff of the politics of transition in Cuba. What is yet to be determined is the outcome.

CHANGE IN THE CUBA OF THE 1990s

All the different permutations and combinations of these three possibilities boil down to two interpretations. The difference between these interpretations is not whether change will occur, but whether it is going to be gradual and orderly (even if it results in a new or drastically altered regime) or turbulent, and spin out of control. Which is likely to be the case?

In 1993, four years after the collapse of the socialist bloc and two years after its cliency relationship with the Soviet Union had come to an end, the Cuban regime remained in place. To be sure, a sense of urgency was palpable in much of the formulation and implementation of domestic policy. Levels and styles of citizen mobilization were more reminiscent of the turmoil and experimentation of the 1960s than of the more structured and predictable patterns of the late 1970s and early 1980s. Open massive unemployment and underemployment had become a reality. In its edition of April 2, 1992, the weekly *Bohemia* reported that, by that time, about 155,000 workers had been reassigned to chores in agriculture and construction. By January 1993, roughly 75 percent of Cuban factories had simply stopped producing anything because of the lack of raw materials. In agriculture, animal traction had all but replaced tractors and combines. Workers' dining halls were shut down. In spring 1993, the quota of food that could be purchased through the official rationing system did not cover the entire month. All of these factors seemed to be pulling the regime away from its blueprint for re-equilibration. Following a violent storm in March 1993, the Cuban government broke precedent and asked for international donations to help repair the extensive damages. From that point onward, Cuban officials pointed to adverse weather conditions as a major contributor to their inability to fulfill commercial contracts and meet their own production goals for the "special period." On June 3, 1993, Alberto Betancourt Roa, director of CUBAZUCAR (the state sugar corporation), announced that due to *force majeure*, Cuba would have to suspend its sugar deliveries and that sugar production would not surpass the 4.2 million metric ton mark.

Externally, the regime had embarked on a worldwide campaign aimed at forcing an end to the U.S. economic embargo, first imposed in 1962. Passage of the Cuban Democracy Act, signed into law by President George Bush in Miami in October 1992, had tightened the provisions of the embargo on the ground that this would accelerate a transition to democracy.[17] Cuban officials were utilizing this stated purpose to denounce the United States. On their own, most of Cuba's traditional trading partners, including steadfast U.S. allies (members of NATO and the EEC) and countries not particularly sympathetic to the regime, denounced the Act and/or announced countermeasures of their own.[18] Even before final approval of the Act, on October 8, 1992, the European Community filed a formal complaint with the U.S. government on the ground that this violated international law. Canada and Britain issued orders imposing fines on any company complying with the Act. On November 24, 1992, the United Nations General Assembly approved a non-binding resolution condemning the expansion of the embargo; only the United States, Romania, and Israel voted against it. On December 2, 1992, the final declaration of a meeting of the Group of Eight in Buenos Aires included language criticizing "attempts to confer extraterritoriality to the laws of any country." International controversy about the Cuban Democracy Act put the Cuban problem back in the venue of the nationalism-imperialism debate, to the detriment of the reality of a besieged dictatorship steadfastly refusing to negotiate a reconciliation with its opposition and determined not to entertain any policy options except its own.

In terms of the relationship between rulers and ruled, there was a palpable estrangement between state and society, and the government was increasingly unable to provide services that the population had grown accustomed to. This, in no small measure, was a direct result of miscalculations and obstinacy on the part of the ruling elite, particularly Fidel Castro. But it would be hard to underestimate the very overwhelming impact of what was probably the worst economic crisis in the country's history. What had begun in the mid–1980s as a disguised program of economic austerity, the "campaign to rectify errors and negative tendencies" (*rectificacion*), had evolved into a desperate struggle for survival, which the government euphemistically described as "a special period in time of peace."

The population's response to these conditions was complex. The kingdom of dissimulation that ordinary Cubans had built for themselves was giving way to increased social disorganization, open discontent, and some isolated instances of formal protest. The crime rate soared as Cubans found it impossible to make ends meet without engaging in petty thievery. Expressions of discontent were more open than ever before. For example, in the municipal elections of December 20, 1992, about 31 percent of the 7,546,194 voters invalidated their ballots or left them blank. There was increasing disbelief in the government's insistence that the United States might invade and that the economic depression that the country was experiencing was a direct result of the U.S. embargo and the collapse of the Soviet system. But there was also considerable resentment at the United States for making things worse by tightening the embargo.

Dissidents ventured where they rarely had gone before, openly criticizing the regime on live interviews with Miami radio stations and in statements to international media. The Catholic Church became more openly critical. In October 1991, Archbishop Jaime Ortega Alamino asked Cuban Catholics not to join the rapid reaction brigades organized by the government to intimidate people and conduct acts of street violence against dissidents and protesters. In May 1992, Archbishop Ortega criticized the official media for openly espousing an attitude of "us versus them" when referring to Cuban Christians. He added:

When we seem to be marching towards a lay state, it is hardly convenient to continue talking about Marxism as a religion and about the encounter of Christians and Marxists as an ecumenical meeting between two churches.

In late October 1992, the Cuban Episcopal Conference issued a statement condemning the Cuban Democracy Act and reiterated the opposition of the Catholic hierarchy to the U.S. economic embargo.

Intra-elite relations seemed to be experiencing considerable turbulence. Despite official proclamations, the PCC was far from united. Disunity within the party had been a problem for the past ten years. In December 1985, due to a lack of consensus on a number of issues, the last session of the Third Congress of the PCC had to be postponed. Shortly after concluding its delayed session, in February 1986, Castro went ahead on his own and launched the so-called process of rectification on April 19, 1986.

Moreover, there were very complicated maneuvers involving preparations for the Fourth Congress of the PCC in October 1991. A number of ad hoc procedures were put in place so that the top leadership would be able to control the process of delegate selection and, by implication, the agenda and the debate. On the one hand, many of the base leaders of the PCC elected by secret ballot earlier in the year were not considered completely reliable. But these did not reach the Congress in large numbers. On the other hand, the *llamamiento* process, which was the leadership's call for an open and sincere debate leading to the Congress, produced far too many controversial suggestions. The Politburo had to issue a declaration that the revolutionary project and its historic leadership were beyond questioning.

Before the Congress took place, its organizing commission implemented a number of important changes on the ground that they would have been approved anyway.[19] Even so, the issue of the free peasant market, one of the first and most controversial aspects of the policy of rectification, was hotly debated at the insistence of "the right," with many people openly calling for its restoration. For their part, "left" elements did not concede the point about the inclusion of believers in the party without a fight. Structural and personnel changes approved by the Congress included the elimination of the Secretariat; the promotion of "safe" younger politicians (Maria de los Angeles Garcia, Alfredo Hondal Gonzalez, Alfredo Jordan Morales, Carlos Lage, Abel Prieto, Roberto Robaina, Nelson Torres Perez), technocrats, and trouble-shooters (Concepcion Campa Huergo, Yadira Garcia Vega, Candido Palmero Hernandez) to an expanded Politburo of twenty-five members; and the elimination of deputy positions up and down and across the entire party structure. These changes were not trivial. If anything, they were put in place to help implement the strategy of re-equilibration with which the government intended to pull the regime out of its state of deterioration and prevent its breakdown. In addition, the Congress gave the Politburo carte blanche to rule the country through exceptional mechanisms for as long as this was made necessary by the "special period."

What this cursory review of the evidence seems to suggest is that there has been opposition in Cuba, but that it has not been able to establish and consolidate itself either at the level of the leadership or within the ranks of the mass public. Is this state of affairs likely to continue? Will the government strategy of re-equilibration somehow merge with or assimilate some of the demands of the opposition? Are the dynamics of officially sponsored changes and of their unanticipated consequences likely to complement or collide with each other?

A SOCIALIST APERTURE TOWARD CAPITALISM

Changes in the configuration of international political blocs left the regime scurrying to find not only new trading partners but also ideological moorings. This posed a double-barreled threat to its legitimacy. Keeping a trading economy afloat was a tall order; managing the deepening contradiction between an official rhetoric of "socialism or death" and the everyday practice of state capitalism was no panacea. The top leadership strained to put the best possible face on this glaring contradiction. In September 1991, Castro stated that Cuba could have both a socialist economy and society and wide cooperation with foreign capital. In a November 1992 interview that received national television and radio coverage, Carlos Lage, secretary of the executive committee of the Council of Ministers, described current economic policy as "a socialist opening to the capitalist world." This, he hastened to add, would not sacrifice the political, economic, and social project chosen by Cuba.

In short, government policy calls for a mixed economy of sorts, combining foreign capitalist enclaves, primarily in the export sector, with socialist production and distribution predominating in the domestic sector.[20] This was an enclave-based economic restructuring, unaccompanied by political liberalization.[21] It is likely that any successful reorganization of Cuban political economy will require massive foreign investment and a reorientation to export-led growth in non-traditional sectors.[22] While this strategy is probably correct, it poses serious problems of legitimacy to a leadership that has made the rejection of capitalism and market economics a central tenet of its economic model.[23]

Two additional problems loom large. One is that, despite very generous terms and facilities offered to foreign capital, the latter has yet to take full advantage of them. While the amount of foreign investment received thus far is substantial, it is insufficient to pull the country out of its deep recession and to make the official strategy of re-equilibration successful. By spring 1993, there were close to 300 foreign firms operating in Cuba, including giants like BASF, Bayer, CIBA-GEIGY, Komatsu, Nissei Sangyo, Rhone-Poulenc, Sandoz, and Volvo.[24] But many had yet to make an investment commitment, and new investment remained heavily concentrated. For example, in 1992, reports of a massive infusion of fresh Canadian capital used the figure of U.S. $1.2 billion to describe what Sherrit Gordon intended to invest in modernizing nickel plants at Las Camariocas and Punta Gorda.

Linkages among these new resources/activities and Cuban foreign trade and domestic economy activity remained tenuous. One major factor was its enclave nature. Another was the collapse of the Council for Mutual Economic Assistance (CMEA), which took the lion's share of Cuba's trade. Between 1984 and 1989, Cuban exports to and imports from CMEA countries were roughly 70 percent of the total (See Table 3.1). In dollar terms, the amount of Cuban imports from the Soviet Union was U.S. $5.2 billion in 1989. This dropped to $1.7 billion in 1991. Accordingly, the economic Commission for Latin America (ECLA) reported that between 1989 and 1992, Cuban import capacity had declined by 73 percent.[25] As a result of this drastically reduced import capacity, Cuba's gross social product fell precipitously, as vital imports could not be purchased elsewhere because of a lack of foreign exchange and Cuba's low credit rating. (The latter was due to its unilateral moratorium on servicing its foreign debt with hard-currency countries in 1986.) Input shortages had a serious impact on all of Cuban industry. Sugar production declined from 8.1 million metric tons in 1989–1990 to 4.2 million in 1992–1993.

Whatever trade this new investment is generating with the Western Hemisphere and Europe cannot come close to filling the void left by the Soviet

Table 3.1
Cuban Foreign Trade, 1984–89 (millions of Cuban pesos)

EXPORTS

	1984	1985	1986	1987	1988	1989	84/89 TOTAL
Hemisphere	111.2	72.9	85.4	81.6	98.1	248.2	697.4
% of total	2.0	1.2	1.6	1.5	1.8	4.6	2.1
Canada	43.5	32.2	37.2	36.0	38.5	54.8	242.2
all other	67.7	40.7	48.2	45.6	59.6	193.4	455.2
Nicaragua	31.2	19.9	30.1	26.6	20.1	19.6	147.5
Venezuela	2.0	7.8	2.1	1.5	21.8	31.1	66.3
Mexico	10.7	1.9	1.7	2.0	4.9	17.8	39.0
rest	23.8	11.1	14.3	15.5	12.8	124.9	202.4
EEC	137.7	184.4	245.6	269.6	393.2	437.7	1668.2
Spain			88.2	84.9	81.5	86.0	
Eastern Europe	4686.4	5161.5	4627.2	4689.2	4518.2	4069.0	27751.5
USSR	3952.2	4481.6	3935.8	3868.7	3683.1	3231.2	23152.6
% of total	72.2	74.8	74.0	71.6	66.7	59.9	69.9
World Totals	5476.5	5991.5	5321.5	5402.1	5518.3	5392.0	33101.9

IMPORTS

	1984	1985	1986	1987	1988	1989	84/89 TOTAL
Hemisphere	318.6	379.5	297.4	294.3	360.4	514.8	2165.0
% of total	4.4	4.7	3.9	3.9	4.8	6.3	4.7
Canada	56.5	58.8	53.4	33.0	28.5	37.1	267.3
all other	262.1	320.7	244.0	261.3	331.9	477.7	1897.7
Argentina	149.9	193.3	162.2	124.3	127.5	179.2	936.4
Mexico	72.7	77.1	29.7	72.0	108.0	80.0	439.5
Venezuela	7.5	5.8	10.2	19.1	28.9	56.5	128.0
Peru	4.7	3.0	3.7	3.6	8.4	19.1	42.5
rest	27.3	41.5	38.2	42.3	59.1	142.9	351.3
EEC	396.0	366.9	473.0	411.0	398.4	480.0	2525.3
Spain			147.4	165.4	146.1	184.9	
Eastern Europe	5784.8	6507.0	6297.4	6530.0	6432.5	6636.3	38188.0
USSR	4782.4	5418.9	5337.6	5446.0	5364.4	5522.4	31871.7
% of total	66.2	67.4	70.3	71.8	70.8	68.0	69.1
World Totals	7227.5	8035.0	7596.1	7583.7	7580.0	8124.2	46146.5

Source: Computed from Direccion General de Estadisticas, *Anuario Estadistico de Cuba, 1989*, pp. 253–61.

Union and the CMEA. During 1984 to 1989, Cuban export trade with the Western Hemisphere moved from 2 to 4.6 percent of total exports and from 4.4 to 6.3 percent of total imports. While these figures cover years preceding the free fall of the Cuban economy, they show the enormous gap left by the disappearance of the CMEA. This cannot be filled by new trading partners in a short period of time.

Second, the very generous terms offered by the Cuban government have two negative effects in the short term. One is that Cuban participation in profits is but a fraction of what it could be if the country did not find itself in such a weak position. While this varied somewhat from one sector to another, and from one joint venture to the next, in essence what prevailed was a buyer's market. Extensive concessions in taxation, profit repatriation, and the provision of infrastructure reduced national participation in the surplus generated by these activities and deflated the net diffusion effects of this investment in the domestic sector. For example, according to a March 1993 report by Cuba's Grupo de Turismo, tourism generated U.S. $530 million in gross revenue in 1992. This compared favorably with the U.S. $145 million generated by the sector in 1987 and the U.S. $387 million in 1991. In addition, the sector accounted for roughly 62,000 jobs, or 1.6 percent of total employment, in 1992. These are all impressive numbers. But according to several estimates, Cuba only netted U.S. $245 million in 1992 once profits, commissions, transportation expenses, and direct imports into the sector were discounted.[26] What this means is that this high-priority sector, which seems to be performing fairly well, cannot be counted on to produce miracles or quick fixes. Major gains will require a sustained effort and adaptability to changing market conditions to remain competitive.

In summary, Canadian, Spanish, Mexican, Japanese, and other investors cannot save the regime. Something more is required. Consequently, following the inauguration of Bill Clinton in January 1993, the Cuban government launched a strong public relations campaign to shame his administration into easing the embargo or abrogating it altogether.

The other negative aspect of Cuba's generous concessions to new foreign investment is in the area of labor and community relations. Although these remained enclave operations, their social and political aspects posed a direct challenge to the legitimacy of the regime. The contrast between foreign capitalist affluence and domestic socialist mediocrity is just too strong at all levels. For example, concerning tourism, criticism has emerged from within the party itself over the system of apartheid created by the increasing number of foreign tourists visiting the island, which has resulted in the virtual exclusion of the *criollos* (natives) from the choice spots in the littoral and has put extra pressure on the supply of food in the country. Cubans are practically excluded from the "dollar area," and ordinary citizens cannot make purchases in well-supplied stores reserved for foreign tourists, entrepreneurs, and diplomats. More ominously, prostitution, which Cuban officials had proudly

declared extinct thirty years ago, has reappeared as a direct result of the
upsurge in tourism and of the increasingly narrow employment opportunities
available to a predominantly young and technically well-qualified labor force.
In addition, hundreds of young technicians and professionals are avidly seeking jobs in the dollarized sector of the economy. This is an internal "brain
drain" of sorts.

But employment in the dollar sector entails having to adjust to more
demanding conditions than many Cuban workers are accustomed to. The
government's monopoly of the domestic labor market, and the fact that it
acts as intermediary between foreign capitalists and Cuban workers, create
additional frictions. While some major irritants have been removed, most
workers continue to be paid in Cuban pesos at a fraction of their nominal
dollar salaries. They cannot engage in collective bargaining and, until recently, they could not use whatever dollars came into their hands to patronize
restricted shops. Despite these annoyances and outright injustices, workers
in the dollarized foreign enclaves are considered lucky by those excluded
from them.

A recent study of the impact of this early onslaught of enclave capitalism
concludes somewhat tentatively. According to this work, while direct foreign
investment is undermining Castro in several ways, this effect is being countered by others that may actually help consolidate the system, particularly
if foreign investment increases.[27] This and other sources are beginning to
discover antagonism between Cuban managers in joint enterprises, enjoying
more autonomy, salaries, and working conditions, and those trying to run
state enterprises under all kinds of vicissitudes.

SOME LIKELY SCENARIOS

On the surface, it appears that the almost legendary adaptability of the
historic revolutionary leaders has not deserted them. Through a combination
of official policies, astute manipulation of certain factors specific to the Cuban
situation, and the adroit turning of some unfavorable contingencies to their
advantage, they have managed to disconnect potential links between would-
be leaders and followers, and thereby prevent discontent from turning into
political mobilization and massified opposition.

While these conditions prevail, Castro has no incentive to engage in serious bargaining and negotiation with his Cuban opponents. He can continue
his present course, hoping that he may finesse an accommodation with the
United States, that his ad hoc economic policies will mature and bear full
fruit, and that the number of imponderables shall remain a manageable few.
Given the trends afoot in mid–1993, this is probably too much for him to
ask. As suggested above, he needs major qualitative changes in terms of
access to fresh credit and major levels of direct foreign investment to jump-
start a restructured economy and put it in the path of self-sustained growth.

This is unlikely without some major changes in the domestic configuration and international relations of the regime.

While a relaxation of the U.S. embargo remained possible—particularly with respect to food, medicine, travel, and communications—there was very little to indicate that, short of drastic change in the nature of the regime, the United States would abrogate it altogether. Without this, Castro's own idiosyncrasies and concern for his own political survival are likely to prevent him from allowing the more drastic and rapid conversion to market mechanisms that the Cuban economy requires to be able to feed and employ the population, particularly in the absence of a new external patron. In either case, with or without a patron, and even barring any new complication, the vicious circle in which the Cuban economy is trapped is likely to get even worse. Castro will have to make some additional concessions on the economic front.

Elite and popular reactions to these concessions are hard to gauge. Dissent on economic policy alone is not likely to fracture the elite in a regime-threatening fashion, whether to demand or protest changes. However, the issue of repressing the population, which could arise if economic conditions continue to deteriorate unremittingly, would probably produce such a split. Absent a sustained dialogue with the opposition or a previous tacit elite agreement, this split may not bring about a crucial realignment of forces or the emergence of a new winning coalition capable of managing a transition. But it would force the regime to engage in continued repression of spontaneous, sustained popular protest. Ironically, given extant mechanisms of political control, spontaneous protest may be more likely and, with the absence of prior elite agreements and clearly formulated alternatives, the potential for violence and anarchy will increase.

In the short term, however, there are no likely candidates to play the role of connecting the elite and masses into a coherent opposition. Military officers are less likely to lead a dissenting faction and to play a prominent role in managing the transition than the party *apparatchiki*. The existence of only one party makes it easier for the politics of dissent to become the politics of opposition within that party, than for a military conspiracy to crystallize. A military coalition would require the active collaboration of the intelligence apparatus, which was effectively gutted and purged in the aftermath of the Ochoa affair. At present, the MININT is under the receivership of a trustee of FAR Minister Raul Castro, General Abelardo Colome Ibarra.

For the most part, the present leadership of the dissident movement has not made any decisive move to mobilize the population. Those who have tried to recruit more aggressively, such as Yndamiro Restano of the Movimiento Armonia, have quickly found themselves in jail. Those who remain free do not seem to be contemplating a change of tactics; therefore, it does not appear that they will lead an active campaign of civil disobedience any time soon.

Without a leadership willing to lead, there may not be a mass willing to follow. The strategies of survival evolved over the years are not likely to be revised at a time of extreme hardship and duress. People are too preoccupied with subsistence to engage in the kind of spontaneous combustion that might produce a massive blow-up. Cubans have always worried about not becoming martyred in sterile causes; consequently, there is quite a lot of apprehension about "starting anything." However, Cubans are also known to mobilize through anger in the face of blatant injustice and abuse of power. It is not out of the question that we could witness incidents of looting hard-currency stores (*diplomercados*), hotel commissaries or even local groceries. It is also likely that mistreatment of ordinary citizens by an abusive official or mob could spark violence.

Castro may know more about the psychology of ordinary Cubans than the rest of us, but, in the early 1990s, those Cubans posed a greater potential threat to him than anyone at the elite level. He demonstrated his concern by vigorously campaigning during the weeks leading up to the election of February 1993. He cannot rest on his laurels, however. He is spread too thin over too many projects and crises. Soon he may be confronted by the most difficult choice of his career: whether to preside over a more genuine process of change or to eventually engage in massive repression of ordinary citizens.

In conclusion, given the very narrow margins for success of the present strategy of re-equilibration, the prospects for the future seem to cluster around two options. One is a deepening of the process of change, led by the government; the other is the continuation of current policy, with increasing chances of violence and turmoil. That Fidel Castro remains the key player in determining which of the two courses will prevail seems to suggest which is more likely. That he has never put his supremacy on the auction block does not augur well for the future of his country.

NOTES

1. For a recent, well-documented exercise in predicting change, see Andres Oppenheimer, *Castro's Final Hour* (New York: Simon and Schuster, 1992).

2. For a contrast, see Edward Gonzalez, "The Beginning of the End for Castro?" in *Cuba Roundtable, Cuba in the Nineties* (New York: Freedom House, 1991), pp. 7–22; Susan Kaufman Purcell, "Collapsing Cuba," *Foreign Affairs*, Vol. 71, No. 1, 1992, pp. 131–145; and Andrew Zimbalist, "Teetering on the Brink," *Journal of Latin American Studies*, Vol. 24, No. 2, May 1992.

3. This question is addressed squarely elsewhere. See "Introduction" in Enrique A. Baloyra and James A. Morris, eds., *Conflict and Change in Cuba* (Albuquerque, N.M.: University of New Mexico Press, forthcoming), pp. 4–5.

4. For a sample of these reactions, see "Our Most Sacred Duty: Save the Fatherland, the Revolution, and Socialism," *Granma*, August 29, 1991. Consult any of

Castro's speeches during this period, for example, the September 5, 1992, anniversary speech delivered at the Juragua nuclear power plants in Cienfuegos.

5. For an expanded discussion on these points, see Marifeli Perez-Stable, " 'We Are the Only Ones and There Is No Alternative': Vanguard Party Politics in Cuba, 1975–1991," in Baloyra and Morris, eds., *Conflict and Change in Cuba*, pp. 68–70, 76–84.

6. For description and discussion, see J. Richard Planas, "The Impact of Soviet Reforms on Cuban Socialism," in Baloyra and Morris, eds., *Conflict and Change in Cuba*, pp. 246–56. Also see Jorge I. Dominguez, "The Political Impact on Cuba of the Reform and Collapse of Communist Regimes," in Carmelo Mesa-Lago, ed., *Cuba After the Cold War* (Pittsburgh, Pa.: University of Pittsburgh Press, forthcoming), Chapter 4.

7. This was the first time in which, in a confrontation with the Soviet leadership, Castro had to explicitly defend his position on the ground that he was not favoring Stalinism. For details and discussion, see Enrique A. Baloyra, "Socialist Transitions and Prospects for Change in Cuba," in Baloyra and Morris, eds., *Conflict and Change in Cuba*, pp. 48–55.

8. For a more complete discussion on this topic, see Peter Johnson, "The Nuanced Lives of the Intelligentsia," Baloyra and Morris, eds., in *Conflict and Change in Cuba*, especially pp. 140–48.

9. Abrantes died in jail later, allegedly of a heart attack while he was exercising.

10. For more details on the Ochoa-de la Guardia-Abrantes case, see Enrique A. Baloyra, "The Cuban Armed Forces and the Crisis of Revolution," in Louis W. Goodman et al., eds., *Civil-Military Relations in Latin America* (Lexington, Mass.: Lexington Books, forthcoming). For a discussion of political control of the Cuban military, see Phyllis Greene Walker, "Political-Military Relations Since 1959," in Baloyra and Morris, eds., *Conflict and Change in Cuba*, especially pp. 115–28.

11. Adam Przeworski, "Some Problems in the Study of the Transition to Democracy," in Guillermo O'Donnell et al., eds., *Transitions from Authoritarian Rule. Part III. Comparative Perspectives* (Baltimore: Johns Hopkins University Press, 1986), pp. 50–53.

12. Leonardo Morlino, *Como Cambian los Regimenes Politicos* (Madrid: Centro de Estudios Constitucionales, 1985), pp. 245–73.

13. Jorge I. Dominguez, "Secrets of Castro's Staying Power," *Foreign Affairs*, Vol. 72, No. 21, Spring 1993; Samuel Farber, "Castro Under Siege," *World Policy Journal*, Vol. 9, No. 2, Spring 1992; Edward Gonzalez and David Ronfeldt, *Cuba Adrift in the World*, RAND–4231-USDP (Santa Monica, Calif.: Rand Corporation, 1992).

14. For a critique of this point of view, see Carollee Bengelsdorf, "Cubanology and Crisis: The Mainstream Looks at Institutionalization," and Nelson P. Valdes, "Revolution and Paradigms," in Andrew Zimbalist, ed., *Cuban Political Economy: Controversies in Cubanology* (Boulder, Colo: Westview Press, 1988), pp. 212–23 and 196–206, respectively.

15. This was certainly the case until 1975. For discussion and description, see Frank T. Fitzgerald, *Managing Socialism: From Old Cadres to New Professionals in Revolutionary Cuba* (New York: Praeger, 1990), pp. 111–31; K. S. Karol, *Guerrillas in Power* (New York: Hill and Wang, 1970), pp. 451–76; Jose Luis Llovio, *Insider: My Hidden Life as a Revolutionary in Cuba* (New York: Bantam, 1988), pp. 206–

13, 237–51; Rhoda Rabkin, *Cuban Politics: The Revolutionary Experiment* (New York: Praeger, 1991), pp. 50–52, 59–62, and 101–104; Sergio Roca, "The *Comandante* in His Economic Labyrinth," in Baloyra and Morris, *Conflict and Change in Cuba*, pp. 89–91; Andres Suarez, *Cuba: Castroism or Communism?* (Cambridge, Mass.: M.I.T. Press, 1967), pp. 237–41.

16. Cuba's revolution has frequently been compared to Mexico's. For a discussion of how the Mexican revolutionary regime preserved and improved on some of the key features of the *porfiriato* (the long reign of Porfirio Diaz), see Lorenzo Meyer, "Historical Roots of the Authoritarian State in Mexico," in Jose Luis Reyna and Richard S. Weinert, eds., *Authoritarianism in Mexico* (Philadelphia, Pa.: ISHI, 1977), p. 4.

17. In its final form, the Act was included at Section 1701 *et seq.* of the National Defense Authorization Act of 1993 (H. R. 5006/S. 3114).

18. These included Argentina, Canada, Chile, France, Germany, Mexico, Britain and Venezuela.

19. The Secretariat was abolished, as well as the positions of second secretaries and alternates. Party departments were cut to nine and the party bureaucracy was reduced accordingly.

20. For a comprehensive discussion of those policies and of their probable outcome, see Carmelo Mesa-Lago, "Cuba's Economic Policies and Strategies for Confronting the Crisis," in Mesa-Lago, ed., *Cuba After the Cold War*, Chapter 6.

21. I am aware of changes in the platform of the PCC and of the 1992 constitution, but neither of these represents a political liberalization.

22. "Non-traditional" is utilized here in reference to the revolutionary period, during which tourism and non-sugar exports were neglected, and Cuba's insertion into the world economy relied very heavily on its participation in the now-defunct Council for Mutual Economic Assistance, which joined the economies of the Soviet bloc. Cuba's role within that order was one of providing agricultural (sugar, citrus) and mining (nickel) products.

23. For discussion of adequate future strategies, see Jan Svejnar and Jorge Perez-Lopez, "A Strategy for the Economic Transformation of Cuba Based on the East European Experience," in Mesa-Lago, ed., *Cuba After the Cold War*, Chapter 9.

24. Taken from Amaya Altuna de Sanchez, "Cuba mayo 1993, analisis informativo de la realidad." Paper delivered at the Annual Congress of the Partido Democrata Cristiano de Cuba, Miami, June 4, 1993, pp. 19–23.

25. Naciones Unidas, Comision Economica para America Latina y El Caribe, *Balance Preliminar de la Economia de America Latina y El Caribe*, LC/G.1751, December 18, 1992, p. 8.

26. "Bridging the Gap? Cuban Tourism in the 1990s," *La Sociedad Economica*, Bulletin No. 29 (London), April 19, 1993, p. 1. Also see Mesa-Lago, "Cuba's Economic Policies," in Mesa-Lago, ed., *Cuba After the Cold War*, p. 224.

27. Gillian Gunn, "The Sociological Impact of Rising Foreign Investment," *Cuba Briefing Paper Series*, No. 1, January 1993, p. 15.

4

Why Does Castro Survive?

J. Richard Planas

The question, "Why does Castro survive?" has drawn considerable political interest following the collapse of Marxist-Leninist socialism in Eastern Europe. Many, from the layman to the scholar to political leaders and exile political figures, believe that Fidel Castro should never have, and should not now continue to defy the socialist law of gravity. Indeed, quite a few prominent figures have staked their credibility in predicting his demise.

Many who continue to predict Castro's fall from power have a compelling moral reason for wishing the collapse of the regime: They regard it as oppressive and unjust. In most instances, their forecasts go hand-in-hand with a set of attitudes and behavior patterns indicating, as it might be expected, a strong opposition to the regime. Throughout the years, these attitudes and behavior have had a considerable impact on, and likely will continue to affect, the course of Cuban politics. Analyzing why Castro has not yet fallen can be helpful to the extent that it draws attention to the interplay among the inner workings of the current Cuban system, the impact of the above attitudes and behavior toward Cuba, and Castro's continued ability to remain in power.

By way of initial explanation, predictions regarding Castro's imminent fall have failed to materialize largely because they have relied on imprecise interpretations of events in Eastern Europe, the Soviet Union, and China; they have failed to take into account certain aspects regarding the internal dynamics of the Cuban political system; and they have overlooked certain political realities that inadvertently have contributed to the stability of the regime.

One of those political realities is that, as the history of the modern state suggests, with few exceptions, national political leaders overall have enormous staying power. Such power is magnified when leaders exercise an authoritarian style of leadership, and more so when their style is accompanied by a totalitarian political system that reaches into the innermost aspects of people's social, economic, and personal lives. We may cite simple authoritarian models like the Somoza or the Duvalier regimes, which remained in power for years, the first in spite of having to wage a long war against insurgent guerrillas, the second despite keeping its people in extreme poverty and hunger. Or we may observe Iraq's Saddam Hussein, whose country has experienced worse economic decline and political turmoil than Cuba, the result of two costly wars and a worldwide embargo that makes the U.S. embargo of Cuba seem minor by comparison. These examples suggest that there are not sufficient grounds to sound too optimistic, since Cuba is not yet confronting any of these situations. Moreover, if Cuba had to face more difficult times one day, the above cases also suggest that an obstinate and clever political leader can survive in power for long periods of time.

An examination of predictions about the collapse of unjust political regimes suggests that we tend to overemphasize the role of the masses that spontaneously rise in protest to overthrow their tyrannical leaders. The modern historical record does not lend much support for this belief. Popular uprisings, such as the one that led to the dethronement of Louis XVI, or the Bolshevik revolt against the Russian czar, require a minimum degree of free expression, communication, and education for the masses to be able to spearhead a successful revolution or counter-revolution. Otherwise, the spontaneous convergence of thousands of unorganized, despairing individuals into a unified force of opposition at a specific point in time that is strong enough to topple a totalitarian regime is not a social phenomenon that occurs easily.[1] This act requires the coalescing of various elements—not the least of which is overcoming fear—within people totally unrelated and without previous communication and planning with each other. Further, success is predicated upon the assumption that resistance by the established regime will be less than swift and brutal.

The recent experience in Eastern Europe, rather than being the exception, adds to the rule. What is being overlooked in these countries is the fact that the masses did not bring down communism; communist governments did that to themselves. In all cases, including Romania, the civilian leaderships failed to prevent the spread of public demonstrations at the outset, something that was perceived by the masses as a sign of weakness on the part of the regimes. The masses took only the opportunities that were conceded to them by weakened and tired bureaucratic leaderships that lacked the determination to do what the Chinese did in order to safeguard their system. Only in China and Romania did the leadership order the armed forces to strike back at the population. In China, the armed forces obeyed orders and succeeded. In Romania, the armed forces did not follow Ceausescu's orders initially, and although they did so later, their response was not as ruthless as that of the Chinese.

Some, including Cuba's optimistic forecasters, seem to believe that the best prospect of toppling Castro from power lies with the armed forces. While the possibility does exist, one would have to say that it is slight. Due to educational training, but mostly to the effectiveness of the Communist armed forces' complex counter-intelligence networks and the nature of the system itself, military coups d'etat have been rare in the Communist world. In addition, significant differences between the armed forces in the former Communist countries and those in Cuba do not seem to be taken into account.[2]

Thus, by relying on a historically weak thesis that expects too much of the spontaneous capability of the masses, as well as on an exaggerated view regarding the conspiratorial possibilities within the military in Communist regimes, some people misconstrue the lessons of Eastern Europe to recommend policies or make statements in the hope of seeing the events in those countries duplicated in Cuba. Unfortunately, in Cuba the possibility to meet, plan, and organize at the level of the masses is very small. When a heroic political dissident tries to gain that much political ground within the regime, "spontaneous" acts of repudiation by the masses or swift action by state security tend to be enough to dissuade others from joining the protests. In Cuba, small, violent outbreaks and popular protests have taken place in the past several years. But unlike China's Tiananmen Square episode, they have been rapidly quelled. Castro seems to understand that patience is a popular uprising's worst enemy, and he intends to project the image that resolve to save his revolution is not something he lacks.[3]

THE MAN AND THE SYSTEM

This brings us to the political leader. When we speak of a totalitarian system, it is usually Stalinism that we have in mind. Stalin invented it, and Castro refined it and made it politically acceptable to the world. A self-centered and violent personality who uses people as a survivalist uses all the resources of his environment, Castro is a leader of extraordinary political skill. His thirty-four years in power tend to support a tacit principle in politics: Whether in a democratic or totalitarian system, survivability indicates political skill, not fortuity. Very few leaders, after all, can neutralize a U.N. human rights commission investigating his regime for abuses of power, then turn around and begin to systematically eliminate the human rights movement in his country, and still be elected to a U.N. subcommission on human rights.

But nowhere is Castro's political ability shown best than the way he manages the system to retain political control. The frontline defense—which makes the system efficient in preventing discontent from coalescing into an effective opposition force—is not state security, the armed forces, the party, or any of the mass organizations. The first line of defense is a byproduct of the system itself, namely, the individual's need to feign loyalty and adherence to the revolution's policies as a means of survival. All too often, pretending to support the revolution has become necessary in order to continue receiving privileges and deriving benefits that only the system can provide, and to escape punishment that affects not only the individual but one's family as well.

True, simulation poses a problem for Castro in that he cannot identify his enemies. But this limitation is outweighed by the fact that simulation makes it difficult for any meaningful latent opposition to organize, because to a large extent it is not easy for those who oppose the regime to identify each other. It is not only a matter of overcoming fear. The problem is that the system, because it is based on mistrust, renders even courage ineffective.[4] Simulation permeates not only the masses but the security and armed forces as well, making middle- and high-level conspiracies within these two sectors extremely risky. While the system may fail at fostering the attitudes of the "New Socialist Man," insofar as fear prevails, the system does what Castro wants it to do, especially at this time: It fosters conformity among the masses and acquiescence to revolutionary behavior.

Yet, as effective as the system's frontline defenses are, lately they have been pierced in ways that would have previously been unimaginable, thrusting the regime into a crisis. Human rights groups have emerged; the Catholic Church has at times taken stronger stands; there are indications of increased subversive activities; and some people are venting their frustration at official authority, as evidenced by the increasing number of murdered police and Interior Ministry members. For the first time since the late 1960s, the regime has acknowledged the existence of enemies within the revolution and the party. There are even some indications that people are overcoming their fear: for instance, they are being more critically outspoken in public.

The forces that have precipitated this recent crisis involve political "dissonance"—that is, events of such magnitude that, by opposing the established beliefs and political ideology, have brought into question the regime's credibility and forced party militants and revolutionaries to reexamine their loyalty. The causes of political dissonance were not the collapse of socialism and its resulting social and economic decline, but rather Gorbachev's *perestroika*, *glasnost*, and his new political thinking—in other words, Soviet reforms. Gorbachev's reforms not only effectively neutralized Castro's internationalist rhetoric broad; far more important, they also created uncertainty and doubt among believers at home, and among doubters, the justification to oppose the regime and to question (some more openly than others) its course.[5] As a result, a significant phenomenon appears to have taken place in recent years: the evolution of a large segment of the population from being dissatisfied to becoming a latent—yet still atomized—opposition, which makes the current crisis potentially even more threatening.

At the same time, past and present circumstances indicate that the repressive features of the system become most effective when it feels most threatened. At that point, Castro activates an array of measures intended to inhibit or repress dissenting behavior and to encourage conformity and passivity with only the necessary minimum of physical confrontation that circumstances would allow. Some degree of public criticism has been allowed, to vent political pressure and to identify potential enemies. Nonetheless, other manifestations of discontent signal a partial loss of credibility by the regime, in its ability to instill fear and to garner traditional revolutionary support.

Castro is taking adequate action to confront the crisis. Feeling that his own survival may be at stake, he has implemented a series of measures to strengthen the regime's frontline defense. The objective is to prevent any latent opposition from coalescing into an active force. Among the techniques being used at present are the following:

- Reporting the message through the media that the regime is determined to crush any opposition to the revolution.

- Keeping in check high-level officers in the armed forces and the Ministry of Interior through a widened network of counter-intelligence mechanisms, including the activation of a central control that monitors their location twenty-four hours a day.

- Lowering the age of people who can travel abroad in an effort to encourage good behavior, and allowing almost anyone who travels to the United States to return with consumer goods as a means to reduce discontent at home.

- Enhancing a climate of mistrust by erasing the distinction between acts of delinquency and counter-revolutionary behavior, and linking the code words "counter-revolutionary activity" to former revolutionaries who have gone over to the opposition.

- Neutralizing dissidents in their early stages through imprisonment or physical confrontation by workers and neighborhood brigades.

These types of control mechanisms have allowed Castro to travel abroad and play host to the Pan-American Games with relative assurance that nothing will happen at home. His success in controlling events similar to those that resulted in mass uprisings in Eastern Europe—people seeking refuge in foreign embassies, and continuing to hold mass political rallies at the same time that he dictates more austerity measures—should not be overlooked.

MANAGING EXTERNAL EVENTS

Such apparent efficacy in keeping the dissatisfied masses atomized is not entirely the result of the system's mechanisms. Somehow, external events have a way of protecting the regime. By exploiting some of these events to his advantage, Castro manages to neutralize potentially increasing discontent. He accomplishes this in part by recreating and reshaping reality in a very clever manner. Traditionally, life in Cuban society has been conditioned by distorted reality, the product of censorship and disinformation. But now the strategy calls for lifting censorship of events in Eastern Europe and the former Soviet Union. The purpose is to show the Cuban people that unemployment, chaos, civil strife, and hunger are the results of free-market reforms, of governments abandoning socialism and one-party rule.[6]

Through the use of the media and in his speeches, Castro presents a powerful argument: Despite all their problems, both the regime and socialism are still the better alternative. He warns Cubans about being seduced by siren calls from abroad (i.e., the United States). Then he points to Nicaragua and Panama and tells Cubans that the people of those countries are no better off now than they were in the past because U.S. promises to reconstruct those countries have fallen short. Cuban media also constantly relate to the population the number of people who die of hunger in Latin America every day, contrasting these reports with conditions on the island, and promise that, despite the decline in food availability, people will not be allowed to starve. Such propaganda may be highly effective because some aspects of these arguments coincide with real conditions, and it is difficult to refute them from abroad.

Another way that the regime reshapes reality is by presenting new scapegoats and reviving old ones in order to redirect blame and thereby avoid responsibility for the current "special period." Thus, the regime has not mentioned that ideological decisions and the failure of the policies of the 1960s—which led to economic dependence on the Soviet Union—were especially responsible for Cuba's inability to seek alternative trade partners and internal economic diversification. Instead, it constantly blames the U.S. embargo and the collapse of Soviet relations for the shortages that make life so unpleasant for Cubans.

THE IMPACT OF STATEMENTS AND ACTIONS FROM ABROAD

Soviet reforms and the ensuing discontent brought about by the decline in social and economic living conditions have created a state of political turmoil unprecedented in revolutionary Cuba. In almost any modern society, such a state of affairs normally creates strong desires for political change. Cuba appears to be no exception. Nonetheless, statements and actions generated abroad are inadvertently strengthening the regime's stability. These statements and actions bolster the government because they neutralize and extinguish the existing turmoil among the dissatisfied masses while providing a sensible justification for loyalists and supporters to continue to defend the regime.

An assessment of the impact of these statements and actions is based on in-depth personal interviews conducted during the last two years with people who have left the island during that span of time as well as with others who have gone back—people from all walks of life, including party militants. In analyzing the possible effects of these elements on the Cuban population, I have relied on traditional theories of social behavior with regard to the way basic needs and desires condition the interpretation of events, which in turn can lead to the formation of specific images; the role of political communication among enemy groups; and the unintended and often contradictory effects that statements and policies sometimes have on their targets.

Predictions about Castro's certain fall from power, and those well-intentioned measures emerging from U.S. political circles and exile leaders aimed at eliminating Communism and promoting Cuba's prompt social, economic, and political recovery after Castro's fall, have one serious drawback: They convey implicit messages that the Cuban population constantly interprets within a context of its most basic needs—survival, safety, esteem—and its cherished desires—liberation from oppression by the dissatisfied masses or the successful defense of the status quo by loyalists and backers of the regime.

A political interpretation of these statements and actions by a large segment of the population is almost inevitable for one compelling reason. These highly politicized statements and actions become relevant to the lives of Cubans because, given the uncertainty that prevails on the island, they either threaten or promise fulfillment of the people's most basic needs. Such relevance owes a great deal to the fact that, in terms of the political debate, those statements and actions originate in "enemy" territory, that is, the United States. This means that the behavior of both the dissatisfied masses and of supporters toward the regime is likely to be affected by the manner in which they interpret Cuba-related events; that is, individuals will decide whether to sacrifice, delay, or seek fulfillment of their needs and desires in accordance with how they interpret the events.

What then do Cubans hear from abroad? They hear that Castro's downfall is imminent; that although Washington says it will not invade Cuba, the U.S. government emits subtle signals that it might; that a U.S. policy aimed at worsening economic conditions in order to accelerate Castro's demise is being formulated; that Cuban exiles support an American invasion or are pushing to have the U.S. president allow them to invade. Other rumors are that plans by several exile organizations are being drawn regarding the reconstruction of a post-Castro Cuba, including a new constitution; that discussions take place abroad regarding how collective property should be privatized and how property should be returned to its "rightful" owners; and that proposals are made for immigrants from all over the world to be allowed to enter the island to improve the quality of the labor force.

Others say that the future Cuban leadership should be constituted in exile in the form of a provisional government, which those on the island will join after Castro is removed from power; that exile groups are seeking to control the opposition inside the island, and that the criteria for Cuban leadership chosen by the external opposition is that of exile seniority; and that acts of repudiation also take place in the streets of Miami.

If it is hinted to the masses, over and over again, that the solution to their problems will come from abroad and in a short period of time, that the future of Cubans is being decided abroad, and as a consequence there will be hardly any role for those inside the island, can the masses be expected to take to the streets to oust Castro? Are the messages providing them with reasonable motives to risk their lives in the process? Or will they instead act sensibly and behave in accordance to the message—that is, wait until the man falls from power by himself or is brought down by external forces?

Both interviews and social theory suggest that it is likely that the dissatisfied masses and any latent opposition within the armed forces will rely on the "law of minimum effort" because they are receiving the message of "gain without pain," the ultimate in slick advertising. The above beliefs have a misleading effect because they misinform the masses and the armed forces about the true course of events, which is uncertain and unknown. Further, these messages foster passivity among the masses and the Cuban military, thereby relieving them of their civic duty to decide the future of their nation because they are being conditioned to assume that someone else will do it for them, whether a mysterious force or the U.S. Marines. The paradox in these cases is that, invariably, all who identified with these predictions and actions strongly believe and advocate that the Cuban problem should have a Cuban solution, that is, that change in Cuba depends on, and should be the responsibility of the Cuban people inside the island.

From Castro's standpoint, these statements and the messages they convey facilitate two important objectives. They render latent opposition to the regime ineffective by fostering political passivity, and solidify his support by rallying his people behind him.

In effect, these messages are likely to promote political inertia among the masses and entrenchment among Castro's base of support. Nearly all of the sixty-two persons interviewed related that the prevailing attitude among many people within Cuba nowadays is one of hope and waiting for the inevitable to happen. This attitude is precisely what Castro needs, because hoping and waiting are manifestations of passive behavior.[7] Two former Ministry of Interior officers pointed out that even disgruntled personnel from the ministry who had been replaced in their jobs following Minister Abrantes' purge and who are highly trained in subversive activities are not likely to move against the regime because they expect that eventually, something will happen.

Castro's supporters, however, may dislike the current living conditions because they are also beginning to be affected by them. Nevertheless, within the context of their basic needs and desires, the above beliefs would likely be perceived as threats to those needs rather than as a solution to their problems. To them, an external solution implies a threat to their jobs, their homes, and in many instances their lives, because it denotes political persecution and revanchism. For these people, the slogan "socialism or death" acquires a different meaning than it has for the dissatisfied masses. Indeed, for them, the alternative to socialism and to support for Castro and his regime may be death.

To procure the allegiance of party militants, the regime is employing a clever tactic. Two independent sources have confirmed that in an effort to get revolutionaries to assume a defensive posture, news stories about the above statements and actions by U.S. political and exile leaders are presented as topics for discussion at party cell meetings. Lately, Castro and media have even extended the presentation of these "external-threat scenarios" to the population at large, something quite without precedent.

Moreover, these messages from abroad appear to have created a negative image of the external opposition, promoting fairly uniform views on the part of the masses and supporters of the regime alike. In some ways (though certainly not in others), Cubans relish the idea of transforming the island into a small-scale version of the United States. Cubans would enjoy the increased availability of consumer goods as well as certain aspects of the American lifestyle, such as social and political freedom, entrepreneurial rights, and access to technology. Nevertheless, those interviewed indicate that these messages have contributed to an image that Cubans on the island have of their counterparts in exile. Cubans, it seems, want the best that the United States has to offer but without the "Miamian," and many tend to believe that one does not come without the other. The image of the "Miamian" is that of someone with a neocolonialist mentality—someone who believes that long years spent opposing the regime from abroad and that professional and political experience gained in the United States give him the qualifications and the right to guide Cuba's political, economic, and social development in the future.

In Cuba, the "Miamian" would confront a nationalistic attitude that has been conditioned by years of government propaganda. While they may be technologically inferior, Cubans would say they are too proud to accept an exile elite telling them what to do. Similar social tension is taking place today in the former East Germany regarding West Germans, a phenomenon that is retarding social integration in the newly unified country.

In conclusion, antagonistic attitudes by U.S. political and exile leaders toward the Cuban regime have generated belligerent statements and actions. These statements and actions are understandable from an ethical standpoint. Many feel a sense of personal indignation at the injustices committed by the regime, as well as a sense of frustration over a man who continues to defy both his enemies and historical events. The prevalence of these feelings among U.S. political circles seems to be a major reason that the traditional approach—creating the necessary adverse conditions, thereby providing an external push to bring down the regime—continues to be considered valid.

Nonetheless, these statements and actions have inadvertently helped to create a mind-boggling situation. An external opposition made up of U.S. political and exile leaders is pushing hard to bring down the wall of Castroism. The opposition, however, has failed to notice that the wall, which is indeed falling, is leaning in its direction. Thus, by pushing instead of pulling, the opposition abroad is actually propping up the regime. It bolsters the regime because its attitudes and behavior generate events that foster political passivity among the dissatisfied masses and entrenchment among Castro's supporters. In essence, the external opposition is suffocating the effects of the crisis brought about by the Soviet reforms by creating an artificial sense of hope that the nightmare will disappear on its own, while providing supporters of the regime with the necessary reasons to defend what they think is their only alternative.

NOTES

1. Lenin understood this point well, even to the point of contradicting Marx. The irony is that anti-Marxists are now seeking to prove Lenin wrong by relying on a Marxist assumption regarding the spontaneity of the masses.

2. It is not only the case that the training and education of Communist armed forces strongly emphasized the concept of civilian rule. Ideologically, the armed forces were educated and warned about the evil of "bonapartism" (military intervention in the political arena). Moreover, a distinctive feature of the Cuban armed forces, as well as of the Ministry of Interior, is that all of the high-level military officers are men who have been emotionally close to the Castro brothers since the early years of the revolution. In other Communist regimes, there used to be a much wider affective gap between the civilian and top military leaderships. To some extent, the familiarity that exists between Cuban generals and the Castro brothers works in the latter's favor, since the military have to overcome the emotional bond in order to commit treason.

3. Descriptions of several recent mass protests in Cuba obtained from personal interviews indicate that people do not hesitate to manifest their displeasure against the regime when state security personnel are not present or when the latter are easily outnumbered. When swift action is taken by an imposing presence of state security, however, resistance quickly wanes. Moreover, although it remains to be seen whether the Cuban armed forces will attack the populace, Castro is using tactics similar to the Chinese in that he has brought detachments from the Eastern Army to be used as shock troops in the capital. Some of those interviewed who have relatives in the armed forces believe that their relatives would not want to participate in attacks against the population, although they may find themselves in a situation in which it would be difficult not to do so without risking their own lives. Other interviewees have stated that the government has inculcated the idea that revanchism

will take place by the internal and external opposition should the revolution die, thereby fostering a defensive attitude against the enemy.

4. Even those who have assumed an overt posture of resistance to the government, such as the human rights and political dissident groups, operate under the assumption that they have been infiltrated by the regime. Moreover, if people have overcome fear to a certain degree, it has been largely because the government has allowed and instigated public criticism both as a means to vent discontent that could otherwise build political pressure and as a tactic to identify potential enemies. Several who participated in the Calling to the Fourth Party Congress, the party call to militants to rid themselves of their masks, stated that some party members lost their jobs when they made their criticism against the regime in public meetings. Nevertheless, widespread fear continues to be the rule of the day. A recent orchestra director who deserted in Spain noted, "There is a great fear in Cuba due to the lack of trust that prevails even among family members, who do not dare to share among themselves their rebellious attitude against the regime" (Marlene Urbay, "Directora de orquesta recientemente exiliada busca reeditar en Miami lo que hizo en Cuba," *Diario las Americas*, January 12, 1992).

5. Both the political leadership and recent defectors acknowledge that the Soviet reforms dramatically weakened revolutionary fervor. Some recent Cuban defectors have related an internal crisis that many of their countrymen have undergone as they struggled to reconcile their desire to continue supporting the revolution and the reality confronting them with the crumbling of socialism in Eastern Europe and the Soviet Union.

6. See "Castro Engages in Crisis Management," *Cuba Situation Report* (a USIA-Radio Marti publication), No. 3, Vol. 5, December 1989, pp. 100–102.

7. Two former MININT officials described the degree of passivity that exists on the island by pointing out that many disgruntled MININT personnel who are highly trained in counter espionage and subversive activities and were replaced in their jobs following the Abrantes purge are not likely to act against the regime. They add that such an attitude is the product of a sense of expectation that "somehow, something will happen."

5

The Cuban Armed Forces and Transition

Phyllis Greene Walker

The momentous changes that have swept the socialist world since the late 1980s have had a dramatic impact on the Cuban people as well as on the nation's armed forces. Buffeted by the loss of critical economic and political support provided by the Soviet Union and its Eastern European allies, Cuba has been plunged into its gravest economic crisis since the early 1960s. At the same time, its increasing political isolation—it has one of the world's last Marxist-Leninist governments—has enormously complicated its prospects for the near future. As a result of these changes in the global environment, the situation of the Cuban military institution is now, perhaps more than at any other time in the history of the Revolution, in a state of flux. It has been hard hit by the loss of foreign military assistance and training once provided by the Warsaw Pact nations and has witnessed the effective elimination of its "internationalist mission," as former Third World allies have abandoned Marxism for democracy. In addition, the crisis has led not only to personnel and spending cuts, but also to a reorientation in the armed forces' domestic role that has emphasized the attainment of economic goals as part of their revolutionary mission.

Cuba's Revolutionary Armed Forces (Fuerzas Armadas Revolucionarias, or FAR) has thus far maintained its loyalty to the defense of the Revolution. Nevertheless, it is being obliged to redefine its national role in order to adapt under the new circumstances. In what ways, then, has the FAR been affected by the changing environment? What have been the implications for the role of the military as an institution? And more important, how have these developments affected the military's long-prominent role as a national actor? In addressing these questions, this chapter considers the present situation of Cuba's Ministry of the Revolutionary Armed Forces (Ministerio de las Fuerzas Armadas Revolucionarias, or MINFAR) and the personnel under its command, and focuses on the impact of these recent changes on the institution.

THE CURRENT SITUATION OF MINFAR

The changes affecting the military institution may be examined by considering two broad and somewhat overlapping areas: mission-related changes, which have related directly to the armed forces' assigned functions as a professional military institution; and institutional/administrative changes, which include those pertaining to budgetary and personnel matters as well as to the military's institutional position within the government and in relationship to the Communist Party of Cuba (Partido Comunista de Cuba, or PCC).

Mission-Related Changes

From 1975 through at least 1990, the Cuban armed forces were assigned three professional missions: to provide for the island's territorial defense against external threats; to help maintain domestic security; and (in what has become known as the internationalist mission) to provide military aid, advice, and combat assistance to selected foreign countries or groups. The first two missions, providing for external defense and domestic security, represent institutional responsibilities that by tradition have been reserved for armed forces throughout the world and have been assigned to the FAR since the beginning of the Revolution. The third mission, however, was added only after the commitment of combat troops in Angola in 1975. It has been the one most dramatically affected by the shift in the international environment and consequently, it merits special consideration.

The New "Internationalist" Mission. While the armed forces' internationalist mission may not yet have been wholly eliminated as a part of Cuban military doctrine and foreign policy, it has for all intents and purposes been suspended. This suspension has affected not only military aid and advisory support, which Cuba began providing to foreign insurgencies in the early 1960s, but also the more direct military support that was represented by providing combat personnel to fight on behalf of its Third World allies. In January 1992, shortly after the collapse of the Soviet Union, President Fidel Castro publicly redefined this mission, declaring that henceforth, "internationalism begins at home," and abjuring Cuba's further support for revolutionary movements abroad.[1]

Indeed, the thirty-third anniversary of the insurrection's victory in 1992 marked the first time in fully half the history of the Revolution that Cuba did not have combat troops stationed abroad. This represented the culmination of a trend that had begun several years before with the gradual withdrawal of troops and advisers from a number of Third World nations.

In Angola—where, as late as 1988, Cuba had had as many as 50,000 troops stationed—the last 116 soldiers departed in May 1991, a month earlier than required by the Tripartite Agreement, which had provided for an end to the Angolan civil war and for Namibian independence.[2] In the case of those returning from duty in Angola, the arriving soldiers were greeted with heroes' welcomes, medals, and much fanfare. Other Cuban departures were less publicized, however. In April 1991, some 1,500 military personnel were withdrawn from Congo, an action prompted by the African nation's decision to embrace multiparty democracy and which signaled the end of Cuba's fourteen-year military presence.[3] The end of the Sandinista government in another former close ally, Nicaragua, also brought to an end the Cuban presence in that country, when shortly after President Violeta Chamorro's electoral victory, the final 160 Cuban military advisers were sent home in March 1990.[4] Six months earlier, in September 1989, MINFAR's remaining troops in Ethiopia—which were believed to have then numbered fewer than 3,000, down from a peak of 12,000 in the late 1970s—were withdrawn at the behest of that country's government in a span of only ten days' time.[5]

The timing of these troop withdrawals may be linked with the Soviet decision to limit its role as a sponsor of Third World revolutionary causes, as well as with these nations' own nascent commitments to democratic processes. Yet regardless of what had spurred the withdrawals, the impetus behind Castro's January 1992 announcement of the decision to halt aid to insurgencies appeared to have been solely pragmatic. It reflected the formal abandonment of a two-track foreign policy that Cuba had pursued since at least 1961, when Ernesto "Che" Guevara spearheaded Cuba's revolutionary adventurism in Venezuela. Clearly, the global region most directly affected by Castro's pronouncement was Latin America, where into the 1980s Cuba had frequently sought to gain political and economic support from governments while covertly supporting efforts to undermine them.[6] Granted, this decision was influenced by the shift in the international correlation of forces and the loss of Soviet economic assistance, and begs the question as to whether it came about only because Castro was no longer capable of supporting foreign insurgents. But more important, it may also be explained by Castro's realization that the best hopes for his regime's survival are tied to achieving economic and political reintegration within the region and the world. With this new aim in mind, the armed forces appeared no longer to be a useful tool of foreign policy.

Reorganization of the Security Apparatus. In late 1989, following the courts martial of Generals Arnaldo T. Ochoa Sanchez and Jose Abrantes Fernandez, a major reorganization of the state security apparatus was carried out that brought the previously independent Ministry of Interior (Ministerio de Interior, or MININT) under the direct command of MINFAR, which is headed by General of the Army Raul Castro, Fidel's younger brother. The rationale for the restructuring was presumably prompted by Abrantes' failure, according to the official explanation, in having bungled a drug-trafficking investigation so badly that his mistakes appeared deliberate.[7] Its real objective, however, was to bring the powerful yet wayward MININT under tighter, more centralized control. Following Abrantes' removal, Army Corps General Abelardo Colome Ibarra—the third-ranking officer in the armed forces after the Castros, a Politburo member, vice minister of the Council of State, and widely regarded *raulista*[8]—was appointed the new Minister of Interior.

Under the command of MININT are a number of forces with paramilitary, military, and intelligence-related responsibilities. These include approximately 4,000 Border Guard Troops (Tropas de Guardafronteras); the 10,000-strong National Revolutionary Police (Policia Nacional Revolucionaria, or PNR); and a 2,000-member elite force, the Special Troops, that is organizationally part of the MININT, yet under Fidel Castro's direct command. Another 10,000 to 15,000 personnel are employed under the Department of State Security (Departamento de Seguridad del Estado, or DSE), the principal organization responsible for domestic intelligence, and the General Directorate of Intelligence (Direccion General de Inteligencia, or DGI), the primary foreign intelligence service. The number of personnel assigned to these various bodies fluctuated little during the 1980s. While data are still unavailable to indicate how these organizations have been affected since the onset of the current crisis, the regime's recent increased emphasis on internal security would suggest that at least the DSE has managed to hold its ground.

Prior to Abrantes' brief four-year tenure, MININT had had only two ministers, Ramiro Valdes Menendez and Dr. Sergio del Valle Jiminez, who alternated in the position after MININT's creation in 1961. Both were *comandantes* of the revolution and were honored veterans of the insurrection, but had little association with the FAR, the Rebel Army's institutional successor.[9] After the 1989 reorganization, FAR officers were appointed to head the ministry's key departments and directorates. At lower levels in the organization, however, even though MININT officers also may hold military rank, they have undergone specialized training and are not viewed as members of the regular armed forces.[10] Over the years preceding the reorganization, an intense rivalry developed between MINFAR and MININT, with the latter increasingly seen as a repository for corruption and an undeserving beneficiary of the regime's largess. The problem of corruption and Raul Castro's personal goal of subduing the organization were the key factors that prompted the reorganization in 1989. What remains unclear is whether the reorganization has succeeded in resolving the longstanding institutional rivalry. The ensuring changes in the international environment and Cuban domestic policies suggest that this problem may still not be wholly resolved.

With the continuing deterioration in economic conditions since 1990, a number of efforts have been made to bolster internal security and enhance political control. Most of these have only marginally involved members of the regular military, if at all. In early 1991, the Committees for the Defense of the Revolution (Comites para la Defensa de la Revolucion, or CDRs), under the charge of Division General Sixto Batista Santana, were restructured by reducing the size of the local block committees, presumably to improve their political reliability. Rapid Response Detachments were formed in mid–1991, the first having been created in Havana only weeks before the opening of the Pan-American Games. These units, composed of civilian volunteers who work in conjunction with the local block committees, have been placed under the purview of MININT and are specifically assigned to deal with public expressions of dissent, whether in the form of group demonstrations or, in what are known as "acts of repudiation," coordinated action carried out against "individuals with political and ideological problems."[11] Human rights advocates have most frequently been the target of these "acts of repudiation."

While the incidence of common crime has risen with the deteriorating economic conditions, a broader notion of crime is often used as an excuse for cracking down on dissidents. Havana police, for example, were called upon in 1991 to pay increased attention to identifying and acting against so-called "pre-criminal conduct," an ambiguous preventive measure that can easily be turned against regime opponents.[12] In December of that year a new Unified Vigilance System (SUV) was put into operation in the capital in an effort to coordinate with the local PNR the sundry "vigilance" activities being carried out to fight crime—mainly economic crime—as well as "anti-social" behavior.[13] Only weeks earlier, hundreds of MININT officers were detailed to work with Havana's PNR in the so-called "fight against crime."[14] All in all, dating from the first police raids carried out under "operation Cascabel" in late 1990,[15] the emphasis on these anti-crime organizations—whether to prevent criminal activity or, as is often the case, to suppress dissent—bespeaks the leadership's concern for maintaining internal order as a means to prolong, if not guarantee, regime stability.

The Return of the "Civic Soldier?" In the midst of the new preoccupation with domestic order, the armed forces' role in providing internal security has been redefined. As stated by Fidel Castro in a March 1991 interview: "[O]ne of the Armed Forces missions at this time is to help the economy."[16] This redefinition seems to suggest a return to the model of the "civic soldier,"[17] which was prominent prior to the inception of the Soviet-sponsored military professionalization effort in the early 1970s.

One of the first indications of the military's redefined role was the MIN-FAR command's decision in mid–1990, taken in the wake of the collapsing Communist governments in Eastern Europe, to prepare the armed forces for self-sufficiency. The decision was meant to entail not only the armed forces' employment in agricultural work—primarily to feed the troops and alleviate the drain of resources from the national economy—but also efforts to build, maintain, and recycle spare parts. As discussed in the popular military publication *Verde Olivo*, the plan's objective was for the armed forces to attain self-sufficiency by 1995. Well before 1995, however, there appeared to be few options other than self-sufficiency.[18] By late 1991, planning was already underway for the so-called "Zero Option," a time when there would be no fuel, energy, or other supplies arriving from abroad, obliging a wholly autarkic existence.

MINFAR's Youth Labor Army (Ejercito Juvenil de Trabajo, or EJT), which in 1990 was composed of some 100,000 personnel, has since its creation in 1973 traditionally been the force employed in agricultural work as well as in construction projects. The rationale behind the EJT's creation was to free the more qualified MINFAR troops for professionalization and specialization in military affairs. It is important to note here that since the onset of the economic crisis and the withdrawal of Cuba's forces from Africa, regular military troops, along with EJT personnel, are now once again being used in agriculture. As a result of the economic crisis, the military has been largely obliged to earn its way by virtue of what it produces. In addition, the value of up to 10 percent of various units' harvests—as much as 12 percent in one instance in 1991—is routinely dedicated toward supporting the civilian Territorial Troops Militia (Milicia de Tropas Territoriales, or MTT).[19] The redefinition of MINFAR's "professional" role is rumored to have generated some grumbling and discontent in the armed forces. Only because that redefinition has been necessitated by a common national crisis are military officers not yet thought anxious to become traitors to the Revolution.

Institutional/Administrative Changes

MINFAR has also been witness to a variety of institutional and administrative changes that have been provoked by the economic crisis, which have included, most significantly, personnel cuts and reductions in the military's budget. Furthermore, concomitant with these more recent changes has been the continuation of a gradual shift in the relationship between the FAR and the PCC.

Personnel Cuts. In 1990, the International Institute of Strategic Studies estimated that the size of the regular armed forces, including activated reservists and draftees carrying out their military service, was around 180,500.[20] Since that time the government has demobilized most of the returning Angola veterans, the majority of whom were thought to be reservists, and has cut the Active Military Service (SMA) requirement from three to two years. Information regarding the extent of the demobilization and the proportion of draftees affected by the new service requirement remains difficult to obtain. It is also impossible at this time to determine the number of Cuban youth still being called up for military service. Nevertheless, it is clear, regardless of the lack of precise numbers, that the size of the active-duty regular armed forces, which includes the army, navy, and air force, is being cut. All indicators point to a gradual return to what may be described as the regular armed forces' historic level, which has hovered at around 100,000 members.[21]

The official rationale for reducing the SMA requirement, announced in March 1991, was that the general educational level of Cuban youth had so improved since the introduction of conscription in 1963 that training, which formerly took three years, could be completed in two. A contributing factor was that some posts formerly filled by SMA soldiers were being "professionalized," with responsibilities being turned over to regular military personnel.[22]

According to SMA regulations, all male youths are required to register for military service with their municipal military committee before they reach the age of sixteen. Following induction calls, held twice a year, conscripts complete a basic training program and are assigned to service with the regular armed forces, the EJT, or the MININT. During the early 1980s, an estimated 30,000 youths were being called for military service each year.[23] For those who chose "Order 18," which provides incentives for maintaining an exemplary record, SMA improved a young man's odds of gaining admission to a university, representing a second chance for those who had failed to meet admission standards before being drafted. Prior to the reduction in the service requirement, youths were frequently able to gain an early release from the military based on good behavior or the completion of their internationalist duty. The FAR has since maintained that the early-out option would be continued, pending completion of training.

These cuts do not necessarily imply that, since the end of the Cold War, Cuba has decided to downgrade its defensive capabilities. On the contrary, the doctrine of the War of All the People (Guerra de Todo el Pueblo, or GTP), adopted in 1980, continues as the keystone of Cuban defense planning. Since the early 1980s, defense exercises are regularly conducted that incorporate all segments of the civilian population as well as reservists, retired officers, and members of the 1.3-million-strong MTT. The government and the MINFAR, jointly with the civilian population, also continue to carry out military maneuvers and war games on a regular basis. To facilitate these efforts, the country is still organized in defense zones, coordinated by a National Defense Council, that would be activated in the event of an attack.

In addition, in view of the large numbers of combat veterans who have entered the reserve forces since the withdrawal from Angola, a new Association of Combatants of the Cuban Revolution was organized in western Pinar del Rio province in late 1991. Composed of active-duty troops, reservists, and retirees with combat experience, the Pinar del Rio group was envisioned as the prototype for the provincial-level organizations that would be organized throughout the island during 1992. According to one report, the new association's objectives were "joining together the different gen-

erations of combatants for the unconditional defense of the nation, the revolution, and socialism, as well as promoting patriotic, military, and internationalist education."[24] While the new organization's ostensible aim might
be to keep morale high and the veterans ready for defense, its more practical
purpose might simply be to keep track of them.

   Budget Reductions and the Loss of Soviet Support. According to data
published in September 1990 by the International Institute for Strategic
Studies (IISS), military expenditures fell from a peak of $2.24 billion in 1988
to $1.83 billion in 1989. For the first time in recent memory, Cuban defense
spending had declined both in absolute terms and as a proportion of gross
social product (roughly, the socialist equivalent of gross national product).
Between 1984 and 1987, annual defense expenditures averaged approximately $1.5 billion, ranging from 8 to 13 percent of the government's budget.
The $2.24 billion figure for 1988 capped a trend toward increasing military
expenditures that dated from the mid–1960s. Since then, spending on the
armed forces has declined dramatically, given Cuba's economic situation and
the military's effort to become self-sufficient. The most significant and publicized development that has accompanied the shift in the Cuban military's
economic fortunes has been the virtually total loss of Soviet military assistance. The Soviet military assistance program, initiated in the early 1960s,
encompassed direct financial aid, the provision of military trainers and advisers, and scholarships for the Cuban officers who received advanced professional and technical training at various Soviet and Eastern Bloc military
schools. According to the U.S. Department of State, the Soviet Union had
provided Cuba with a total of some $5 billion in foreign economic assistance
during 1990, of which nearly one-third, $1.5 billion, was earmarked for the
military. During 1991, as the Soviets began to back away from their Cuban
commitments, questions were raised among U.S. analysts as to whether it
had been overvalued. Even at that time, however, there was little doubt
that additional assistance would be a fraction of what it had been, if it were
forthcoming at all.

   Former President Mikhail S. Gorbachev's announcement in September
1991 that the 2,800 Soviet troops making up a "special training brigade"
would be withdrawn was less than welcome in Havana.[25] The brigade, introduced in 1962 in the wake of the Cuban Missile Crisis, was viewed by
the Cubans as symbolizing the Soviet commitment to the island's defense
against the threat of a U.S. invasion. At the time of Gorbachev's announcement, Castro harshly criticized the decision as having been "unilateral," and
angrily alleged that he had not been consulted beforehand. Talks with the
Soviets to negotiate the terms for the brigade's phased withdrawal began in
November 1991, but stalled by December because of Castro's insistence in
linking the brigade's withdrawal with the dismantling of the U.S. Naval Base
at Guantanamo and the departure of the 6,000 U.S. troops stationed there.

The Soviet government, however, was explicit in refusing to accept the legitimacy of such linkage.[26]

The talks continued through early 1992, and by the end of the year, only 750 of the former Soviet brigade members were left on the island. All personnel were scheduled to have departed by mid–1993.[27] Nevertheless, by late 1992 there were also signs that Cuba's military relations with its old Russian ally were beginning to improve somewhat. According to the trade pact signed in Moscow that November, the first major economic accord reached since the demise of the Soviet Union, the Russian military agreed to pay "rent" in exchange for its use of the signals intelligence facility at Lourdes, of which a portion would be in the form of much-needed spare parts for the FAR.[28]

The FAR and the PCC. The "construction" of a party apparatus within the armed forces was initiated in December 1963. Almost continually since then, the role of the party in the FAR has been a source of tension. The strain has contributed to one variant of the cleavages thought to exist within the armed forces[29]—that between the PCC-oriented "political" officers, whose careers have been built almost exclusively around their activities in the FAR's Central Political Directorate, and the more mission-oriented "professional" officers, who have ascribed greater import to the fulfillment of their role as trained specialists in military science. For both "political" and "professional" officers, the maintenance of a proper ideological orientation has been a major factor in determining a successful military career. For this reason, what is surprising is that party-military tensions have persisted in spite of the fact that most commissioned officers are party militants.

By contrast, a much smaller proportion of the troops and non-commissioned officers are party members. Political officers are assigned to all units in order to improve the troops' political preparation, support development of the politically correct spirit of "moral combativeness," and, incidentally, serve as conduits for intelligence regarding the soldiers' behavior and attitudes. The Union of Young Communists (Union de Juventud Comunista, or UJC) is organized within each branch of service and, as in the civilian world, serves as the stepping stone to full-fledged party membership. Yet, despite the glowing reports that regularly appeared in *Verde Olivo*,[30] party fervor among the troops was thought to be on the decline, especially after the execution of the popular and decorated General Ochoa in 1989. Given the challenge that the FAR as a whole has represented for party militants, it thus becomes easier to understand why the military institution's influence within the PCC has gradually declined over the past twenty-odd years.

As indicated in Table 5.1, only twenty-five, or 12.5 percent, of the 200 party militants elected for membership on the Central Committee at the Fourth Congress of the PCC in October 1991 were men with military rank. Six of these twenty-five officers were affiliated with MININT. By contrast,

Table 5.1
Officers' Representation on the PCC Central Committee, 1981–91

	Individuals Listed with Military Rank*	Size of Central Committee**	Percentage with Military Rank
1981	62	225	27.6 percent
1987	45	223	20.2 percent
1991	25	200	12.5 percent

*Included are officers holding rank in either the MINFAR or the MININT.

**The figures listed for Central Committee size in 1981 and 1987 include those individuals designated as "alternates." In 1991, the position of alternate was eliminated, and the size of the Central Committee was expanded slightly.

Sources: Central Intelligence Agency, National Foreign Assessment Center, *Directory of Officials of the Republic of Cuba: Reference Aid*, Report No. CR 81–11988, Washington, D.C.: National Foreign Assessment Center, June 1981, pp. 3–9; the Central Intelligence Agency, Director of Intelligence, *Directory of Officials of the Republic of Cuba: A Reference Aid*, Report No. LDA 87–12438, Washington, D.C.: Directorate of Intelligence, June 1987, pp. 3–7; and the Foreign Broadcast Information Service, "List of Central Committee Members Reported," *Daily Report: Latin America*, November 13, 1991, pp. 1–4.

20.2 percent of the Central Committee members (including alternates) elected at the Third Party Congress in February 1986 were individuals holding military rank. After the Second Party Congress, which was convened in December 1981, 27.6 percent of the Central Committee members were officers. The 12.5 percent level following the Fourth Congress indicates a general decline in which the military's proportional representation on the Central Committee has been reduced by more than half over a ten-year period.

By contrast, the military's representation on the PCC's Political Bureau (Politburo) suggests that the institution still retains considerable influence at the apex of the leadership structure. Upon the 1991 decision to expand the Politburo, two new military officers—Division Generals Julio Casas Regueiro and Leopoldo Cintra Frías—were elected, with six of the twenty-five-member body being men with military rank. In absolute terms, this represents one officer more than was represented on the old Politburo.[31] Excluding Fidel and Raul Castro, the two remaining officers on the Politburo are Army Corps General Abelardo Colome Ibarra, the head of MININT, and Division General Ulises Rosales del Toro, the FAR's chief of general staff. Yet, despite the prominence of officers at this level in the party hierarchy, two considerations need be kept in mind. Only three Politburo members—Rosales del Toro, Casas Regueiro, and Cintra Frias—could be said to speak exclusively for the interests of the regular armed forces. And more important, with the possible exception of Rosales del Toro, who was 49 years of age at the time of his election, none of the officers represents the "new" generation of leadership within the ranks; all are veterans of the guerrilla campaign in the Sierra Maestra. Thus, even though officers do appear to have maintained influence at the top of the party's power structure, the question remains as to how closely they are in touch with the interests of the military institution.

THE ARMED FORCES AND TRANSITION

As indicated by the changes discussed above, the armed forces as an institution are clearly in a state of transition, as reflected in the efforts to redefine the military's role as a national actor. This role is being redefined in terms of the military's missions as well as in terms of the resources, political and economic, that are required to support those missions and maintain institutional autonomy. But the consideration of transition also raises the question of the armed forces' possible role with respect to political change, which is believed by many to be imminent in Cuba. Indeed, the popular questions of the day are whether, if economic conditions continue to worsen, the FAR will intervene against Castro and whether, in the event of a popular uprising, it would move against the Cuban people. Although anticipating how the military would behave in either situation is nigh impossible, since any action would be determined by an unforeseen combination of variables and events, one can discuss in more general terms what its disposition might be.

A widely held view is that the armed forces, being "of the people," would be on the side "of the people" in any political crisis. But Cuban society is not monolithic. However difficult the situation in Cuba today, it must be recognized that, as noted by one recent account, there is still a "substantial, if immeasurable, core of support" among the population for Castro and the Revolution.[32] Neither is the military a monolithic institution, and similar divisions should be expected within it, to be found from the level of the non-commissioned personnel to that of the officer corps. While discontent in the civilian and military worlds may be on the rise, this is not a uniform sentiment within either sector. The difficulty is in discerning between those who are still "true believers" and those, believed to be a majority, who only "go along to get along," given the high cost of dissent. Conceivably, an open challenge to the regime by groups in the military or in the population would reveal this cleavage and could produce conditions that would lead to civil war, as Cubans sided with either the opposition or the government.

It would be an error, then, to assume the FAR would behave as a monolithic institution should political conditions deteriorate. Various currents are present within it just as might be found in any complex bureaucratic organization, and these currents represent varying tendencies for action or inaction. Younger "professional" officers, for example, might be thought more inclined to support a revolt against Castro than the older "political" officers, if only because the latter have made their careers in the existing system and the former, in watching its decline and their own diminished role, might feel that they have little to lose. Similarly, non-commissioned personnel, presumably having closer ties to "the people," might be inclined not to comply with their superiors' orders to open fire on citizens participating in a popular demonstration. No doubt the FAR command's greatest wish is that these eventualities, which would test the unity of the institution, not come to pass. Although there may be displeasure with the current leadership, the military does not appear anxious to act as an initiator of regime change. To judge by the Soviet experience in the transition from Communism, the armed forces would do better to maintain a peripheral, rather than proactive, role. Thus might the integrity of the military as a national institution be preserved.

CONCLUSIONS

The FAR may be distinguished as one of the most stable institutions created by the Revolution. Changes in the international and domestic environments, however, have obliged the military to adapt to the new circumstances. The FAR's missions are being redefined and its resources cut back to the extent that, if current trends continue, the institution will soon become only a shadow of the professional combat-ready force that it was a decade ago. Owing to the economic crisis and the changed global environment, the maintenance of a large standing army can no longer be politically justified. The institution's domestic political significance, as reflected by the declining proportion of officers elected to the PCC's Central Committee, is also being reduced. Although the MINFAR command scored a coup in bringing MININT under its charge, the FAR's regular troops, assigned to agricultural labor, have lost standing in relation to the forces under MININT, who have been given increased responsibility for internal security and, presumably, the resources to support their efforts. The effect of this disparity may be to maintain, if not aggravate, the longstanding rivalry between military men and state security personnel.[33] All in all, these changes suggest that the FAR has experienced a diminution in its role as a national actor.

The Cuban leadership does not appear to be managing the redefinition in the military's role with the political skill that might be expected of it. In large part, this is because the government now lacks sufficient resources to reward continuing loyalty. Some perquisites, such as expense-paid vacations at the island's tourist hotels, are still available, but many are evaporating.

Rewards are important in order to counter-balance the weak appeal that the armed forces' new role represents for military professionals. Although the armed forces reportedly are receiving a share of the government's revenue from tourism—helping to compensate for the loss of Soviet aid—economic conditions still preclude the possibility of increasing either spending or personnel.

Indeed, given the state of the economy, the only rewards available are political ones, but the leadership appears to be chary even with these. It chose not to reward the military at the Fourth PCC Congress, for example, by expanding the number of officers elected to the Central Committee. Such an action would have enhanced the institution's sense of having a stake in the present system. Instead, the government, by relegating regular troops to field work, has created a situation that would aggravate potential political tensions. To judge by its behavior, the Cuban leadership seems to believe either that the political loyalty of the armed forces is a given or that the threat posed by possible disloyalty is insignificant.

What, then, might the armed forces' role in a political transition be? The fundamental issue revolves around the military's perception of its national role. To be more precise, does it perceive itself to be a supporter of the regime or of the state? This distinction is not idle. Its significance has been explored by Robert Fishman in analyzing the differences among the transitions from authoritarianism to democracy in Southern Europe. Clearly, the distinction between the regime and the state is important in identifying the sources of political change and in understanding the varying outcomes effected by such change.[34]

The fusion of regime and state in Cuba complicates the evaluation of the military's role in a political transition, but it does not make such an analysis wholly impossible. To the extent that the military recognizes itself as an institution of the state, and not as a creature of the regime, the possibility that it will play a constructive national role is enhanced, as exemplified by the Soviet armed forces' behavior after the 1991 coup attempt, when they did not attempt to block the popular current for reform. At the same time, the resistance to political change demonstrated by the Cuban regime makes the military's choice more difficult and increases the likelihood that any change will take the form of rupture rather than reform. Given this official resistance, the best that can be hoped for is that the armed forces, in executing their redefined missions, will manage to gain a degree of autonomy, thus bolstering the military's awareness of its role as a state institution. The worst, on the other hand, is that continuing pressures will lead to increased factionalism. The open development of schisms within the armed forces could pave the way for a move against the regime, which would also compromise the future integrity of the institution. While in the aftermath of such an action the prospects of a peaceful transition might not completely disappear, they would surely become more elusive.

NOTES

1. Pascal Fletcher, "Cuba to Halt Military Aid to Revolutions," *Washington Times*, January 14, 1992.

2. For details regarding the terms for Cuba's phased withdrawal from Angola, see Bureau of Public Affairs, United States Department of State, "Tripartite Agreement on Southwestern Africa: Blueprint for Peace and Namibian Independence," *Southwestern Africa: Regional Brief*, December 1988. The parties to the Tripartite Agreement, which was signed in December 1988, included Angola, Cuba, and South Africa, with the United States serving as an "honest broker."

3. "Cuba to Withdraw Troops from Congo," *Washington Times*, April 2, 1991.

4. Lauren Weiner, "Cuba Sends Advisers in Nicaragua Home," *Washington Times*, April 2, 1990.

5. "Cubans Leaving Ethiopia," *Washington Times*, September 9, 1989; "When Fidel Comes Marching Home," *Washington Times*, September 26, 1989.

6. The most prominent Latin American insurgent movements that benefited from Cuba's support in the 1980s were those active in Colombia, El Salvador, and Guatemala. Cuban support also was a critical factor in the 1979 victory of the Sandinista National Liberation Front (Frente Sandinista de Liberacion Nacional, or FSLN) in Nicaragua.

7. Abrantes was sentenced to 20 years' imprisonment for negligence and misuse of government funds. He died of a heart attack in prison in January 1991.

8. The term *raulista* denotes someone who is politically closely aligned with Raul Castro.

9. Valdes' closest connection to the military was his organization of Rebel Army Intelligence during the insurrection. Del Valle, a physician who also is commissioned as a division general, served as one of MINFAR's vice ministers during the mid–1960s.

10. Distinguishing between MININT and MINFAR personnel can be confusing, because MININT has used the same system of ranks as MINFAR, yet their insignia are different. Armed forces personnel tend not to consider their MININT cohorts to be "real" military officers. Nevertheless, assignment to MININT has been one of the options available to Cuban youths who are conscripted for active military service (Servicio Militar Activo, or SMA).

11. " 'Thought Militia' Readied in Havana," *Washington Times*, July 12, 1991.

12. Office of Research, Radio Marti Program, *Cuban Media Summary*, October 1991, p. 7.

13. According to the Cuban Attorney General's office, the main economic crimes are the theft of food, money, and consumer goods and the forging of documents. See "Government Concerned about Economic Crimes," Foreign Broadcast Information Service, *Daily Report—Latin America* [hereafter FBIS], November 19, 1991.

14. "Minint Joins Police to Fight Crime in Havana," FBIS, November 25, 1991. Just under one-fifth of the country's population resides in the vicinity of Havana; comparatively few references, however, are made in the Cuba media (as represented in selections that are published in the FBIS *Daily Report*) regarding the status of the "fight against crime" in other major regions of the country. The "fight," nevertheless, is being carried out as part of a national campaign.

15. Ibid.

16. "Castro Views Agricultural, Military Issues," FBIS, March 21, 1991.

17. The model of the "civic soldier" is associated with the work of Jorge I. Dominguez. As employed in this chapter, the concept is narrowed to include only regular military personnel who are engaged in nominally non-defense tasks related to agriculture or economic production. In contrast to Dominguez's usage, this consideration does not address the notion of "fused" roles, as might be represented by officers assigned to administrative duties in civilian agencies. For Dominguez's discussion of the concept, see his *Cuba: Order and Revolution* (Cambridge, Mass.: Harvard University Press, 1978), pp. 341–44.

18. With respect to resources available to the armed forces, the military's rumored majority stake in La Gaviota, a joint venture with holdings in the tourism industry, should be noted. Given the loss of Soviet foreign aid, it is not unreasonable that the government has decided to support the military budget with earnings from the lucrative tourism sector of the economy.

19. "Soldiers' Productivity in Agriculture Praised," FBIS, June 3, 1991.

20. International Institute of Strategic Studies, *The Military Balance: 1990–1991* (London: IISS, 1990), p. 192.

21. Jorge I. Dominguez has pointed out that the "size of the truly professional forces . . . apparently remained constant" from the late 1960s through at least 1975 (for which the latest data were available at the time of his book's publication). See Dominguez, *Cuba*, p. 348.

22. "Reduction in Active Military Service Explained," FBIS, July 5, 1991.

23. An expanded discussion of the military service requirement is presented in Phyllis Greene Walker, "The Cuban Military Service System: Organization, Obligations, and Pressures," in *Cuban Communism*, Irving Louis Horowitz, ed. (New Brunswick, N.J.: Transaction Publishers, 1989), pp. 599–623.

24. "Raul Castro Attends Veterans Group Meeting," FBIS, December 18, 1991.

25. Miguel Barberena, "La situacion internacional es diferente'," *Excelsior* [Mexico], September 12, 1991.

26. "Troop Withdrawal Talks with Soviets to Begin," FBIS, November 15, 1991.

27. "Soviet Armed Forces," *CUBAINFO Newsletter*, December 4, 1992, p. 7. Contrary to the initial accounts published when negotiations began, the newsletter indicated that the Soviet infantry brigade was made up of only 1,500 troops.

28. Douglas Farah, "Improving Trade with Russia Bolsters Cuba's Economic Outlook," *Washington Post*, December 26, 1992. As of mid–1992, some 2,000 Russians and Ukrainians were reported to be working at the Lourdes facility. See Michael G. Wilson, "Hastening Castro's Downfall," *Heritage Foundation Backgrounder*, July 2, 1992.

29. See Dominguez, *Cuba*, p. 369, for a brief discussion of cleavages within the military. Another cleavage, not mentioned by Dominguez, that has become noteworthy of late is that between junior and senior officers.

30. The publication of *Verde Olivo* was suspended in 1991 because of the economic crisis.

31. At that time, five of the twenty-four Politburo members (including alternates) held military rank. Based on information published in the Central Intelligence Agency, Director of Intelligence, *Directory of Officials of the Republic of Cuba: A*

Reference Aid, Report No. LDA 89–10094 (Washington, D.C.: Directorate of Intelligence, June 1989), p. 3.

32. "Castro's People Try to Absorb 'Terrible Blows,' " *Washington Post*, January 11, 1993.

33. To better appreciate this, it is important to recognize that MININT was placed not under the command of the FAR General Staff, which has primary responsibility for the military forces, but under MINFAR command—that is, under the direct authority of Raul Castro. Just as interservice rivalries are known to develop among military forces, it seems reasonable that rivalries may exist between the FAR General Staff and its new MININT counterpart, particularly as each competes for a share of the already diminished MINFAR budget.

34. Robert M. Fishman, "Rethinking State and Regime: Southern Europe's Transition to Democracy," *World Politics*, Vol. 42, April 1990, p. 432.

6

Informal Politics and the Crisis of Cuban Socialism

Damian J. Fernandez

This chapter will focus on informal accommodation and resistance at the grass-roots level in Cuba from the mid–1980s to 1993. The period is characterized by political and economic crisis, underscored by the fall of Communism in the Soviet Union and throughout Eastern Europe and the breakup of the Soviet Union. In Cuba this period initially coincided with the Campaign to Rectify Errors and Negative Tendencies, which Fidel Castro launched in 1986. In 1990 stricter austerity measures and tighter political control followed under the banner of the Special Period in Times of Peace. After presenting a general discussion of political informality on the island, and its importance to understanding politics in general and Cuban politics in particular, I will analyze how everyday forms of accommodation or resistance are evidenced in two ways: in the behavior of youth and in the rise of "economic crimes" after the mid–1980s. The impact of such informal expressions of social politics on state-society relations in the short and medium term will also be examined.

Although political informality has always coexisted with political formality in Cuban socialism, everyday forms of accommodation and resistance have thrived after the mid–1980s. The politics of informality at the grass-roots level have had, and will continue to have, an important, if contradictory, impact on governability and legitimacy, placing in question the practical and ideological roots of Cuban socialism. As a consequence, informal political behavior will contribute to the shaping of the island's future.

FORMALITY AND INFORMALITY: A REVIEW OF THE LITERATURE

The scholarship on Cuban politics has portrayed a political system far more formal, institutionalized, and monolithic than the situation any visitor encounters on the island. Regardless of the author's ideological perspective and his or her evaluation of the political regime, studies of Cuba have focused on the mechanisms of formal power, whether elite leadership or institutions. Two general perspectives on the articulation of political power—top-down and bottom-up—are evident in the literature. The top-down perspective highlights the authoritarian, coercive aspects of the system. The level of analysis is the executive elite and the institutions that exert hegemonic social control. Within this perspective, popular participation is formalistic (i.e., mobilization). Participation is coerced into mass organizations and the single party. Mass organizations serve as transmission belts for state-directed initiatives rather than for the representation of interests from below. The political system is centralized, rigid; the state is strong, all-encompassing. Civil society is nonexistent. Individuals and groups are subject to the political will of the state—meaning here, the legal arrangement in which authority (leaders and bureaucracy) is vested. This view of the political system resembles that of the totalitarian model, in which the private and the public are meshed and coercion is enforced through the police, popular mobilization, and the militarization of society.[1]

The bottom-up view of Cuban politics focuses on the participation of the masses in the political system—in the *poder popular* ("people's power" assemblies), unions, militia, rallies, voluntary work, elections, mass organizations, and in the struggle that brought about the social revolution. The point of departure is that popular will and national consensus are the backbone of the radical agenda of equality and nationalism. The political system, therefore, has been created by and for the Cuban people. As such, it is legitimate and responsive to the needs of the population, in spite of structural limitations imposed by exogenous political-economic factors (e.g., underdevelopment, the U.S. embargo, low world prices for sugar, and recently, the collapse of the Soviet Union). From this vantage point, the Cuban state reflects, represents, and responds to the society.[2]

Neither perspective considers the informal transactions in private and public spheres. Both neglect the fact that Cubans break the official code of conduct on a daily basis, in spite of the state's attempt to coerce, and at times accommodate, society. In the first perspective, there is little, if any, space for individual and collective resistance. What space is available falls largely in the private sphere (in the family and small circles of friends) and in public forms of dissimulation. Individuals are portrayed as subjects, not agents, of politics. According to this view, manifestations of autonomous participation are not worthy of study because, all in all, they are ineffective in altering the pillars of the system. In contrast, the second perspective, which is more favorable to the regime, disregards or, at best, discounts the meaning of activities outside the state-sanctioned institutions, and perceives Cubans as agents, not subjects, of the state. The alternative view that I propose here depicts Cubans as both agents and subjects of politics.

Few scholars have taken into account the informal ways of accommodating and resisting the state's authority in Cuba. For our purposes, informality is defined as practices that run counter to the state's prescribed code of conduct. Informal behavior escapes the "territoriality" of the state, though it may exist even within the components of the state; that is, one can find informality inside state bureaucracies.

That Cubanists have neglected such a pervasive phenomenon is surprising on several counts, although understandable given the methodological and epistemological difficulties involved. Informality is not alien to the political culture. As elsewhere in Latin America and throughout the world, it has a long tradition. The less powerful have always found mundane ways of getting some of what they want, or feel entitled to, without overt defiance of the status quo, by circumventing the officially prescribed patterns of behavior. In colonial times, the axiom "obdezco pero no cumplo" ("I obey but I don't comply") came to symbolize a political culture in which legal formalities were often bypassed. In the Cuban case, the roots of everyday resistance to and accommodation of state authority predate 1959. Consider, for instance, the ways that slaves devised a syncretic hagiography that guaranteed the survival of their religion. When the masters saw their slaves celebrating a patron saint's feast, little did they know that their servants were paying homage to Chango, Oshun, or Obatala.

THE POLITICAL CULTURE OF INFORMALITY IN CUBA

Since 1959, the popular culture of accommodation and resistance has remained alive, below the monolithic facade of stability, order, and acquiescence. The state's inability to get Cubans to behave in ways officially prescribed testifies to this. From labor absenteeism to low productivity, to the persistence of gay life and religious devotion, Cubans have both accommodated and resisted the system by breaking official codes of conduct.

Informality has permeated the Cuban experience during the Castro era. The initial years of the revolution were characterized by improvisation, personalism, and experimentation, reflected in myriad ways, from leadership style (charismatic authority) to economic strategy (mass mobilization for production). Scholars have addressed the non-institutional dimensions of this period, emphasizing the role of Fidel Castro and his modus operandi.[3] After the 1970s, during the so-called phase of institutionalization of the revolution, the informal seems to have "disappeared" (with the exception of some sketchy discussions of the lider maximo's (maximum leader's) continued personal involvement in policy making in spite of institutions and technocracy).

Furthermore, informality is a feature of the Cuban "character." Nowhere is it epitomized as in the Cuban choteo. As Gustavo Perez-Firmat has noted, choteo (mockery) is a way of both accommodating and resisting the "forms" imposed, whether political or social.[4] One could even argue that the most daunting task the Cuban state has undertaken has been the attempt to "formalize a culture of informality." *Ser informal* ("to be informal") is within the spectrum of characteristics with which Cubans still describe themselves and others.

To understand politics in Cuba in a broad sense, and at the social base, one must tackle *lo informal* (the informal) head on. Otherwise, one would miss what happens on a daily basis and what constitutes "the political" at a personal level for most Cubans. Studying informal participation highlights several important aspects of Cuban politics: the limits of the state and state capabilities; latent pluralism in the polity; the dynamics of change and conflict in state-society relations and the repercussions for legitimacy and governability; and the average Cuban's view of politics as projected on behavior and discourse.

Cuban politics is a combination of formality and informality from the top elite to the grassroots of society. The personalism of charismatic authority has coexisted with a bureaucratic, centralized, and militarized regime. The tension between the two is at the heart of formality and informality at the highest level of Cuban politics. Such contradictions are typical of revolutionary societies. In the early 1960s, the issue was expressed in a series of divergent options for constructing the new state. For instance, the army could be structured as a regular professional force (as Raul Castro proposed) or as a popular militia of the armed people (as Guevara preferred). In this struggle of (and for) forms, the traditional models and those who supported them eventually won.

One of the purposes of the Rectification Campaign that Castro launched in 1986 was to eliminate the formalism that permeated Cuban socialism. The result was precisely the opposite of what was intended: An even greater formality prevailed at the institutional level. Institutions that were supposed to represent the people (e.g., the Committees for the Defense of the Revolution) fell under the direction of the military. Militarization (one of the tenants of Castroism in theory and practice, according to Andres Suarez) is anathema to informality. Yet, informality has thrived in Cuba, fueled by the adverse political and economic situation since the late 1980s. Popular vernacular, such as *inventarsela, sociolismo, resolver, buscarsela, pinche, mayimbe,* and *socio* express the ingenious ways that Cubans find to cope with the situation of shortages and adversity. [Editor's note: Precise translations of these terms are difficult. *Inventarsela, resolver,* and *buscarsela* refer to creative ways of making ends meet, usually outside the system. *Sociolismo* is a play on words and suggests a kind of crony system within socialism. *Pinche* and *mayimbe* are your high-level contacts. Your *socio* is your buddy.]

CONCEPTUAL CONSIDERATIONS

Recent scholarship has addressed everyday forms of accommodation and resistance in a variety of historical and geographic contexts. James C. Scott is one of the pioneers of this level of analysis, focusing on "weapons of the weak," the "moral economy" of peasants, and the arts of domination and resistance.[5] From a different angle, Joel Migdal has addressed the challenges that society poses to Third World states.[6] Both scholars question traditional notions of power relationships in which the strong always get their way. In Latin American studies, in addition to historical analysis on forms of accommodation and resistance, the informal economy has recently received considerable attention. Moreover, since the mid–1980s, the dramatic changes in the former Communist world have pushed Sovietologists in search of civil society in Communist and post-Communist systems. In many instances, the roots of civil society are to be found in informality and in the tradition of popular resistance.

The methodological point of departure for this analysis stems from the works of Scott and Migdal. Scott defines everyday forms of resistance as a constant struggle between those relatively powerful and powerless groups "short of collective outright defiance." The forms of this struggle are "foot dragging, dissimulation, false compliance, pilfering, feigned ignorance, slander, arson, sabotage and so forth." These activities "multiplied many thousandfold . . . may in the end make an utter shambles of the policies dreamed up by 'would be superiors.'"[7] Although Scott focuses on peasants, everyday forms of resistance are available to all social groups. While he tends to limit his discussion to resistance, techniques of accommodation are also important to a full understanding of how politics works for the common people.

Everyday forms of resistance and accommodation are part of the attempt to deal with the state's impositions as well as with its rewards. Situations of scarcity may be particularly conducive to these modes of behavior. The concept of moral economy sheds light on this. Scott argues that "any claim on peasants by elites could have no justice when it infringed on subsistence needs."[8] The perception of injustice springs from the infringement on the right to subsistence. This right is more than merely economic, justifying resistance, "illegality," and even rebellion. Resistance and accommodation are not always diametrically opposed. Individuals may accommodate political reality through strategies that the state considers illegal, dissident, and/or counter-revolutionary. In short, accommodation is a tool of survival, not an explicit acceptance of the prevailing mode of governing. As such, it can take place outside state-sanctioned arenas.

Migdal argues that, by and large, Third World states have been weak in that they have not been able to make people "in even the most remote villages behave as state leaders want." The reason for this is that state capabilities "to *penetrate* society, *regulate* social relationships, *extract* resources, and *appropriate* or use resources in determined ways" (emphasis in original) have been low. "The failure is also a result of unrealistic standards for state behavior," he states. Ultimately, this weakness "affects the very coherence and character of the states themselves."[9] We will show that this is true in the case of Cuba.

   Migdal differentiates between strong states (those with high capabilities
to complete the tasks of penetration, regulation, extraction, and appropri-
ation) and weak states (those with low capabilities). Strength and weakness
run in a continuum. Between the poles, Migdal, in passing, portrays Cuba
as a strong state. He is not alone in depicting the Cuban regime as powerful;
that is the consensus that emerges from the literature. In comparison with
other states, Cuba has high capabilities to perform the tasks of statehood.
Nevertheless, such a portrait misses significant nuances and limitations. The
Cuban state has not performed all of its tasks with equal efficiency and
effectiveness. It has not been successful (or strong) in getting all Cubans to
act in ways deemed appropriate. It has, for example, had greater success in
extracting and appropriating resources (in spite of the common practice by
workers of diverting materials from the workplace) than in regulating social
relations. For instance, the family code that prescribes that men share in
household chores has had limited impact.
   Where should one look to find informal politics? The answer is broad:
everywhere. The issue is not where to look but what to look for, because
informality coexists and operates even within formal bureaucratic institutions
and processes. Among the areas where one is likely to locate everyday
expressions of informal accommodation and resistance are: discourse (public
versus private transcripts); humor; the black market (or the second economy);
dissimulation and formalism; informal neighborhood networks; fashion
(clothes, hairstyle); arts (music, films, painting, literature); sabotage; religion;
labor (low productivity, absenteeism); the daily life of women; and
"criminality."
   For the scholar these arenas for research present conceptual and methodological challenges ranging from definition (e.g., is pilfering resistance?)
to operationalization (i.e., how do you measure formalism?).

FORMALISM AND INFORMALISM IN STATE-SOCIETY
RELATIONS

   The Cuban government, recognizing the insidious effects of "formalism,"
has on several occasions called for the "deformalization" of political participation. (See, for instance, Fidel Castro's series of speeches of the mid–1980s
collected under the title *Por el Camino Correcto*.[10]) But when deformalization threatens to shake the system, the government resorts to control once
again. The rallying cry of the Fifth Congress of the Union de Jovenes Co-
munistas (UJC) in 1987 was *sin formalismos*, while in the Sixth Congress
(1992) the banner was *resistencia*. The *llamamiento* (the call) to the Fourth
Congress of the Communist Party of Cuba (1990) was another example of
the attempt to reinvigorate the political process by eschewing formulaic
participation and opening the space for contending perspectives from the

grass roots. The debate came to naught, as the Party Congress foreclosed the possibility of reforms from above.

The reasons behind deformalization are twofold. First, the state and its leaders recognize that Cuban society is far more pluralistic than the official discourse has indicated. In response, the state has attempted at times a partial and slow accommodation of some of these interests (e.g., religion). Second, in trying to address the society, the state has been trying, particularly since the 1980s, to modify its own structures by broadening and invigorating them with the purpose of attracting and keeping followers, substantiating Migdal's thesis that the character of the state itself changes as a result of its failure to achieve its goals.

The Cuban state's reaction to formalism is contradictory. While it decries the pernicious effects of formalism, it continues to embrace democratic centralism, to resort to a brand of nationalism that is superficially homogeneous, and to combat expressions of informality in a variety of ways (including repression). The campaigns to eradicate economic crimes, homosexuality, and other forms of "deviance" are cases in point. What the state is trying to do is inject revolutionary fervor, commitment, and vivacity into top-down institutions and processes that are out of sync with the social base. That is, the state wants to undo formalism with forms both old and new. Changes in the constitution, the Rectification (Campaign to "Rectify Errors and Negative Tendencies," launched in 1986), the Communist Party and the National Assembly of Peoples Power reflect a desire to reformulate the existing system, while sustaining traditional methods and institutions. Mass mobilization persists as a mechanism for dealing with dissent. Rapid Response Brigades, the recently created Ministry of Interior-directed groups that harass human rights activists, are the latest syncretic concoction of formality and informality. (The government claims that the brigades are spontaneous organizations.) Above all, the state opposes informality because it is a sphere outside its reach. A state that has defined itself in a maximalist way perceives informal space as an ideological and practical challenge.

During the Special Period, an informal economy (of which the black market is just one manifestation) has flourished on the island. As the state becomes less able to produce and deliver goods, citizens resort to mechanisms outside of state control to find the necessary goods to live. The black market, or the informal economy, is considered illegal in Cuba, for it runs against the basis of the centrally commanded socialist economy. (However, pockets of capitalism are officially sanctioned in some areas of the economy, principally tourism.) Participating in the black market is not only an economic crime, but a political one as well. From the official standpoint, economic crimes are counter-revolutionary, for they undermine stability. Officials perceive economic "criminality" as a security threat to the state.

According to Cuban sources, economic crimes have soared: "In 1991, those most frequently committed were embezzlement, misappropriation, failure to protect the property of government economic units, receiving stolen goods, and illegal economic activity."[11] The severity of the situation is evidenced by the state's response. In late December 1991, during the session of the National Assembly, the debate over "the struggle against crime and counter-revolutionary conduct" took center stage. Officials complained of a widespread "social indiscipline" that had to be combated. To eradicate social indiscipline, the government has established a series of para-policing structures: the Consejos Populares (a decentralized bureaucracy to deal with municipal issues in the Special Period, including crime); the National Commission of Social Prevention and Attention; the Unified Vigilance and Protection System; and the *patrullas campesinas* (peasant patrols), to protect crops in the countryside.[12] In addition, the court system has been overhauled to expedite processing cases, and the police have orchestrated several campaigns to arrest participants in the informal economy.

Two cases of economic crimes offer insights into the socio-political as well as economic implications of these activities in a socialist context. The first case is that of Manuel Suarez Rodriguez (also known as Manolito Cafe). Manolito Cafe was accused of heading a group that sold coffee, "living high on the hog due to enrichment from that activity," and organizing several gambling operations.[13]

The second case is that of "Golden Feathers." Nineteen workers of a transportation enterprise that distributed chicken were indicted for stealing and selling for private profit the feathered cargo. Many of the birds never reached the state's slaughterhouse because they were slaughtered in other houses. While Manolito Cafe had a long rap sheet, those arrested in Golden Feathers did not have "previous criminal records, have a good cultural level, and even seemed like exemplary workers."[14]

These two cases are but the tip of the iceberg. Not only are "exemplary workers" involved, but government officials participate in such activities as well. Perhaps most revealing is that these sorts of activities require coordination and collaboration among groups of people. As a result, informal networks among co-workers, family members, and friends emerge. In a society that has been characterized by some as "atomized," the solidarity and cooperation embodied in these associations are important politically. They indicate the possibility of collective organizing, on the one hand, and the decrease in governability, on the other. (By the same token, they also demonstrate a greater willingness of citizens to participate in actions that can result in sanctions.)

A police major in Havana attributed the rise in economic crime to "lack of control in institutions," among other factors.[15] The case of Golden Feathers, according to the government's report, uncovered "constant violations of the law" throughout the slaughterhouse. If the law is being continually violated, what is the capability of the government to penetrate the society and regulate social relations?

The economic crisis alone (particularly, the shortages of food and basic items) does not explain the spread of illegal economic activities. The state's concern with economic "crimes" also stems from the fear that the "seeds of capitalism" are budding at the grass-roots. The regime's tourism policy has fueled behavior that is unpalatable to the official code of conduct. Since the mid–1980s, the regime has courted foreign investors (principally from Spain and Latin America) to invest in hotels and tourist-related enterprises in Cuba. As a result, islands of capitalism and luxury open only to foreigners coexist side by side with the shortage economy in which most Cuban nationals have to survive. The tourist sector operates in a dollar economy. Dollars can buy any item at the *diplotiendas* (or tourist stores, accessible only to the foreigner or to the Cuban who has a *socio*, a buddy, who works there).

The tourism policy has generated resentment—called tourism apartheid—and created economic and social linkages with sectors of the population who find ways to plug into these capitalist outlets to get dollars, consumer goods, access to food or entertainment, and even a way out of the island (if a foreigner marries a Cuban national, making possible an exit visa). A dynamic economy surrounds the hotels and the *diplotiendas*, from prostitution to contraband in Cuban tobacco. A new version of the Cuban picaresque figure has emerged: the *jineteros* and *jineteras*. The *jineteras* are prostitutes that escort foreigners in exchange for dollars or consumer goods; the *jinetero* is closer to an intermediary or hustler.

The evidence points, on the one hand, to a society that has been less malleable than the state expected, and, on the other, to a state less able to shape the behavior of the people that it had assumed. The case of the youth-state relations is revealing.[16]

Since the 1960s, but particularly since the early and mid–1980s, the behavior of youth has been a matter of serious concern for the state. The number of juvenile criminals, unemployed, and dropouts has increased (about 200,000 in total by the mid–1980s). The rise in crime among the youth is an indicator of "desocialization," if not resistance. Whether crime is a political act or not is an important question. In the case of Cuba, and given the extent of the mechanisms of control, the government literally "creates crime." The definition of "political" is maximalist; the political is all. In this sense, mundane activities such as participating in the black market or wearing an earring are also "criminal." Such a definition cannot help but create dissidents and deviants. Young people have continued to behave in an "extravagant" manner. Long hair, rock and roll music and punk fashion have alarmed many conservative elements in the regime. The official response has been an attempt to create a new style to accommodate the young, since political institutions were out of touch with that sector. The Fifth UJC Congress in 1987 reflected this change through its slogan *Sin Formalismos* ("Without Formalism"). Formalism had stifled the energy of the youth and was eroding the legitimacy of the political system. The campaign's purpose, much in accord with the process of Rectification, was to reignite the revolutionary ardor of the young by providing openness and flexibility. Cuban socialism was to be rejuvenated, making it attractive to the youth.

Even the "exemplary youth" seemed to be infected by attitudes that challenged the official code of conduct. Indiscipline and lack of control were not exclusive to those at the margins. In a 1979 speech to the National Assembly, Fidel Castro criticized the *blandengueria* (weakness or softness) of the youth in general and within the UJC in specific. He chastised UJC militants who skipped classes and UJC base organizations that were careless in matters of principles. In short, some Communist youth did not act like Communists. Castro called for greater militancy and combativeness against all the *chapuceria* (sloppiness) of the organization and the society at large.

The informal expressions of youth politics represent a struggle that has been expressed in semiotic and material ways: in discourse, fashion, hairstyles, music, and alternative lifestyles. Consumerism and capitalist influence within the youth have flourished, a development that is of great concern due to expressions of individuality through material consumption. The adoption of styles from the capitalist countries flew in the face of the values of collectivism and egalitarianism espoused by the state. In short, these "extravagant" youth were challenging the state's authority and control. Their affront had costs attached: expulsion from schools, harassment, incarceration.

The young both accommodate and resist governmental demands. For instance, on the one hand they might be willing to defend the Socialist Homeland, but "at the moment of participating in [agricultural] work evade it." Official socialization is undermined by the private sphere: "The school must direct its work to soften and counteract the negative aspects inculcated by the nuclear family."[17] Dissimulation is a widespread form of resistance and accommodation, as is dodging the military draft, a common pastime for the young. Medical excuses and personal contacts are used to evade the obligatory service in the Revolutionary Armed Forces. The family and the *socio* network, once again, play vital roles in shielding their own from the state's demands.

The government and the youth have both accommodated and resisted one another. The state has adopted a variety of mechanisms to respond to the demands of the young, from "modernizing" the UJC's style of work and its language to establishing discos; from rejuvenating the Central Committee in the Third and Fourth PCC Congresses to allowing, at some moments, greater room for self-expression—for example, the Fifth UJC Congress, and *el llamamiento* (the call for an open discussion and criticism) for the Fourth PCC Congress. The state has also resisted the youth organizations through a language and world view that, by and large, close the door to, or at best co-opt, the "agenda" of young Cubans. This suggests, on the one hand, the limits of the state and, on the other, the latent pluralism of Cuban society.

THE POLITICS OF INFORMALITY: CONTINUITY AND CHANGE

Informality has implications for the nature of the state, for continuity and change in the political system, and for governability and legitimacy. In terms of continuity, everyday forms of accommodation and resistance are functional. Informal politics gives the regime a flexibility that governmental forms do not have. When people find ways of coping with their daily problems and create solutions outside the state-sanctioned mechanisms, they are not *directly* challenging the state. Citizens' needs are being met. The second economy is probably the premier example of the functionalism of informality. This is not to say that there are no costs either for the state or the individual associated with informality. For the latter, these costs range from possible sanctions to the added inconvenience, energy, and resources needed to carry out transactions in the informal sector. For the state, the costs are mixed in relation to governability and legitimacy.

The Cuban state, which defines itself through a maximalist political, economic, and social agenda, must respond to social informality in some way. Otherwise policy choice, implementation, and efficiency will be haphazard at best. Can the state expect a specific result if along the way the process is diverted by a host of informal actors, such as absenteeism and the diversion of resources? With time, the regime's own survival will be at stake. The rift between state and society undermines the former's ability to accomplish the tasks that it has set for itself. The process is not as dramatic as a tidal wave; it is closer to a slow erosion of governmental authority and legitimacy.

At the same time that this erosion is taking place, informality also, paradoxically, enhances governability and legitimacy. The functionality of informality allows the status quo to persist without major shake-ups. The facade of governmental power is sustained, while behind it the daily practices of citizens indicate the state's inability to make them conform to officially prescribed patterns. As for legitimacy, the fact that informality is shrouded in secrecy and that the powerless "act" or conform in public points to an acceptance of the legal authority. Continual repetition of the "performance" may subtly but substantially contribute to the acceptance of the political order as well. Informality can serve as a shock absorber for overt defiance of the powers that be, thereby securing governability and legitimacy at a macrolevel.

In the short term, the government responds to informality through rewards for appropriate behavior, selective repression (for it cannot combat every case of resistance and accommodation that is deemed undesirable), ideological campaigns, and also by turning a blind eye. However, in the long run, the state must redefine itself by reforming institutions and tailoring its ideology to mesh with the social base. For society, breaking the code of conduct is a small way of questioning the legitimacy, pushing the limits, challenging the governability of the regime, and occasionally contributing to reforms as the state responds to the social base.

The state also resists and accommodates the society. Through mechanisms of coercion, ideology, and mobilization, it attempts to plow ahead, even when the social terrain is arid and rocky. When confronted with social challenges to its policies and ideology, the Cuban state has opted for reforms, renewal, and co-optation. (Witness the changes in the working style of the UJC, with its recent emphasis on entertainment to attract youth and the relative opening to dissent in the mid–1980s.)

Informal politics is not only an individual phenomenon. Informal groups and networks operate on the island outside the state's hegemony. Popular religions, particularly of the Afro-Cuban and *espiritista* variety, are examples of non-institutional and non-state associations that have experienced a renaissance since the 1980s. Informal neighborhood networks composed of *socios* operate as lines of information, instruments to facilitate bureaucratic processes, and mechanisms of exchange and solidarity, coexisting with the Committees for the Defense of the Revolution but outside the CDR's purview. These networks are based on friendship and reciprocity.[18]

Forms of behavior deemed deviant by the state, such as wearing certain fashion styles, are far from eradicated. Evasion of military and voluntary service is also common. The consequences of all these individual and collective actions are many and remain to be explored. What is clear, though, is that the informal groups, whether *freekis* (disaffected youth who dropped out of society, much like hippies), gays, or religious practitioners, are seeds of civil society and change, posing serious challenges to the one-party socialist state.

Informal political participation brings into question the tenets of Cuban socialism. If charismatic authority, the vanguard party, and popular mobilization have been the structures with which to pursue the agenda of social equality, the practice of going outside the official channels to seek an alternative mechanism for resource allocation undermines the practical foundation of the political system.[19] The charisma of the *lider maximo* (maximum leader) no longer seems to command the ability to deliver the nation from crisis. Party politics and popular mobilization appear discredited and useless in accomplishing this task. Furthermore, as individuals and informal networks pursue their interests to survive, the ideological base of the socialist welfare state is shaken. Social equality does not reign supreme in the underground economy, although all Cubans share the hard times of economic shortages and political malaise.

NOTES

1. See, for instance, Juan del Aguila, *Cuba: Dilemmas of a Revolution* (Boulder, Colo.: Westview Press, 1984). For a discussion of models of Communist politics, see Rhoda P. Rabkin, *Cuban Socialism: A Case Study of Marxist Theory in Practice* (Ph.D. dissertation, Harvard University, 1982). For an analysis of participation in Communist societies, see Donald E. Schulz and Jan S. Adams, *Political Participation in Communist Systems* (New York: Pergamon Press, 1981).

2. A recent example of this school is Linda Fuller's *Work and Democracy in Socialist Cuba* (Philadelphia: Temple University Press, 1992).

3. See, for instance, Edward Gonzalez's *Cuba Under Castro: The Limits of Charisma* (Boston: Houghton Mifflin, 1974).

4. Gustavo Perez-Firmat, "Choteo as Informant," paper presented at the colloquium "Lo Informal: Everyday Accommodation and Resistance in Cuba," Florida International University, April 10, 1992.

5. See, for instance, James C. Scott's *Weapons of the Weak: Everyday Forms of Peasant Resistance* (New Haven: Yale University Press, 1985); *The Moral Economy of the Peasant: Rebellion and Subsistence in Southeast Asia* (New Haven: Yale University Press, 1976); and *Domination and the Arts of Resistance: Hidden Transcripts* (New Haven: Yale University Press, 1990).

6. See Joel S. Migdal's *Strong Societies and Weak States: State-Society Relations and State Capabilities in the Third World* (Princeton: Princeton University Press, 1988).

7. Scott, *Weapons of the Weak*, p. 29.

8. Scott, *The Moral Economy of the Peasant*, p. 33.

9. Migdal, *Strong Societies*, pp. 4–5.

10. Fidel Castro, *Por el Camino Correcto* (La Habana: Editora Politica, 1987).

11. *Foreign Broadcast Information Service: Latin America (FBIS)*, March 12, 1992.

12. *Granma*, December 27, 1991.

13. FBIS, February 28, 1992.

14. FBIS, February 24, 1992.

15. Ibid.

16. The following discussion is based on my chapter on "The Politics of Youth," in Enrique Baloyra and James Morris, eds., *Contradiction and Change in Cuba* (Albuquerque: University of New Mexico Press, 1993).

17. Miguel Barreiro Valcarcel, "Importancia de la Participacion de los Estudiantes en el Trabajo Productivo Agricola," *Juventude Rebelde*, January-March 1987, p. 51.

18. For a discussion of informal networks in a different context, see Larissa Lomnitz and Ana Melnick's *Chile's Middle Class: A Struggle for Survival in the Face of Neoliberalism* (Boulder, Colo.: Lynne Rienner Publishers, 1991).

19. Marifeli Perez Stable, "Charismatic Authority, Vanguard Party Politics, and Popular Mobilizations: Revolution and Socialism in Cuba," *Cuban Studies*, Vol. 22, 1992, pp. 3–26.

7

Political Changes and Social Attitudes in Cuba During the Special Period: Implications

J. Richard Planas

Fidel Castro has stated numerous times in recent years that Cuba will not make political concessions during the "Special Period in Times of Peace." Nevertheless, the regime has officially approved reforms that carry a calculated risk while allowing other changes to take place unofficially. Some changes are already being experienced by the population; others appear to be in the planning stages. There are still others of which, although they have been approved, there is little awareness of their implications because the regime has failed to publicize them adequately. Many of these changes are less perceptible to the eye of the casual observer and have gone unreported in the Western media, yet they encompass significant social and political implications that heighten understanding of Cuba today.

Among the most significant changes are the recent constitutional modifications approved in July 1992. While these modifications do not necessarily translate into immediate visible political changes, they represent a potential basis for evolutionary or revolutionary transformations in the island, depending on the level of political activism and infighting they inspire. Anomic social attitudes, such as acquiescence, resignation, and escapism, present to some degree throughout the revolutionary period, have now become more prominent and are retarding both the peace and the level of change in Cuba.

These changes and the anomic attitudes in Cuba today are the result of the need to cope with severe difficulties under Castro's Special Period. The circumstances that led to these changes and to the pronounced development of these social attitudes were heavily influenced by the political and ideological collapse of the socialist bloc and Cuba's subsequent loss of preferential treatment by Moscow following the disintegration of the Soviet Union. As a result, Cuba embarked on the Special Period. This stage of the Cuban Revolution may be seen as the transition process of a nation that was ideologically, politically, and economically interrelated with a system that was different from the present international order. Such a transition involves the regime's overall adaptation to very demanding circumstances and the pursuit of two basic objectives: Cuba's economic survival and its own political re-definition. Whether these changes will last beyond the Special Period—assuming there will be a recovery phase—and affect institutional Castroism remains to be seen.

In this chapter, descriptions of general conditions provided by foreign journalists and academicians who have recently visited the island are com-bined with interviews with Cuban emigres and with information derived from the Cuban media in order to get a wider and more realistic perspective of Cuba today. The objective is to go beyond the visible reality to identify and analyze the implications of that reality. The chapter will deal with sys-temic changes that have come about by decision as much as by default on the part of party officials, although at times it is clear that the regime has been permissive of certain conditions with full awareness of their repercus-sions. Because of their importance in conditioning individual and aggregate behavior, the chapter also focuses on social attitudes toward the regime and analyzes their possible implications.

PRELIMINARY OBSERVATIONS ABOUT SYSTEMIC CHANGES

Official pronouncements do not reveal why the regime is now willing to allow change. It appears to have acquiesced out of sheer political necessity and survival. Weakened by internal divisions at the grass-roots level within the party and by the visible increase in social discontent, the regime is seeking consensus regarding the future course of the Revolution among both its supporters and a large segment of the population that has grown disen-chanted following the collapse of socialism in Europe.

The regime's policies appear to be aimed also at persuading foreign gov-ernments that meaningful reforms are taking place in Cuba. While these reforms might not prove convincing to a U.S. administration, governments with an inclination to extend assistance to Cuba might conclude that Havana has met minimum acceptable political requirements and might find them-selves in a stronger position to disregard U.S. pressure and establish stronger commercial ties with the island.

The prospect of changes taking place in Cuba should not be based on the assumption that the regime is pushing the Cuban people toward reforms, but that—out of political necessity—it has taken a calculated risk: that by making changes but failing to inform the population adequately about their political implications, at the same time that it resists the pressures resulting from them, it will be able to control the situation politically in its favor. Nevertheless, the regime has provided reform-minded people with the con-stitutional tools and the opportunity to forge even more radical social and political reforms. Moreover, by approving the constitutional changes, the regime has placed itself in a more vulnerable international position, one akin to the Soviet Union's at the time of the Helsinki Conference on Security and Cooperation in Europe in which Western governments were able to exact Moscow's commitment to individual civil rights.

SYSTEMIC CHANGES TAKING PLACE DURING THE SPECIAL PERIOD

The regime's political and legal boundaries have narrowed, as indicated by, first, the measure of governmental decentralization that is taking place. Mass organizations have gained a measure of official autonomy insofar as they are no longer regarded as transmission belts of state policy and are described as no longer under the protection of the state. Constitutionally, they have become advocates of the interests of the groups that they represent. There is also talk that these organizations might have to provide for most of their own funding.

The Union of Young Communists is constitutionally no longer under the direction of the Communist Party and is no longer the primary source of party members. Moreover, local governments and enterprises have greater influence in social and economic issues as well as in making political decisions that were previously issued by the central government. New governmental organizations, the Peoples' Councils (*Consejos Populares*), are assuming responsibilities regarding solutions of problems at the workplace that were previously assigned to the party.

Second, while organized dissident activity or violent individual opposition are actively resisted and persecuted, less attention is being paid to other individual manifestations of defiance, such as open criticism of the regime, listening to foreign media, reading forbidden books or watching forbidden movies, prostitution, some illegal economic activity, and absenteeism at party and mass organization meetings.

Black market food production and allocation has grown in scope and now provides from 75 percent to 85 percent of the population's food supply. The scope of black market activities dealing with personal services and production and distribution of consumer goods that the regime does not offer the population has expanded as a result of increased misappropriation of state resources.

Intellectuals have wrested a somewhat greater social, cultural, and political space, as evidenced by greater possibilities of travel, extended stays abroad, and the May 1992 National Union of Cuban Writers and Artists' (UNEAC) document revealing a more critical posture toward the regime.

Youth are being granted a wider cultural space. The regime is paying less attention to ideological diversity or indifference among youth in exchange for political support.

In the constitution, the state's regulatory powers over "religious activities" have been substituted for powers regulating the *state's* "relations with religious institutions."

The regime has also diluted the ideological value of Marxism-Leninism. Ideology is the political backbone of a totalitarian system. Ideology communicates the regime's policies, justifies its actions, promotes its goals, and educates its citizens. Although for the last three decades Cuban political culture has developed within a Castroist framework, symbolically and legally it has identified itself with Marxism-Leninism. Over these years, Marxist-Leninist doctrine has been the primary justifying element of the political system. The media, education, political discourses, and mass organization meetings have all been impregnated with this ideology.

Nevertheless, the worldwide crisis affecting Marxist-Leninist socialism has had a negative impact on Cuban political ideology. The regime now finds Marxism-Leninism less useful because the answers it provided in the past are less credible to the population and thus less valid. Political legitimacy now appears to be based less upon Marxist symbols ("the new man," Communist society, internationalism) and more upon a nationalist rhetoric (resistance, survival of the Revolution, Marti, and independence from "the northern Goliath") and, on a second level, upon the fulfillment of material promises (security, food, health, employment).

Although the regime cannot discard Marxism-Leninism entirely overnight because that might have a negative impact on its political credibility, it has taken steps that in fact contribute to the erosion of Marxism-Leninism. For example, in the constitution, the regime has dropped Marxism-Leninism from its premier position as the official ideology. Marxism-Leninism is no longer considered victorious or elevated as a doctrine. Regarded instead as a political philosophy, the ideas of Marx and Lenin have been placed after the ideas of Jose Marti in the prologue. The Communist Party ideology is no longer based on Marxism-Leninism alone. Now, it is based first on the ideas of Jose Marti and second on those of Marx and Lenin.

The duties of the Union of Communist Youth no longer include those of educating young people in the ideals of Communism. Instead, the organization is responsible for promoting the active participation of youth in the political process and for their civic education.

The regime has eliminated from its constitution one of the most important ideological tenets upon which the philosophical foundation of Marxism is based—the determining influence of a society's relations of production over its superstructures—by eliminating from its constitution the following statement: "The Constitution and laws of the socialist State are the juridical expression of the socialist relations of production."

The irreversible character of socialist property has been eliminated. In redefining socialist property, the concept has been considerably narrowed, even allowing for the possibility of its transfer into the hands of private nationals or entities.

The regime has also extended a prominent role to the family and to patriotic and pedagogical approaches as means of strengthening the moral fiber of society through three constitutional changes. First, it recognizes—for the first time—the family as "society's fundamental cell" and gives it "essential responsibilities and functions in the education and formation of new generations." These functions and responsibilities were previously in the hands of the state. Second, it has eliminated the Marxist theory of scientific materialism from the foundations of its educational and cultural system. Such foundations now include scientific and technological knowledge on education, Marxist and Marti's ideas, and Cuban and universal progressive pedagogical traditions. Third, it has placed "patriotic" education of new generations ahead of Communist formation. The previous duty of society to "educate children and youth in the communist spirit" now becomes the responsibility of the state.

To co-opt alienated youth, the regime has resorted to de-ideologizing its political slogans and allowing youths more room to express themselves.

The Marxist theory of scientific materialism no longer is dominant over religious activities, and the introduction of foreign capitalist ventures has inserted a high level of ideological dissonance with Cuba's political culture that likely will contribute to eroding Castro's political discourse and Marxist ideology.

PRELIMINARY CONCLUSIONS REGARDING SYSTEMIC CHANGES

First, the regime's totalitarian features have loosened, as a result of which Cubans have gained a measure of "illegal freedom," that is, freedom not recognized by civil or constitutional law. From a constitutional standpoint, moreover, other freedoms have been approved.

Second, the constitution has abandoned Marxism-Leninism as a doctrine and has sought to redefine socialism and Communism by taking into account other ideas than those of Marx and Lenin. From an ideological standpoint, the constitution has incorporated a more pluralistic outlook.

Through indoctrination, rewards, and fear of repression, a totalitarian regime seeks to conform external and internal individual behavior to its political program. If, by definition, a totalitarian system is one in which governmental power successfully controls most aspects of social and individual life, on the basis of the previously outlined indicators, the regime's repressive controls over some areas of society have weakened during Cuba's Special Period. Despite the fact that Cuba remains a highly authoritarian society, Cubans have wrested a measure of social, political, and economic space from the government, most of it illegal. The creation of a legally defined civil space may have to await energetic action from the citizenry, because it is doubtful that the regime will willingly allow it.

In the past, freedom to act outside the regime's permissible boundaries was strictly limited. The great majority of the people dared not, or were not willing, to step out of the narrow, officially imposed guidelines for several reasons:

- The regime's psychological and emotional tools operated effectively.
- The regime had been partially successful in fulfilling the population's basic needs.
- Neither the government nor the population regarded economic and social problems as insurmountable. The slogan "no hay salida" (there is no way out) had not yet become part of the political culture.
- The regime had not evoked sufficiently strong foreign criticism to force internal changes. Its political image abroad was generally perceived in Cold War terms as part of one of the two political alliances contending for world supremacy, and as a stubborn, radical actor on Third World issues.
- To some extent, the political discourse (Marxist ideology and Castro's rhetoric) were effective in reassuring cadre and masses that, despite problems, Cuban society was better off and more just than other political systems.

Why are systemic changes taking place now? The conditions arising from the Special Period overloaded an already burdened central government, whose habitual responsibilities have been to keep the system functioning organically. To prevent the system from a complete breakdown, the center has had to divert its attention to more pressing matters, thereby precluding the regime from exercising traditional social controls. Reports from the Western press and Cuban media suggest that the regime is concentrating on four primary concerns:

- Guarding against counter-revolutionary political activity within the party apparatus, the military and state security institutions, and dissident groups.
- Trying to produce as much food as possible for the population by harnessing and allocating very scarce resources (40 percent to 50 percent of the 1989 oil level; 30 percent of 1989 import level; 20 percent to 30 percent of the 1989 agricultural equipment, parts, and other resources), and reassigning the labor force in an effort to keep the economy afloat. The government is also trying to attract private capital and ventures while keeping capitalist values away from the population.
- Maintaining national cohesion, while planning the distribution of power from the center to local areas, as the country becomes more regionalized because of the energy crunch and the crisis in transportation and communications.
- Cultivating a new international and domestic image—the former as a means to secure credit, loans, and investments, and the latter to reassure the populace that changes will come through resistance.

In addition to diverting its attention to more pressing matters, other elements seem to be responsible for allowing a devolution of power to take place on an official and quasi-official basis, as indicated by the constitutional changes and the planned transfer of some powers from the center to governments and mass organizations at the local level. These elements are, first, international pressure and the need to improve the regime's external image. In exchange for possible economic assistance and political acceptance, individual governments, regional groups, and personalities have pressed Castro to make political changes. The second element is the need to build consensus at home, to shore up support within the party, and to create expectations that change will come, thus buying time until economic conditions improve. Finally, the lack of resources is forcing the regime to localize previously held central functions.

Other manifestations of illegally attained freedom have not come about through devolution of power; instead, they have been the result of further erosion of legitimacy due to rising discontent and apathy, ideological confusion, and increased "fending-for-oneself" behavior. These conditions have brought about a breakdown of authority, on the part of both government workers and citizens, resulting in increased illegal activities and behaviors that encounter little or no retribution. Another contributing factor is the considerable decline of fear, which has resulted in bolder acts of political resistance, in part because the availability of material goods and the possibilities of obtaining rewards for compliance with governmental policy have dwindled. As a result, there is less fear of not obtaining them or of losing them when anti-government behavior is manifested.

IMPLICATIONS OF SYSTEMIC CHANGES

A totalitarian system maintains political control through a unified, command approach in which decisions emanate from the top, in which uniformity of policy is highly regarded and sought (democratic centralism), and in which diversity at the local level is not usually recognized, much less stimulated. Hence, a governmental policy of recognizing differences and stimulating solutions at the local level introduces new social and political dynamics that tend to affect the status quo. Recognizing grass-roots voices and allowing the populace to establish priorities—no matter how insignificant the issues— may bring about the formal creation of a political space between the local groups and the center (local autonomy) that previously did not exist—a step toward a civil society.

Giving the grass roots a voice may also contribute to the potential institutionalization of political decentralizing practices that would make their reversal more difficult in the future. If the process is allowed to take root, people may end up obtaining a larger measure of political influence, which can be reversed, but only at a greater risk of triggering people's resistance, and a loss of legitimacy and credibility. Such policy implies a tacit recognition that governmental power can no longer be held in a centralized fashion, a step that exerts a dissipating force on totalitarian rule.

The Special Period has contributed to the extension of the black market and the contraction of socialist economic practices and controls. As a result, Cuba remains a socialist state whose society nevertheless survives through a successful capitalist black market that reallocates resources and produces goods according to its own demand and supply mechanisms. Such a reality is politically and ideologically disruptive of a totalitarian system. The implication of a successful black market within a centrally planned economy is the realization by the populace that non-governmental economic practices are more effective in providing goods and services than the state. In time, this realization tends to erode individual allegiance to the regime and insert doubt about its political claims, thereby weakening ideological indoctrination.

Since mass organizations officially are to enjoy a more autonomous position, the possibility exists for those seeking change to argue their position from a legal standpoint. Constitutionally, the groundwork has been laid for the potential creation of interest groups of workers, women, students, or private farmers.

That youths are exhibiting a more superficial commitment to the Revolution and indoctrination is becoming less credible imply that the commitment of future generations to the process might be more political—that is, in the form of group interest—and less ideological. Young people may cooperate more in expectation of what the state will give them in return for support instead of the traditional altruistic commitment that the revolutionary process demanded. The UJC will have to overhaul the ideological premises of its educational program.

The regime's need to compromise with the intellectual community signifies that intellectuals have become among the most critical and subversive interest groups. It is likely that intellectuals will not be satisfied with the regime's concessions and might soon press for additional changes.

The party's consent to allow religious believers into its organization, and the constitutional modifications that now make it illegal to discriminate on the basis of religious beliefs, amount to a public message that another official ideology—Marxism's traditional philosophical nemesis—has cultural validity and political legitimacy. Moreover, religious institutions have acquired a degree of constitutional autonomy that, if used, can translate into pluralist inroads in education, politics, and culture.

Since ideology has served as the regime's formal uniform, the dynamics of social and political change suggest that as the uniform is allowed to undergo changes, such alterations are likely to spark modifications in the status quo. For example, those seeking systemic change can now point to constitutional revisions as the basis of reform.

Official constitutional changes carry several implications. First, law and ideology have been formally separated. Laws that do not reflect Marxist-Leninist ideology can now be promulgated. This formulation is reflected in the state's abandonment of its position regarding the irreversible character of socialist property and the endorsement of foreign private-property holders. It is now more difficult for the regime to sustain a Marxist dialogue about Cuban socialism. A first step has been made in widening the space between Marxism-Leninism and the state and separating state and party organizations from the party, a process that may further erode the totalitarian nature of the regime and Article Five of the constitution.

Second, to the extent that law and education are no longer required to reflect official ideology, they are likely to be influenced by other bodies of ideas, thus allowing for the possibility of philosophical pluralism to pierce the dogmatic nature of the political discourse. The ideological premises of the educational system will need to be revised lest they give way to contradictions in the classroom.

Finally, recognition of the family signifies that the institution has acquired a degree of constitutional autonomy that may pit family values against the state.

Constitutional acknowledgement of the reversible nature of socialist property and the possibility of its transfer into the hands of private Cuban citizens signify that the legal road is already paved for such transfers, should the economic crisis worsen.

The welcoming of capitalist work methods, the increasing presence of capitalist entrepreneurs in the island, and the tangible results that the Cuban people observe from capitalist ventures are likely to call into question Castro's continued insistence that capitalism is evil and may neutralize the ideological value of his slogan, "Socialism or Death." For example, in the tourist industry, conflicts have arisen over workers' desires to seek employment at capitalist ventures. Some workers also have demanded that their enterprises adopt capitalist methods. Even more significant, discontent over so-called "tourism apartheid" is not only the result of discrimination. Discontent arises primarily due to the perceived striking differences between what capitalism and socialism have to offer and the resulting awakening of unfulfilled material expectations that such perceptions create. A dose of political instability has been generated by the conspicuous presence of material conditions, goods, and services produced by capitalist ventures.

ATTITUDES OF THE POPULATION DURING THE SPECIAL PERIOD

Among the prevailing attitudes are resignation and acquiescence toward the system, as characterized by:

- Street slogans, such as "no cojas lucha" (don't sweat it); "no es facil" (it's not easy); "esto no se cae, pero no hay quien lo tumbe" (the system won't collapse and no one can bring it down either).

- Statements of emigrants reflecting a passive hope similar to that of Cubans on the island: "It has to come down," or "It can't possibly last long." These comments reveal, however, more a feeling of desire than realistic indications of how their wishes might happen.

- Longer lines and waiting periods of up to seven hours, sometimes more, to acquire goods and services, indicating increased toleration.

- Formalism—that is, going through the motions—which prevails in mass organizations, labor, party meetings, and in military drills.

Another prevailing attitude is escapism, as seen in the increased number of desertions, of people abandoning the island by raft, and in the thousands who have applied for visas to the United States in a short period of time. There has also been an increased level of promiscuity, alcoholism, and suicide, and an increase in the popularity of Radio Marti programs that have an escapist orientation.

As living conditions deteriorate, Cubans find ways to adapt to new situations through resourcefulness and adaptability:

- The extension of the black market.
- The use of *diplotiendas*, where diplomats do their shopping.
- Reliance on assistance from relatives living abroad.
- Producing goods, such as soap, deodorant, shoes, and building shelters from discarded materials.
- Riding bicycles amid the crisis in transportation, bathing in the reefs when access to beaches is restricted, or hand-cutting sugar cane and the use of oxen in place of tractors.
- Cynicism by government officials who support the regime and adapt to conditions, as evidenced by their participation in black market operations.
- Accepting "voluntary" tours of duty to the countryside to harvest vegetables.

The atomization of political relations is evidenced in dissimulation, or feigning loyalty and allegiance to the regime for purposes of survival and protection, by which individuals isolate themselves from one another, hindering the coalescence of independent opposition groups. Atomization is also seen in the development of a survivalist attitude, forced by conditions on the island, that diverts attention and effort from political solutions and toward concerns about the day's food ration or other basic needs.

Passive hope among internal opponents of the regime is fueled by statements from and actions by U.S. government circles and the Cuban exile community that create expectations that an external solution to the Cuban problem is possible. Some of these statements and actions are:

• Subtle signals about the possibility of a U.S. invasion.
• Stiffening the embargo to bring down the regime.
• Predictions of high-level U.S. government and Cuban exile leaders about the demise of the regime.
• Pressure by Cuban exile leaders on the U.S. government to invade.
• The existence of political and economic plans to rebuild Cuba.

The entrenchment of supporters of the regime arises from uncertainty about conditions prevailing in the event that Castro falls from power. It is fed in part by statements and actions from U.S. government officials and the Cuban exile community and by the regime's own propaganda regarding the crisis in Eastern Europe and the former Soviet Union.

A perceived external solution by enemies of the regime—seen as revanchist amid the lack of credible guarantees—implies a threat to the jobs, homes, and lives of Castro's past and present supporters and drives them into a siege mentality. And the perceived neocolonialist attitude on the part of the Cuban exile community leads supporters—as well as opponents—to entrenchment.

Bewilderment about the collapse of the socialist bloc, the disintegration of the Soviet Union, and the failure of Marxism-Leninism has resulted in political and ideological disorientation among revolutionaries and sympathizers of the regime. This feeling created uncertainty and doubt among revolutionaries who are now being accused by Castro of wavering in their loyalty. Those who previously expressed misgivings about the regime's policies, and who now utilize events in Europe to justify their opposition, are called traitors by Castro.

Discontent is evidenced in the increased absenteeism, labor indiscipline, and low productivity as a means of passive resistance on the part of workers.

As a result of the Abrantes affair, hundreds of State Security personnel who were removed from the revolutionary process are bitter and disappointed with Castro. Thousands of Armed Forces veterans and officers are likely feeling resentful about the execution of General Arnaldo Ochoa.

There are also signs of increased defiance of authority and greater personal anger, such as the considerable increase of public criticism of conditions along with a rise—although to a lesser extent—in criticism of the regime and of Fidel Castro. Incidents of political graffiti appear to have increased considerably. The fact that government and social repression (imprisonment, street trials, Rapid Response Brigades, job firings, and so on) have increased indicates that people are more willing to step outside those boundaries and are doing so more often.

Anger is easily triggered by incidents of little importance, such as challenging looks, pushing, or critical remarks. It appears that the number of scuffles among citizens and the lack of respect toward policemen is without precedent.

There have also been noticed an increase in organized dissenting behavior and in the anger of revolutionaries, coupled with a prompting disposition to repress counter-revolutionary behavior.

PRELIMINARY CONCLUSION

Fear, the lack of realistic alternatives and solutions, and perceived images from abroad may be responsible for channeling increasing anger and discontent into passivity, entrenchment, and adaptation. Attitudes conducive to adaptation and passivity have gained both in intensity and scope during the Special Period, thereby weakening political activism. However, the level of political activity by those who support the regime has increased. This is indicated by heightened repression and revolutionary commitment on the part of some, although it must be noted that people opposed to the regime participate in revolutionary activities against their will, a trademark of dissimulation.

A low level of political activism (passivity) is being encouraged by perceived signals from abroad and is reinforced by an attitude of resignation compounded by the lack of a realistic alternative. Moreover, resourcefulness, an attitude with revolutionary potential, is being channeled away from political activism by the lack of alternatives.

IMPLICATIONS OF PREVAILING ATTITUDES

Given that discontent and anger are essential elements of violence and political opposition, one of the most intriguing aspects of the current Cuban political scene is that a considerable increase in public dissatisfaction with social conditions has failed to translate into a major threat to the regime. To be sure, the regime has interpreted the present situation as potentially volatile to the extent that it has approved constitutional and political reforms and allowed certain other conditions to prevail, both for reasons of prevention and appeasement.

Dissidents themselves admit that the level of active opposition to the regime—although perhaps at an all-time high—remains ineffective and is well penetrated by state security. Moreover, despite the increase in social anger and acts of defiance of the law, these manifestations are being channeled toward survival and adaptation. Cuban political reality appears even more puzzling in that the above attitudes seem to prevail in the population, including the military and state security, at the same time that the regime has shown signs of weakness by implementing constitutional reforms.

A partial answer for the behavior of the Cuban population lies in the work of naked repression, which has increased during the Special Period, as evidenced by the creation of the Rapid Response Brigades, the arrest and harassment of dissidents, and the increasingly heavy-handed tactics of the police. Perhaps more important, although Cubans are not under a visible state of siege, and political talk still constitutes the most widely used tool of persuasion, there is an invisible yet very real barrier of mistrust that prevails. The fear that arises out of mistrust—a product of dissimulation—has a neutralizing effect on the masses in that it tends to isolate individuals politically from one another.

Dissidents have adduced that political opposition is not more visible and active because people simply do not want violence. Cubans, however, do not lack a tradition of political violence or political activism. Historically and culturally, they have regarded themselves as courageous, and they have never considered themselves as pacifists. Cubans must also be aware that peaceful opposition tactics, such as civil disobedience and general strikes, do not rely on violence, although they entail a measure of personal risk depending on the regime's response. Thus, insofar as acquiescent and passive social attitudes prevail, it is likely that political changes stemming from constitutional reforms will be mostly cosmetic and aimed at solidifying the present political leadership in power. The dynamics of social change, however, suggest that once certain fundamental political aspects of the regime are altered, they are likely to bring about significant changes. There is, for example, the possibility that more meaningful changes—although still within the framework of the present system—can take place in the long run, if citizens' awareness of the implications of their own attitudes and of the hidden political implications of the reform spur a level of political activism and infighting that the regime is not able to contain.

In the final analysis, however, systemic changes, including the type of economic and political reforms desired by the United States, are highly unlikely to take place because of the forces countering such change. At the every least, several conditions must be met before a more radical process of change occurs:

• The circle of passivity and entrenchment must be broken.
• Political repression must be neutralized or overpowered.
• Attitudes of resignation, adaptation, and escapism must be overcome.
• Dissimulation must end.

For the above to happen, there is an important consideration that Cubans must weigh, both individually and collectively: They must perceive that political conditions can ensure an outcome in which their actions and risks are worthwhile. Cubans, including the armed forces and state security, live in a psychological and physical state of political isolation. If, despite this condition, they continue to perceive that their political reality is both threatening and uncertain, or if they perceive that external forces might solve their problems for them, their collective response will not be any different from what it is now. They will continue enduring Spartan conditions, or try to escape (physically from the island, or psychologically), or acquiesce and adapt to their political and social circumstances, sensing that they have less to lose this way than by confronting the regime.

8

The End of the Affair: Moscow and Havana, 1989–1992

Stephen Blank

The collapse of Communism between 1989 and 1991 has isolated Cuba and led to a profound domestic crisis. This chapter will examine recent Soviet-Cuban relations and focus on the Soviet debate on Cuban policy, as well as the debate in both countries over their relationship and over domestic reform.

These debates encompassed all aspects of Soviet-Cuban relations and reflected Moscow's broader internal struggle over power and policy. Although the Soviet crisis and Moscow's relations with Havana intersected in August-September 1991, the roots of the crisis in Soviet-Cuban relations lay in partly hidden differences that first emerged in the 1980s. These allies increasingly diverged over domestic political and economic reform, as well as over policy in the Third World. Each had an increasingly unilateral orientation on these issues that led to ever-sharper ideological discord. Indeed, an unintended byproduct of *glasnost* was that it enabled Soviet satellites and allies, like Cuba, which were encouraged to reform, to speak more openly against Soviet policies. That openness introduced a growing dissonance into the once harmonious Red orchestra.

PRELUDE TO CRISIS: MOSCOW AND HAVANA IN THE MID–1980s

It is easy to see how struggles to restructure socialist economies and polities would engender intense ideological conflicts, since these reforms had to be formulated along ideologically sanctioned lines. However, the virulence of the debate over Third World policies requires more explanation. Long ago, Adam Ulam observed that ever since 1956, the fundamental justification and sign of vitality of the entire Soviet project was its ability to expand into the Third World.[1] Until Gorbachev, such expansion remained a high and per-

sisting priority. Sino-Soviet rivalry and the Cold War provided particularly
strong impetus for that expansion. Thus, until quite recently:

The Third World remained the area of Soviet foreign policy that most acutely raised
the validity of Marxist-Leninist ideology. It was the only part of Soviet diplomacy
that retained any describable ideological impetus but was also the only part that
could *in*validate the ideology. This risk may be the principal source of much of
Moscow's attraction/repulsion in dealing with the Third World. It represents an
ideological parallel to the place of the Third World in Soviet security policy. On
security issues the Third World is the only arena for scoring big *successes*, but over
the past two decades it has also been the main arena in which Soviet policy can
sustain major *defeats*[2] (emphasis in the original).

An expansive Soviet Third World policy seemed to validate the Soviet
project, but it was only feasible if Soviet security policy did not encounter
serious resistance. In the 1970s, events seemed to go Moscow's way, but by
1981, and the 26th Party Congress, difficulties that ultimately undermined
Soviet allies and the Soviet Union itself were seriously limiting Soviet flexibility and power. The imminence of a succession and power struggle in
which Third World policy became a major issue of factional rivalry only
intensified these problems.[3]

Soviet caution regarding the Third World became evident after 1980. In
Central America, arms transfers to Nicaragua and the Salvadoran FMLN
assumed the form of a complicated series of cut-outs, third parties, and
buffers whose aim was to shield Moscow and Havana from U.S. retribution.
Similar caution took place vis-à-vis Grenada.[4] After 1982, Soviet wariness
increased. Failure to aid Syria during its war with Israel; refusal to defend
Grenada in 1983; abandonment of Mozambique to a security regime led by
South Africa, and the rejection of its application to the Council of Mutual
Economic Assistance (CMEA); and Andropov's skeptical remarks concerning
Third World states all indicated a growing desire to shun riskier security
and economic commitments.[5] During Chernenko's rule, substantial Soviet-
Cuban discord occurred over the failure to protect Grenada or give Nicaragua
more aid and over Cuba's declining contributions to CMEA and to Soviet
economic progress.[6]

These trends led Castro to reorient his domestic and foreign policies. At
home, he turned economic policy away from the liberalizing reforms of the
late 1970s and early 1980s. Politically, he reasserted his detailed supervision
over all Cuban policies and reclaimed power from the technocrats who had
dominated planning policy for over a decade. The rectification campaign
that began in 1986 represented a move away from Soviet advice and models
toward a more personalized rule over the economy.[7]

From 1983 to 1987, dynamic policy shifts also took place in the Soviet
Union. In contrast to Chernenko, Gorbachev showed much greater willingness to use force and military aid as an instrument of Soviet Third World

policies. Between 1985 and 1987, Soviet allies and forces in Cambodia, Angola, Nicaragua, and Afghanistan launched repeated major offensives. This was the period of the most successful and brutal Soviet drives in Afghanistan. Arms aid to Nicaragua and Vietnam reached its peak despite repeated Soviet criticism of those states' ineffective and inefficient use of that aid. Civil and military aid to Cuba increased.[8] These policies, though still tactically cautious, were less so than before. They also invalidated many Western predictions by analysts who had accepted the growing Soviet disenchantment with Third World revolutions at face value. In fact, that disillusionment only affected policy after 1987, when Moscow irrevocably decided to get out of Afghanistan.

Gorbachev's early policies, coming at a time of increasingly open pressure on Castro to reform his economy, introduced a curious dichotomy into Soviet-Cuban relations. On the one hand, Castro's increasing freedom of maneuver at home led him to reject *perestroika* in favor of his own neo-Stalinist emphasis on moral incentives and rectification. On the other, in foreign policy, he reoriented Cuba's approach to the Third World.

Even as his ties to Moscow improved between 1985 and 1988, Castro had to limit his foreign policy goals to saving endangered revolutions where Cuban interests were at risk. In Angola, substantially increased Cuban military action funded by Moscow in 1987–88 enabled Havana to undertake bold offensives that forced South Africa to negotiate a treaty ending the wars in Angola and Namibia. Thus, the $450 million Soviet grant to Cuba in November 1987 was conditioned, not on widening the war as Castro had earlier threatened, but on his using it to bring about a negotiated solution more in tune with the evolving Soviet approach to settling conflicts. This approach aimed to preserve pro-Soviet regimes while de-linking that issue from superpower contestation. Cuba's participation in the ensuing four-power negotiations over Angola was a diplomatic triumph, a textbook example of crisis management and the judicious use of force to secure limited political goals.

The Angolan example and the U.S. invasion of Grenada seem also to have influenced Cuban thinking on Nicaragua in the mid–1980s. Overtly, Cuba continued to support a "political solution" that would leave the Sandinistas in control and terminate both the civil war and hostile U.S. actions against Nicaragua. But Castro was skeptical about the Sandinistas' acceptance of the 1987 Esquipulas agreement. He was particularly worried that the Sandinistas had accepted democratic elections, fearing rightly that they would lose them.

Covertly, however, military concerns came to play an increasing role in Cuban policy. Although Castro refused to send Cuban troops, as the Sandinistas requested, in 1985 he personally led the drafting of a contingency plan against an expected U.S. intervention. The plan called for coordinated ground and air attacks against Nicaragua's neighbors to broaden the conflict and inflame all of Central America. All Cubans in Nicaragua would be organized into military units to invade southern Honduras, while Sandinista forces invaded El Salvador and Costa Rica. Because Nicaraguan leaders by 1987 had come to see the termination of the war as their priority, while Castro remained skeptical about a political outcome, after that year Nicaragua slowly began to diverge from Cuban policy. This breach was also inspired by declining Soviet aid to Managua.[9]

At this time, Soviet economic aid to Cuba increased.[10] (Reports alleging a decline in assistance were part of a Cuban disinformation campaign to evade international debt payments.)[11] Even so, Castro foresaw the challenges that the Soviets would pose to Cuba's economic and international position. At his November 1987 meetings in Moscow, he expressed concern to Gorbachev that the technocratic elites in power there would be less tolerant of Cuba's inefficient use of Soviet aid. He told Gorbachev that Soviet economic reforms could devastate developing socialist countries. He was especially concerned that Soviet firms might divert their trade from Cuba to hard-currency customers as they became more autonomous. Gorbachev replied that economic reforms and liberalization were merely tactical moves to revive the Soviet economy and allow it to meet commitments to developing socialist states. Soviet firms would still depend on state priority orders to fulfill international commitments.[12] Castro also feared the Kremlin's weakening ideological commitment and the priority that it placed on ties to Washington. Moves toward detente would, he knew, lower Cuba's value to the Soviets and raise questions about the utility of massive loans and aid. The $450 million loan and the support for a limited offensive in Angola that were given at this time represented the high point of Soviet-Cuban relations under Gorbachev. They were also probably an attempt to allay Castro's concerns.

These aspects of the relationship illustrate both its nature and the importance that Third World revolution played in it. In the mid–1980s, W. Raymond Duncan observed that the Soviet Union would continue to be active in the Third World and that Cuban aims and policies did not simply replicate Soviet ones. However, he noted, "Cuba's economic and military dependence on the USSR make Havana's foreign policy highly vulnerable to sharp reductions in aid from Moscow."[13] A substantial decrease in Soviet economic and military aid would increase various regional actors' ability to deter Cuban support for foreign revolutions in the Caribbean and Central America. Cuba would then become economically dependent on those states for vital resources and energy supplies. Duncan also hypothesized that, should the Soviet Union substantially reduce aid, the regional balance of power would greatly incline toward those "deterring" states. Finally, he suggested that Havana's reaction to major shifts in its relations with Moscow would greatly depend on its perception of U.S. policy towards Cuba. (Since Cuba has not materially changed its perception of U.S. policy despite everything that has happened since 1985, its reaction to the breakup of Communism has been, as Duncan expected, still more repression and rigidity.)

On this basis, Duncan concluded that stresses in the relationship during 1984 to 1987 alarmed Castro about reduced Soviet economic and military support for Cuba and foreign revolutions. It also was clear that substantial diminution of that aid would put pressure on Cuba to curtail its militancy abroad; moreover, a termination of aid would virtually rule out support for such revolutions.[14] Subsequent events have borne out all these hypotheses.

Given the fact that Cuba's global revolutionary ambition is a projection of Castro's personality, the drastic constraints imposed by the changing Soviet policy were great personal and political blows. Declining Soviet support also undermined Cuban strategies to maximize political space and leverage in world politics. Small states like Cuba, of course, often seek to increase their discretionary capabilities. But Castro's intense personalization and expansion of this ambition to the extent of confronting the United States on a global basis made winning and retaining such space even more central an obsession.

The promotion of Third World revolutions—backed by Soviet subsidies, arms transfers, and strong ties to Moscow and its satellites—were essential components in this campaign for political space and the material basis for conducting a "big country's foreign policy." Castro's ability to leverage Soviet support for his grand design depended on his ability to act as broker, or intermediary, between Third World (especially Latin American) revolutionaries and the nonaligned countries, on the one hand, and the Kremlin, on the other. This broker relationship, reflected in Soviet-bloc relations with Grenada, gave Castro bargaining power and leverage vis-à-vis Moscow and entree into several Soviet institutions concerned with such issues: the Central Committee's International Department, the armed forces, and the KGB. This bargaining power gave Castro great freedom of action in his own policies and the right to conduct initiatives in Angola, Ethiopia, Nicaragua, and Grenada, which the Kremlin might then support. Accordingly, Soviet assistance enabled Castro to play the role of world leader and aspire to Third World leadership on South-South issues (for instance, the renunciation of foreign debts, a major campaign after 1985).[15]

Castro's perception that ideological and economic trends in Moscow endangered his relationship with the Soviets must already have taken shape in 1983–84 with the U.S. invasion of Grenada. By 1985 he was moving his priorities away from revolution. He proclaimed: "Right now, I sincerely believe that the cancellation of that [Third World] debt and the establishment of the New International Economic Order is much more important than two, three, or four isolated revolutions—and I'm a radical."[16]

That view never commanded Soviet support. But such actions were essential for Castro's campaign for leverage because leadership in the Third World boosted Cuban standing in Moscow and allowed it to win concessions and latitude not enjoyed by Moscow's other satellites. Conversely, declining

Soviet support since 1987 has undermined Cuba's standing in the Third World to the point that Castro is now widely regarded as an anachronism, and Cuba is isolated abroad.

As Soviet support dried up, Castro's fears grew that the entire basis of his security policy had been invalidated. Cuba lost its bargaining power and became the object of superpower decisions over which it had little say. Third World revolution became a closed option; non-payment of debts also became a non-starter in Latin America and Africa, not to mention Moscow. Increasingly, Cuban leaders desperately sought a new form of leverage to increase their political space.

SOVIET-CUBAN RELATIONS, 1988–91: STRAINS AND FISSURES

The growing pressure for reform in Moscow widened the gap between Cuba and the Soviets after 1987, but open polemics really began just before Gorbachev's trip to the island in April 1989. Reform in Moscow had stimulated pressures for reform in Havana. That pressure allowed Soviet journalists, undoubtedly with support from above, to depict Cuban economic failures and leadership in unflattering terms. By 1989, Soviet policy toward Cuba and the future of the entire relationship had become enmeshed in both regimes' economic crises, as well as in the struggle for power in Moscow. As Soviet economic decline accelerated, the economic subsidies and military aid for Cuba became prominent examples of what was wrong in the relationship.

Another element of discord was Castro's undiminished ideological militancy in foreign regional conflicts, while Gorbachev decisively turned to end the Cold War. Cuba feared that aid would be reduced and the Third World abandoned, as Moscow negotiated accords with Washington. The Soviets applied considerable pressure on Cuba in 1988–89 to induce it to join the four-power negotiations to end Angola's civil war and give Namibia its independence. Since Moscow clearly wanted to upgrade ties with South Africa, Cuban calls for a war to end apartheid became an embarrassment and a recipe for endless conflict in an area marginal to the Kremlin.[17]

The relationship deteriorated still further, even as Gorbachev visited Cuba. By this time, the Soviet Union had decided to cooperate with Washington in the Nicaraguan civil war, develop new relations with Latin America, and induce Cuba to reform economically. These three issues—revolution abroad, cooperation with the United States in Latin America, and the fundamental reform of socialism—became the subject of mutual polemics until 1991.

On the eve of Gorbachev's visit, Deputy Foreign Minister Raul Roa announced that Cuba would continue supporting foreign revolutions because the United States supported "counterrevolutionaries" in Nicaragua and elsewhere. Castro and other officials upheld this line beyond 1989, even as Gorbachev denounced the export of revolution in Havana.[18] Moscow soon followed up with support for peaceful reconciliation in Nicaragua and El Salvador as part of its new policy of promoting purely business and political ties to Latin America. But Castro rejected that approach and extolled the FMLN's glorious and "extraordinary" feats.[19]

By then it was clear to Moscow's friends that the Soviet model led to a blind alley of technological dependence, doubtful economic returns, and a lack of political support for pressing domestic issues. Therefore, they shifted to a more forthcoming relationship with Washington. It had also become clear that Soviet policy in Latin America had come to accept U.S. dominance there. The Soviet economic crisis ruled out a vigorous revolutionary policy in the region. Moreover, state-to-state ties offered prospective political and economic gains that outweighed revolutionary struggle's marginal and dubious benefits. Finally, the Latin American countries themselves were returning to liberal democracy and capitalism to solve their enormous economic problems. The ideological rightism that had precluded Latin American ties with Moscow was quickly eroding; this allowed the Soviet Union to achieve tangible benefits, as revolutionary dreams receded into the mist. Freed from "the lunacy of ideological stereotypes," Soviet observers increasingly understood that U.S. power and trade were essential to the region's well-being and that they no longer needed to see the area strictly from a Cold War perspective.[20]

All of these factors made for a tense and visibly discordant visit by Gorbachev. Although he tried to restructure Cuban relations on a new basis of internal reform, efficiency, and new thinking abroad, Castro stoutly resisted. In July 1989, Castro expressed open fears of civil war in the Soviet Union. And on October 30, 1989, he stated that *perestroika* contradicted Marxist-Leninist principles.[21] Even though Soviet officials flatly ruled out reducing aid, Cuba already was complaining about late deliveries and Soviet pressures to reform.[22] To add to Castro's discomfort, at the end of 1989 Soviet new thinkers and reformers began publicly attacking Cuba. These attacks represented the public expression of previously suppressed thought, as political reform gathered steam. But they clearly also enjoyed official support and reflected internal Soviet political divisions over Cuba.

Andrei Kortunov's revelations about the extent of Soviet aid were the most shocking of these disclosures and could only have been compiled with access to official sources. Kortunov assessed this aid as at least 3 billion rubles of the total of 12 billion rubles that were allocated to Third World states in 1989. This was a sum one-third greater than the Soviets spent on science and law enforcement. It also nearly equalled the amount earmarked to improve domestic social conditions. Kortunov depicted aid recipients as au-

thoritarian dictators who employed neo-Stalinist methods and who used this
aid to launch foreign military adventures directly contrary to Soviet interests
abroad.[23]

Despite this opening salvo, official policy continued to support Cuba to
roughly the same degree as before. Moreover, important forces also defended Castro. Members of the Ministry of Foreign Affairs criticized Kortunov's figures and estimated the benefits of Cuban food shipments to the
Soviet Union. Nevertheless, it was by now clear that there were elements
at the very top of the Soviet hierarchy who wanted to break with Havana if
the latter did not mend its ways.[24] For the Cubans, the question thus became
one of sustaining the relationship for as long as possible. In the words of
one Cuban source, relations with the Soviet Union were "like an AIDS
patient; we were injecting him with Interferon to make him last a little
longer."[25]

For some time, the administrative routine of Soviet policy continued to
provide aid, trade subsidies, and weapons. Although trade fell in 1990 from
8.66 billion rubles to 7.07 billion rubles, Moscow still accounted for about
70 percent of Cuba's foreign trade. In January 1990, the Soviets delivered
parts for a nuclear reactor that evoked concerns regarding a self-sufficient
Cuban nuclear program. In 1990 and 1991, military aid to Cuba showed no
signs of decline. No significant reduction of naval and air activities took place
for Cuba's air and naval forces or for the Soviet forces stationed there. In
February 1990, Moscow delivered six MIG–29s. The MIG–29s were the
first in an intended shipment of thirty-six, which also aroused U.S. concerns
because defectors had reported that Cuban MIG–29 squadrons are structured in such a way that at least four of the twelve jets are capable of carrying
nuclear weapons.[26]

This patterns held until the failed Soviet coup in August 1991. Although
Soviet domestic pressures led to public polemics, debate, and criticism of
the Soviet relationship to Cuba, pro-Cuban conservatives in key policy positions were able to block major policy changes and sustain a significant, if
reduced, aid and arms transfer program. At the same time, spreading chaos
within the Soviet Union raised the possibility of a spontaneous decline in
Soviet assistance due to the breakdown of the system. Reductions in Soviet
aid considerably reinforced Cuba's hardships and stimulated Castro's concerns about abandonment. But, mindful of the efforts of his "friends" in
Moscow, he persevered, intensifying his apocalyptic warnings of invasion
and his invocations of "socialism or death." In turn, his intransigence led
his Soviet critics to make contacts with Cuban exile forces in Miami, further
provoking him, but not changing this fundamental pattern of struggle.

The Soviet debate and rivalry was often acrimonious. As the extent of
Soviet foreign aid (especially to Cuba) became a major issue, policy differences crystallized. Kortunov and Shmelev, who first raised this issue and
pointedly cited Western figures since no Soviet ones were available, ex-

emplified an uncompromising variant of the "new thinking." They held that military aid and subsidies to leaders like Castro undermined and contradicted the principles that Gorbachev had articulated in his attempt to deideologize and demilitarize Soviet relations with the West. In July 1990, another reformer at the Institute of World Economy and International Relations (IMEMO), Sergei Kazennov, argued strongly that arms sales (about 15 percent of Soviet exports) were actually unprofitable. The weapons were expensive to produce, were sold at discount prices, and, even then, the recipients could not pay for them. The twenty leading importers of Soviet arms also accounted for 96 percent of the Third World's debt to Moscow.[27]

Despite such revelations, Gorbachev's government successfully resisted parliamentary control over aid and arms transfers to countries like Cuba. This left the issue of Soviet-Cuban relations unresolved, as the government tried to evade a public discussion. Within this framework, numerous Soviet factions or lobbies maneuvered over Third World policy in general and Cuba in particular.

Elizabeth Valkenier argues that in 1990–91, the Soviet Union acknowledged a need to "restructure" ties with Cuba and the Third World along more mutually beneficial lines.

> The government's strategy was aimed at gaining incremental economic advantages without incurring excessive political losses. Given this goal, Soviet unwillingness to cut off Cuba was not altogether out of line with the principles of de-politicization and commercialization. . . . Moscow undoubtedly believed that, either through a change in leadership or by force of circumstances, Havana would eventually alter its ways, abate its command economics, and become part of the Latin American and U.S. markets. As a result, the USSR would benefit both directly and indirectly, i.e., it would recoup some of the debt in dollars and extend its commercial presence in the hemisphere.[28]

Soviet policy toward Latin America continued to evolve under the impact of domestic economic crisis. Policy makers increasingly recognized how much economic weakness inhibited Soviet advances in the Third World, particularly in support of states like Cuba. This weakness ruled out a policy of increasing tensions in conflict zones and put a premium on conflict resolution. A comprehensive pursuit of economic ties with the Third World became standard policy. Latin America's significance to the Soviet Union grew, leading the latter to vigorously pursue increased commercial and political ties, especially with major states like Brazil, Mexico, Argentina.[29] Under these circumstances, Cuba's importance to Moscow sharply declined.

Beyond this, Soviet-Cuban institutional relationships apparently fostered a mutual interpenetration that let pro-Castro Soviet figures obstruct reform and maintain a substantial aid program. Conversely, Kremlin reformers made connections with disaffected elements in Cuba and among the exiles. The process resembled postwar Soviet-East European relations, where internal factions on both sides jointly contended against their rivals and their policies. This pattern had something of a history in the relationship. The 1989 trial of General Arnaldo Ochoa and major officials in the Ministry of Interior for drug-running was widely believed to be Castro's version of Stalin's military purge. It also was alleged that Ochoa was perceived as a pole around whom disaffected officials, influenced by Soviet reforms, might gather to demand power and policy changes.[30]

Castro's constant determination to brook no challengers to his power and policies is fierce and long-standing. In 1967–68, the Cuban secret police exposed a so-called "microfaction affair," in which thirty-five party members were arrested, tried, and imprisoned.

The principal charges against this microfaction were that it had opposed Castro's economic and foreign policies; and most importantly, that through its Soviet and Eastern European contacts, it had urged the withdrawal of Soviet bloc support as a means of bringing about Castro's downfall and replacement by trusted old-line Communists. Although Soviet bloc officials were dissociated from the subversive activities of the microfaction, the arrest and sentencing of this pro-Soviet faction nevertheless served as a preemptive warning to Moscow. That is, Havana had signaled its readiness to oppose increased Soviet influence in Cuban affairs, and its readiness to retaliate against cutbacks in Soviet assistance, by its ability to carry out additional actions that would be embarrassing to Moscow.[31]

If one purpose of the Ochoa trial was to thwart reform, Castro may also have sent Moscow the same message as in 1968: that efforts to influence Cuban officials and generals to promote Moscow-inspired policies would be countered ruthlessly. Second, Castro's heightened determination after 1989 to carry on as before may be related to a sense that any reform risked an intolerable ideological and political contagion. While solid proof, of course, is unavailable, this interpretation fits with the evidence of high-level factional rivalry in Moscow over China.

This rivalry and the players' identities are quite apparent from open sources. The pro-Castro Soviet faction embraced the armed forces (which was interested in foreign lodgments), the KGB, and those analysts and policy makers interested in carving out a special Soviet role as a bridge between North and South or as spokesmen for Cuba and the South in world politics. This group included Marshal Yazov, who had a personal tie to Cuba, having been stationed there years ago; KGB Chairman Kryuchkov; Politburo member Evgenii Primakov; elements of the Foreign Ministry such as Valery Nikolayenko, the deputy foreign minister for Latin America in 1990–91; and "certain honest academics" like Sergo Mikoyan and Karen Khacaturov who believed that the policy of disengaging from Cuba was "a dishonorable way to treat a former ally."[32] It was unremitting U.S. hostility that drove Castro to do the things that he did. While his regime was hardly spotless, abandoning it would only further damage the Soviet position in Latin America.

Those recommending disengagement included then Foreign Minister Shevarnadze; Politburo member Aleksandr' Iakovlev; Yuri Pavlov, Nikolayenko's predecessor at the Ministry of Foreign Affairs, and then-ambassador to Chile; important members of the Supreme Soviet such as Nikolai Shmelev; and key members of Yeltsin's foreign affairs team, like the Russian Foreign Minister Andrei Kozyrev and Andrei Kortunov. These critics argued that ties with Castro detracted from Soviet interests and relations with the United States, were of marginal utility in the Third World, and were objectionable on moral grounds and the principles of "new thinking." This group sponsored talks with exiled and emigre factions to avoid repeating what they viewed as a basic policy mistake in Eastern Europe: the refusal to contact the opposition.[33]

The continuation of this internal Soviet debate should not blind us to certain common anxieties that many of these players held concerning Castro. As Jiri Valenta has noted, both groups worried that an abrupt Soviet disengagement followed by a revolution in Cuba might provoke some U.S. counter-action and, in turn, a Cuban attack on the Turkey Point nuclear facility. Cuba had considered that option when the United States had invaded Grenada in 1983—or so prominent Cuban defectors had claimed. (Soviet publication of those reports lent them weight. In addition, Moscow's release of a secret portion of Khrushchev's memoirs concerning Castro's request to launch "a preemptive strike" against the United States at the height of the Cuban Missile Crisis also contributed to their plausibility.)[34]

Such fears restrained even the advocates of disengagement and contributed to a policy that simultaneously supported Cuba and tried to convince the United States to ease regional tensions. Thus, Soviet policies in Latin America in 1990–91 combined lessened support for revolution and violence with growing support for democratic capitalist states, self-determination (including Cuba's "socialist choice"), and the aggressive pursuit of trade. Moscow thereby hoped to escape being held hostage to Castro's policies, while attaining greater standing in Latin America and shifting its Cuban burden onto Washington.

As the conservatives made a comeback in 1990–91, the reformers' assault against Cuba abated. Even so, they were able to publish a scandalous attack on Castro, a withering revelation of his personal life and luxurious lifestyle. This met with sustained opposition from the conservatives, whose arguments persisted beyond the coup, though the policy changed greatly in September.[35]

SOVIET POLICY, 1989–91

It is worth following in sequence the evolution of Soviet policy with regard to the issues dividing it from Cuba in 1989 to 1991. In April 1989, Soviet officials opposed linking conflict resolution in El Salvador to Nicaragua's civil war. By November, they not only supported such linkage, but unceremoniously read Havana and Managua "the riot act" to forestall further shipments of Soviet arms through those states to El Salvador. As I have written elsewhere on the Nicaraguan civil war:

What appears to have prompted this reversal of policy was Moscow's success in securing Washington's pledge to abide by the election result in Nicaragua and its willingness to consider the USSR a real dialogue partner in Central America with regard to resolving conflicts there. These twin objectives weighed heavily in Soviet policy there.[36]

Moscow's quid pro quo for U.S. acceptance of Nicaragua's election results was that the Americans renounce violence in the region. Accordingly, Cuba and Nicaragua strongly remonstrated with Moscow when the United States invaded Panama at the end of 1989, but to no avail. Revolutionary violence undermined Moscow's priority goal of becoming a recognized dialogue partner and interlocutor for the region, a status it then hoped to use as leverage on the Cubans, who would have to accept Latin American integration rather than violent revolution.

In 1990–91, Moscow sought, ultimately unsuccessfully, to induce the United States and Cuba to alter their outlooks. Since both sides in the internal Soviet dialogue grasped the potential risks involved in disengaging from Cuba, the appeal to Havana and Washington to change their policies had to be consistent and reciprocally successful. Many Soviet analysts observed the need for a more economically based policy that promoted regional stability, but for this to occur Moscow could not stay ideologically married to Cuba. As one commentator wrote, Moscow could only acquire a new status when the "little cold war" around Cuba ended. The prerequisite for this was Cuban concord with its Latin neighbors (which might then lead to a rapprochement with the United States).[37] In October 1990, Ambassador Pavlov defended Soviet contacts with Cuban emigres as a way of inducing them to stop pressing Washington to force Moscow to end aid to Cuba. If that was their goal, Pavlov argued, it was senseless to leave the embargo in place, because eliminating it would lead to the reduction, if not cessation, of such aid. Washington knew that Moscow no longer supported revolution in Latin America. Hence, there was no "Soviet threat" to the United States.[38]

At Soviet-Cuban discussions in Havana during November-December 1990, Soviet delegates stressed that it was up to Washington to end the embargo if it desired progress on Cuba. Subsequently, at the superpower summit near the end of the year, they called on the Bush administration to ease Cuba's situation, allow for constructive discussion with the emigres, and stop letting the latter determine U.S. policy. Diminished threats to Cuba, it was emphasized, would evoke a comparable Soviet military response.[39] At the end of 1990, Havana and Moscow finally put together an aid and trade agreement for 1991, thereby easing mutual tensions.

The Soviet line had not changed when Nikolayenko visited the island in April 1991. Moscow, he declared, would maintain its military presence until "the reasons that make it necessary disappear." Again, he urged the United States to initiate cooperation.[40] In a statement not reported by Havana, he revealed that the Soviet Union would work to see that U.S.-Cuban relations "become more predictable, based on an exchange of information on each party's intention."[41] In June, moreover, a senior staffer at the Foreign Ministry's Latin America Department confided that Moscow would scale down military cooperation with Havana only if the United States guaranteed Cuban security and pledged non-intervention. He also offered his "firm conviction" that arms transfers to Latin American revolutionaries were a thing of the past.[42]

In the face of rising U.S. pressure tying aid to Moscow with disengagement from Cuba, Soviet officials continued to espouse this line in official and quasi-official statements. Before the Group of Seven meeting and London summit in June, presidential spokesman Ignatenko said that aid to Cuba "was not subject to discussion."[43] In a July interview, Gorbachev stated that he favored full normalization of ties with Washington, that tension around Cuba was a Cold War anachronism, and that not only was Latin American integration a good thing but that Cuba should participate in it.[44] In discussions in Moscow with Cuban party Secretary Carlos Aldana, it was agreed that joint efforts must be made

to remove the current tension around the island by opening dialogue with the United States, Western Europe, and Latin America. Soviet officials, in this connection, pointed out that Cuba intended to widen contacts with the United States on the issue of normalizing bilateral relations. However, such talks, says Cuba, must be held on the basis of parity and without preconditions that Washington has been setting so far.[45]

The Bush administration, of course, had set these preconditions, demanding political reforms that would have ended Communist rule in Cuba as a prerequisite for normalization. These demands could not have been issued as a serious negotiating position. They merely reflected Washington's inflexibility on the Cuba issue and hardened Castro's position, since he was given no incentives to change. As the August 1991 coup drew nearer, Washington's posture and Moscow's reaction to it both sharpened, increasingly angering Soviet officials who made it clear that they considered U.S. pressure to be blackmail.

On August 9th, a Soviet Academy of Sciences study reported that Cuba was Moscow's biggest debtor. As of November 1989, its debt stood at 15.9 billion rubles, including trade loans and technological and military aid. (One-third of it had been forgiven.) Moscow also paid Cuba annually 2.86 billion rubles to keep troops in Ethiopia and 2.03 billion rubles for troops stationed in Angola. Annual aid was about 4 billion to 4.5 billion rubles, and economic help was "drowned" in preferential trade relations. A Soviet diplomat interviewed on the report denied that the aid was excessive, even in view of Moscow's own economic plight. He justified it on the basis of Cuban influence in the Non-Aligned Movement, the evolution of the Soviet-Cuban symbiosis into a mutually beneficial relationship, the disagreeable shock that would result from any sudden ending of relations with the island, and, finally, threats to Cuban security. He observed:

We feel that Cuba is surrounded by an abnormal situation. . . . There is a certain risk of escalating tensions. A normalization should be reached solely by political measures, through dialogue. And in the first place between the USA and Cuba.[46]

Castro remained unsatisfied. Despite Gorbachev's policy, Washington refused to budge. Pressures for reform were destroying vital economic subsidies and the entire ideological scaffolding of the Soviet and Cuban regimes. Thus, he may well have begun collaborating with Gorbachev's foes. Certainly, his silent response to Gorbachev's restoration after the failed August 1991 coup and his denunciation of the Soviet leader at the 1991 Cuban Party Congress indicates total disaffection. And there were numerous suspicious circumstances preceding the Soviet crisis.

On February 22, 1991, Castro had sent General Juan Escalona, the presiding judge at Ochoa's trial, to Moscow. There he met with many of those later involved in the coup, including Lukianov. On June 27th, KGB chairman Kryuchkov came to Havana at Castro's personal invitation and stayed until July 1st. Kryuchkov urged Castro to "use all his influence in the Non-Aligned Movement so that those countries would support a future return of Soviet policies based on Marxism-Leninism." On June 28th, Aldana met with Vice-President Yanayev as part of a series of meetings with the coup plotters. Yanayev then wrote Castro, urging him not to worry because "the status quo will soon change." In July, in a video for high-ranking leaders, Castro analyzed Cuba's crisis and talked about Soviet leaders who had guaranteed him that "soon the situation will change."[47] Other plotters—Baklanov, Katushev, and Moiseev—also visited Cuba in 1991 and may have discussed it with Castro.[48] An irony of these developments is that Soviet rightists, and presumably the plotters too, viewed ousted Chilean dictator Augusto Pinochet's policies as a model.[49] Conceivably, Castro may have conspired with supporters of a Soviet version of Latin American fascism.

RUSSIA AND CUBA: PRESENT AND FUTURE

Cuba is now almost totally isolated and potentially a source of future conflict and violence. Had this chapter been completed in late 1991, the author might have postulated only the most basic normal future relations between the Soviet Union and Cuba. This is because Russian reformers believe that their country and Latin America face similar problems of building democratic polities and market economies and that Latin America is a promising market for trade and joint projects. Just as the Soviet Right invoked Pinochet, the new elites invoke the liberal democratic winds of change that have swept the continent since the early 1980s. Their main concern is to facilitate transition to a post-Castro regime and develop a purely businesslike relationship with Cuba.

Andrei Kozyrev, now Russia's Foreign Minister, finds inspiration in Latin America's democratization, even going so far as to suggest that such movements could furnish models for Russia's democratization. Proponents of such views repudiate past policies toward Cuba. Kozyrev has stated that even if Russia had the money to support Cuba, it would not do so.[50] Arguments that betraying Castro would be like re-signing the 1939 Non-Aggression Pact with the Nazis have been forcibly rejected. The promotion of Latin American leftism and terrorism is over.

Even prior to 1991, local leftists were getting the message. Ruben Zamora, secretary-general of El Salvador's Popular Social Christian Movement, told a Soviet reporter:

Today, leftist forces on the continent do not have any need whatsoever for the Cuban leadership's discussions of the degree to which the events in Eastern Europe are a departure from Marxism, a betrayal of the socialist cause, and a surrender to American imperialism.[51]

The Nicaraguan elections and El Salvador's conflict resolution are accepted as models and as an opportunity for revising both the form and content of U.S. and Russian relations with Latin America. As Ambassador Pavlov said in February 1991, *perestroika* has freed Moscow from an excessively ideological approach toward the region. Russia can pursue a policy based on mutual interests and friendship regardless of ideology and form of government.[52]

Moscow's renunciation of support for Cuban *Tercermundismo* (Third Worldism) has also narrowed Cuba's room for maneuver. Accordingly, Castro has become ever more a partisan of Third World issues like debt relief and, more recently, Latin American integration. His combination of defiance at home with foreign policy initiatives of regional integration, promotion of large-scale foreign investment, and a belligerent line toward the U.S. embargo represent not strength, but weakness. Increasingly, Cuba is isolated and an object of others' policy deliberations.

Although Moscow's unilateral withdrawal of troops in 1991–92 seemed to herald the end of the military dimension of the relationship, the story is not quite over. As of spring 1993, the Russians were still operating their electronic intelligence-gathering facility at Lourdes. At the same time, they had agreed to seek third-party financing for Cuba's nuclear power plant at Juragua and were continuing to sell the Cuban military spare parts for existing armaments. The two sides had also come to terms on a new trade agreement, continuing their traditional exchange of oil for sugar, though at much lower levels and at less favorable prices for the Cuban side.

In short, Russian policy toward the Castro regime is currently proceeding along two separate tracks. On the one hand, there is a willingness to denounce human rights violations and continue pressing for reforms. On the other, there is the perpetuation, albeit at a much lower level, of military and economic ties. While some have argued that Cuba is of little economic benefit, this has clearly failed to convince the Yeltsin government, which continues to believe that a complete break with Cuba is against Russia's economic interests.

The current trade agreement with Cuba is supposed to make mutual ties more stable and predictable. But it also clearly reflects the current tide in Moscow and the partial resurgence of the military and of Castro supporters like former Ambassador Petrov, formerly Yeltsin's chief of staff. In this respect, as in so many other aspects of Russian foreign policy, a resolution of the domestic debate will largely determine future policy. No doubt too, the character of Cuban domestic politics will also have an influence. But though Cuban officials accept the need for change to deal with the global economy, one cannot take these remarks too seriously as long as Castro retains power, continues to repress dissent, and refuses major structural reform.

Thus, in both states, the final act of the relationship awaits decisive breakthroughs to reform in domestic policy. But whatever the outcome, relations are unlikely to regain their past intensity and will become increasingly a hard-headed business proposition, a marriage of convenience rather than an affair of the heart. Indeed, there appears to be only one way that the past intensity of emotion could be recaptured and that is if Castro, feeling his time running out, really does embark on a kind of Cuban Götterdämmerung, with or without nuclear instruments. There is some evidence that this could occur.[53] However, in that case, the Russian reaction would be one of revulsion, not fraternity. Barring that worst-case scenario, however, these lines from the poet Lermontov would seem an epitaph for the relationship: "The love was without joy, the parting will be without sorrow."

NOTES

    1. Adam Ulam, "The Soviet Union and the Rules of the International Game," in *The Soviet Union in World Politics*, Kurt London, ed. (Boulder, Colo.: Westview Press, 1980), pp. 42–44.

    2. Stephen Sestanovich, "The Third World in Soviet Foreign Policy, 1955–1985," in *The Soviet Union and the Third World: The Last Three Decades*, Andrei Korbonski and Francis Fukuyama, eds. (Ithaca, N.Y.: Cornell University Press, 1987), p. 14.

3. See Robert G. Patman, *The Soviet Union in the Horn of Africa: The Diplomacy of Intervention and Disengagement* (Cambridge: Cambridge University Press, 1990); John W. Parker, *The Kremlin in Transition* (Winchester, Mass.: Unwin Hyman, 1990), Vol. 1; and Pedro Ramet, "Soviet Relations with the Developing World," in *Gorbachev and the Soviet Future*, Lawrence W. Lerner and Donald W. Treadgold, eds. (Boulder, Colo.: Westview Press, 1987), p. 249.

4. Francis Fukuyama, "The Nature of the Problem: A Systematic Soviet Strategy for the Third World?" in *The Red Orchestra: Instruments of Soviet Policy in Latin America and the Caribbean*, Dennis L. Bark, ed. (Stanford: Hoover Institution Press, 1986), p. 41; Jonathan Steele, "Where Brezhnev Fears to Tread," *The Manchester Guardian*, March 15, 1981.

5. Winrich Kuhne, "Nkomati and Soviet policy on Africa in the Eighties: The End of Ideological Expansion?" in *The Soviet Bloc and the Third World: The Political Economy of East-South Relations*, Brigitte H. Schulz and William W. Hansen, eds. (Boulder, Colo.: Westview Press, 1989), pp. 181–96.

6. W. Raymond Duncan, *The Soviet Union and Cuba: Interests and Influence* (New York: Praeger, 1985), pp. 177–201; Jorge Dominguez, *To Make a World Safe for Revolution: Cuba's Foreign Policy* (Cambridge: Cambridge University Press, 1989), pp. 106–11.

7. Duncan, *The Soviet Union and Cuba*, pp. 177–201.

8. Mark N. Katz, "Anti-Soviet Insurgencies: Growing Trend or Passing Phase," *Orbis*, Vol. 30, No. 1, Summer 1986, pp. 385–86; Michael McGwire, *Perestroika and Soviet National Security* (Washington, D.C.: Brookings Institution Press, 1991), pp. 138–59, 171–73.

9. Andres Oppenheimer, *Castro's Final Hour: The Secret Story Behind the Coming Downfall of Communist Cuba* (New York: Simon & Schuster, 1992), pp. 199–217.

10. By an estimated 10 percent. See Susan Kaufman Purcell, *Is Cuba Changing?*, Cuban American National Foundation, No. 28, 1989, p. 9.

11. Clyde H. Farnsworth, "Soviets Said to Reduce Support for Cuban Economy," *New York Times*, March 16, 1988.

12. Purcell, *Is Cuba Changing?*, pp. 8–9.

13. W. Raymond Duncan, "Implications of the Fall of the Soviet Regime on Cuba and Cuban-Sponsored Revolutionary Regimes and Movements in Latin America," in *The Soviet Union and the Challenge of the Future*, Vol. 4, Russia and the World, Alexander Shtromas and Morton A. Kaplan, eds. (New York: Paragon House, 1989), p. 316.

14. Ibid., pp. 316–25.

15. H. Michael Erisman, "Cuban Development Aid: South-South Diversification and Counterdependency Politics," in *Cuban Foreign Policy Confronts a New International Order*, H. Michael Erisman and John M. Kirk, eds. (Boulder, Colo.: Lynne Rienner Publishers, 1991), pp. 144–45.

16. Andre Gunder Frank, "The Socialist Countries in the World Economy: The East-South Dimension," in Schulz and Hansen, eds., *The Soviet Bloc and the Third World*, pp. 18–19.

17. David Remnick and Julia Preston, "Soviet in Cuba Criticizes Export of Revolution," *Washington Post*, April 4, 1989.

18. Douglas Payne, "Fidel Castro Versus Perestroika," *Radio Free Europe/Radio Liberty, Report on the USSR*, January 12, 1990, p. 7.

19. Paul Bedard, "Peru, Fed Up With Soviets, Seeks To Cut a Deal With US," *Washington Times*, July 22, 1988.

20. Payne, "Fidel Castro," pp. 7–8.

21. Ibid.

22. Paul Goble, "Is Moscow About to Cut Castro Loose?" *Radio Free Europe/ Radio Liberty, Report on the USSR*, January 12, 1990, p. 5.

23. Ibid.

24. "Deteriorating Cuban-USSR Relations Viewed," *Foreign Broadcast Information Service—Latin America* [henceforth, *FBIS-LAT*], September 20, 1991.

25. Quoted in Michael P. Fleming, "W(h)ither the Soviet Union in the Third World?" U.S. Naval War College, Newport, R.I., June 1991, pp. 72–75.

26. To say that Cuban planes are nuclear weapons-capable is not, of course, to suggest that the Cubans actually possess such weapons. Stephen Blank, "Soviet Foreign Policy and Regional Conflict Resolution: The Nicaraguan Civil War," *Conflict Quarterly*, forthcoming 1993.

27. Elizabeth Kridl Valkenier, "Glasnost' and Perestroika in Soviet-Third World Economic Relations," *Harriman Institute Forum*, October 1991, pp. 4–5.

28. Ibid., pp. 11–12.

29. David E. Albright, "Soviet Economic Development and the Third World," *Soviet Studies*, Vol. 43, No. 1, 1991, pp. 27–59.

30. Julia Preston, "The Trial That Shook Cuba," *New York Review of Books*, December 7, 1989, pp. 24–31.

31. Edward Gonzalez, "Relations with the Soviet Union," in *Revolutionary Change in Cuba*, Carmelo Mesa-Lago, ed. (Pittsburgh, Pa.: University of Pittsburgh Press, 1971), p. 93.

32. Statement of Professor Jiri Valenta before the Subcommittee on Western Hemisphere Affairs, U.S. House of Representatives, 102nd Congress, Washington, D.C., April 30, 1991, p. 4.

33. Ibid., p. 3.

34. Ibid., p. 4. See also Roger Hamburg, "Soviet-Latin American Relations," *Problems of Communism*, Vol. 39, No. 4, September-October, 1990, p. 107; James G. Blight, Janet M. Lang, Bruce M. Allyn, "Fidel Cornered: The Soviet Fear of Another Cuban Crisis," *Russia and the World*, No. 18, 1990, pp. 21–25.

35. "A Touchy Time in Soviet-Cuban Relations," *Current Digest of the Soviet Press* [henceforth, *CDSP*], December 12, 1990, pp. 11–12.

36. Stephen Blank, "Soviet Foreign Policy."

37. Vladimir Razuvayev, "Between Geopolitics and Ideology," *New Times*, No. 19, 1990, pp. 17–18.

38. "New Ambassador to Chile Views Latin America," *FBIS-SU*, October 26, 1990.

39. "US Summit to Consider Cuban Relations," *FBIS-SU*, December 12, 1990.

40. "Views Military Presence," *FBIS-LAT*, April 16, 1991.

41. "Resolution to US-Cuba 'Mistrust' Proposed," *FBIS-SU*, April 23, 1991.

42. "Diplomat Talks About Aid to Cuba," *FBIS-SU*, June 13, 1991.

43. "Soviet Spokesman: Aid Not Subject to Discussion," *FBIS-LAT*, June 26, 1991.

44. "Mexican Daily Interviews Gorbachev," *FBIS-SU*, July 5, 1991.

45. "Cuba's Aldana Continues Moscow Visit: Meets Gorbachev, Bessertnykh," *FBIS-SU*, July 2, 1991.

46. "Aid to Cuba Costs 4.5 Billion Rubles per Year," *FBIS-SU*, August 12, 1991, pp. 18–19.

47. "Dissident Says Castro Knew of Coup Beforehand," *FBIS-SU*, September 27, 1991.

48. "Article Examines Havana Response to Coup," *FBIS-SU*, September 6, 1991.

49. Tatiana Vorozheikina, "Another Revolt of the Masses," *Twentieth Century and Peace*, March 1990, pp. 11–16; "Passions Over Pinochet," *CDSP*, July 10, 1991, p. 20; "Pinochet Takeover in Chile, Soviet Coup Events Compared," *Joint Publications Research Service—USSR International Affairs* [hereafter, JPRS-UIA], October 8, 1991; "Chilean Economic Revival Seen as Model For USSR," *JPRS-UIA*, July 25, 1991. An alternative interpretation, holding that Castro did not have advance knowledge of the coup, may be found in Oppenheimer, *Castro's Final Hour*, pp. 359–86.

50. "Kozyrev on Relations With Latin America," *FBIS-SU*, October 25, 1991; "Kozyrev on RSFSR MFA, Republic Relations," *JPRS-UIA*, October 28, 1991.

51. "Political Futures of Nicaragua, El Salvador Discussed," *JPRS-UIA*, April 27, 1990.

52. "Soviet Ambassador Views Bilateral Relations," *FBIS-LAT*, February 20, 1991.

53. "DPRK-Cuban Contract for Missiles Export Alleged," *FBIS-East Asia*, March 20, 1991; Eric Ehrmann, "Fallout from the Soviet Nuclear Collapse," *USA Today*, December 3, 1991.

9

Cuba and the United States: Thinking about the Future

Mark Falcoff

Since the future of Cuba itself remains in serious doubt, to discuss the prospect for its relations with the United States is something of an exercise in speculation. Let us begin, however, by grasping the few certainties available to us. First, the Castro regime cannot survive the person of the dictator, but as long as he lives he will probably rule, and as long as he rules, the island will undergo no meaningful political changes. Second, having lost its Soviet patron, Cuba can no longer pose the same sort of threat to the United States and its neighbors; this in turn requires a reexamination of the fundamental premises of U.S. policy. Third, the problems for the United States posed by the end of Castroism are probably potentially as great as its indefinite perpetuation. Each of these propositions invites somewhat more extended analysis.

POWER AND STABILITY IN CASTRO'S CUBA

To posit fundamental political change in Cuba is to think about the island after the death, disappearance, or forcible exile of the Castro brothers. This may happen later rather than sooner, but since all human beings are mortal, it must happen sometime. Whenever it does happen, the existing pressures within Cuba for some sort of political opening are bound to become irresistible. Not all of these pressures will necessarily point in the direction of a Western political and economic model, but they will force the system open and unleash energies and impulses that may be very difficult to contain. President Castro understands this well, which is why he has been so explicit in his rejection of Gorbachev's (and now Yeltsin's) reforms. To date, events in the former Soviet Union have done nothing but bear him out.

To put it bluntly, Castro's interests are first and foremost the perpetuation of his own rule. He understands those interests as best served by the existing system; indeed, he regards the existing system as essential to his continuation in power. Thus, those who speculate on the possibilities of political change growing out of the status quo in an organic fashion—that is, through evolution or "negotiations"—are simply not taking Castro seriously. Or rather, they are refusing to confront the realities of power and survival. The environment in which Castro operates is radically different from that of other Latin American dictators: There are no competing institutions or foreign influences capable of restraining his appetite for power (as they were and are, for example, in Pinochet's Chile). At the same time, the historical-political context within Cuba itself (and within the nearby Cuban diaspora) renders it virtually impossible for Castro to enter into a peaceful retirement. The narrow alternatives, "Socialism or Death," confront the dictator as brutally as they do his hapless people.

This is not, of course, the way the regime itself likes to speculate about the future. Castro frequently refers to the existence of new "revolutionary institutions" that would presumably take over after his death, though in fact for more than thirty years he has been unwilling to allow any of these to acquire a life of their own. The island is still run along the same personalistic lines as it was run more than thirty years ago. Meanwhile, potential rivals (Camilo Cienfuegos, Ernesto Guevara) have tended to disappear, often under mysterious circumstances. Others have been driven into exile (Matos, Del Pino); still others, executed (Ochoa). The only two personalities who have survived mention as possible successors have been Castro's brother, Raúl, and his son Fidel Castro Diaz-Balart, head of the Cuban Atomic Energy Commission. [Editor's note: Since this was written, "Fidelito" has been dismissed for "inefficiency."][1] At best, this holds out the hope for a dynastic-bureaucratic version of Communism whose appeal (and lifespan) would be quite limited.

Spokesmen for the regime frequently insist that even if they cannot predict its precise configuration, some form of socialist continuity is inevitable after Castro. This is so, they believe, because the regime's putative social achievements (particularly in education and health) have won it the support of the vast majority, but particularly from those who remember the "bad old (i.e., pre-revolutionary) days" or who belong to groups (blacks, peasants, cane-cutters, etc.) that were markedly disadvantaged before 1959. Since there are no public opinion polls or elections in Cuba, one cannot know the extent to which these claims are true or false. Nonetheless, the regime's own lack of curiosity—it has resisted calls, for example, for a plebiscite on the Chilean model—does not inspire confidence on the part of most outside observers.

U.S.-CUBAN RELATIONS: THE CONSTRAINTS ON CHANGE

Theoretically, of course, there is no reason that Cuba and the United States must base their relationship on the nature of their internal systems.

After all, for many years the United States maintained normal (sometimes even cordial) relationships with such erstwhile socialist countries as Romania, Yugoslavia, and Poland, and continues to do so with the People's Republic of China. Unlike those countries, however, the regime in Cuba claims to derive a unique legitimacy—one far surpassing its actual economic or social performance—from its active hostility to the United States and all its works. At this point, its sole claim to success as a revolutionary project is its effective liberation of Cuba from the U.S. sphere of influence. Normalization of relations would undercut that claim, and also expose the island and its people to potentially destabilizing influences from expanded trade and tourism. Therefore, one cannot be certain that normalization is something that Castro really wants, however much he may want the United States to want it. What could be a more delicious "high" for Castro, after all, than the opportunity to spurn an outstretched hand, or to maneuver the United States into the position of a humiliated supplicant?[2]

Certainly the record shows that in the not very distant past Havana has spurned opportunities, even very modest ones, to improve relations. In the mid-1970s, a round of talks resolved a number of outstanding immigration and hijacking issues and established interest sections in each capital. For a brief moment it seemed as if normalization of relations was but a matter of time. But though warned by both the Ford and Carter administrations that further progress was contingent upon Cuban non-interference in Cold War battlefields, Castro chose to deploy thousands of troops in the civil wars of Southern Africa (at one point, as many as 50,000 in Angola). From 1978 on, Cuba was also involved in the shipment of arms to Marxist revolutionaries in Nicaragua and El Salvador, and probably also to the terrorist Left in Chile. These developments shaped a decisively anti-Castro policy by the Reagan administration in the 1980s, one so intense as to survive the original provocations.

For its part, the United States has no interest in making life easier for the Castro regime (as it arguably did for similar governments in Eastern Europe during the 1970s, some of which were attempting to distance themselves from Moscow) by widening opportunities for credit and trade or facilitating a massive wave of American tourism. The fact that all three—particularly the latter—might prove ultimately destabilizing over the long term is a moot point, since in the short and even middle run (which could be very long indeed), they would in all probability provide Castro with resources essential to his survival. Liberal critics argue that only by lifting the existing trade embargo is Castro's hold on power likely to be shaken.[3] The Cuban government itself sees matters quite differently, however, since the near-totality of its foreign propaganda these days is oriented toward convincing other countries to pressure the United States to lift the embargo.

An early end to economic sanctions is also ruled out by U.S. domestic politics. One of the more enduring side-effects of Castro's revolution has been the creation in this country of a large, affluent, and well-organized Cuban exile community, overwhelmingly opposed to a policy of "dialogue" with the Castro regime.[4] Cuban-Americans constitute the largest voting bloc in the state of Florida, and are an important constituency in New Jersey, California, New York, Massachusetts, and other states rich in electoral votes. On this issue they possess something of a veto, and not merely within the Republican Party. In recent years, Castro's persecution of writers, artists, labor leaders, and human rights activists has eroded what little support he had managed to hold onto within the American liberal community and greatly weakened the case for normalization within the Democratic Party. President-elect Bill Clinton, for example, has stated that he favors maintaining the embargo, as does Senator Claiborne Pell, chairman of the Foreign Relations Committee, who, until he reversed himself last year, was one of the few congressional supporters of normalization.

To summarize: There is a well-organized, tightly focused, well-funded constituency for firmness against Castro, and there is no real constituency for "dialogue." Thus, for any administration, the short- and medium-term benefits of a conciliatory policy are far from evident, while the high political costs—in the short term at least—are immediately apparent.

U.S. POLICY: THE UNDESIRABILITY OF CHANGE

Apart from domestic politics, what lies behind U.S. Cuban policy today? At one time, that question was easy to answer: Castro had aligned his country with the Soviet Union and pursued policies both within the region and around the globe that were designed to—and often did—undermine U.S. interests. This included the training of revolutionary cadres, the transfer to them of arms, intelligence information, and financial resources, as well as the deployment of a considerable political influence in what used to be called the Third World and at international organizations.

None of these conditions now exists. The Soviet Union has disappeared from the political map; Russian aid to Cuba has fallen far below even the promised (lower) levels for 1990 and 1991; and the prospects for relations with the Commonwealth of Independent States are even more problematic. Even within this hemisphere, the Cuban reach is greatly reduced, thanks to the defeat of the Sandinistas in the 1990 elections in Nicaragua and the recent Salvadoran peace agreements. Cuban influence at the United Nations and other world bodies is greatly diminished. At a recent meeting with former U.S. and Soviet officials and scholars in Havana to discuss the Missile Crisis, Castro even claimed to have abandoned his policy of subversion against his neighbors, though the sheer number of small arms stockpiled on the island suggests a continued capacity to export violence if that is the direction that the leadership decides to take.

Even at its worst, a Cuba of this latter sort would still be a more manageable problem than the kind American policy makers have had to confront over the past thirty years. But to welcome it back to the inter-American family, as it is today and with no questions asked, would fly in the face of U.S. policy in the rest of the region as it has evolved over the past dozen years—from "business as usual" with dictators to a greater concern for human rights and democracy. An unconditional normalization of relations would overturn the bipartisan consensus forged on these issues and undermine the credibility of U.S. policy in other countries where democratic institutions are still fragile. (If we can "live" with Cuba, why then could we not as easily live with re-emergent right-wing military regimes in Central America?) At a minimum, one would have to explain why U.S. policy toward Cuba—a country where there is no free press, where there are no opposition parties, and where elections have not been held in nearly four decades—should be significantly more indulgent than the standard currently applied to other countries. It would in effect allow Castro to determine his own standards for political legitimacy, rather than compel him to conform to those established for the region as a whole.[5] And it would push U.S. policy in a direction very different from that in which inter-American diplomatic opinion has been moving of late—the prime examples being the nearly unanimous support within the Organization of American States for the embargo of Haiti after the 1991 deposition of an elected president, and the sanctions currently being levied against the quasi-de facto government in Peru.

U.S. STRATEGY AND THE CUBAN EXILE FACTOR

Critics of U.S. policy often point out that the embargo and other sanctions do not guarantee political change on the island. Of course this is true, at least in the limited sense that no policy can ever offer iron-clad assurances of success. On the other hand, never have the conditions been more favorable. Until now the effects of the embargo have been blunted by Soviet aid; it will be several years, at least, before the policy has been tested in the new context. The assumption upon which the embargo now operates is that at some point the living standard of the island will drop so dramatically as to encourage elements within the regime, particularly the police and the military, to intervene and reverse the country's political course.

The actual scenarios vary. Some observers foresee popular unrest fueled by shortages, which the armed forces would find themselves morally unable to suppress and which they would eventually join, as in Russia in 1917. Others speak of dissatisfaction within the field-grade ranks of the army—or even the ranks of non-commissioned officers, as in the Cuba of 1933—which would congeal into a palace coup. Still others envision a *coup de main* by the highest ranks of the Revolutionary Armed Forces. It is true that the regime so far has demonstrated that its survival is not dependent upon a satisfactory economic performance, but the end of Soviet aid will for the first time affect the special privileges of the *nomenklatura*, both civil and military, the only group capable of forcing a change of course. [Editor's note: *Nomenklatura* is a Soviet term referring to the list of offices to which Communist party committees at any level have the authority to appoint people.]

A more telling criticism, which even some Cuban-Americans have begun to voice, is that Washington has failed to offer visible incentives to people within the regime, particularly the military, to take action. As long as the crucial second tier of civil and military officials sees its very survival as being associated with that of the leader, it is not likely to rush into precipitous action. There is also a genuine fear of "Miami," a presumptively revanchist Cuban exile community that would take over the island and indiscriminately purge those who have collaborated with the regime, even those in fairly minor positions.

The first of these concerns is wholly valid, and points to a deficiency in American policy for which, however, there may be no correction: the inability to operationalize a transition in Cuba. Indeed, U.S. officials can hardly conceptualize what a transition would even look like. Certainly at a minimum it would mean an end to the rule of the Castro brothers and some gestures toward political liberalization, but who would initiate such changes and under what conditions cannot be confidently foreseen. The United States continues to be guided by the notion that it will know a post-Castro government when it sees it. As for any assurances that would-be Cuban *golpistas* (coup-makers) might seek or want, they may not even be Washington's to grant.

Fear of the exile community is greatly overdrawn, though Washington cannot effectively make that point without appearing to be insulting. No doubt some elements are obsessed by events on the island and dream of returning to resume lives, fortunes, and a sense of place that, in truth, can never be retrieved. Even so, the idea of exiles "taking over" the island (by military force, a boat-lift in reverse or through purchase?) and dispensing favors, justice, and property finds little support among those who presumably would be most intimately involved in the process. The most recent survey of the Cuban-American community in Dade County, Florida,[6] the epicenter of the diaspora, reveals that the majority (64 percent) have no plans to reestablish themselves in their former country (24 percent would, 12 percent are undecided). Some 60 percent also believe that those who have left should not be allowed to simply reclaim homes and properties that they abandoned (33 percent do; 7 percent are uncertain).

Moreover, the sample reveals that Cuban-Americans are sharply divided on so fundamental a question as who should determine the island's political future. Fully 33 percent believe that it should be resolved exclusively by those who have remained behind; 48 percent favor codetermination by the two communities; a mere 8 percent assign this task to the diaspora alone. Significantly, some 79 percent cannot name someone they wish to see as Cuba's next president. Even when supplied with a list of probable candidates, the "winner," Jorge Mas Canosa of the Cuban American National Foundation, drew only 44 percent of the vote. (The "runner-up," Tony de Varona of the Partido Cubano Revolucionario (Autentico) received only 11 percent, and "Don't Know/No Answer" received 25 percent.) Rather surprisingly, in light of the exile community's somewhat unfashionable conservative political image, fully 73 percent believe that "socialized medicine and free education should continue in democratic Cuba"!

It must be conceded that the situation of Cuba and the exile community is utterly *sui generis*. Other revolutions have generated exile populations in the past, but none of them so large in proportion to population, so heavily concentrated in one geographical area, and so physically proximate. Thus, while the United States and the exile leadership may sincerely disavow any intentions of interfering in the internal affairs of post-Castro Cuba, with the collapse of the dictatorship the boundary between the two Cubas threatens to become purely imaginary. This is particularly true in the event of a civil war on the island, toward which not only the Miami Cubans but even the U.S. government would be hard-pressed to maintain a posture of neutrality.

In a broader sense, however, it is far from clear that a close relationship to the United States, or even codetermination with some elements of the Cuban-American community, is something most Cubans would find undesirable. Again, we know next to nothing about the islanders' real feelings, only what we are told through sanitized sources. Thus Cuban government officials often speak disdainfully of Puerto Rico, as if that is the only possible relationship that a Caribbean island might have with the United States.[7] And Cubans available for comment to U.S. journalists often speak of "Miami" as if the Cuban-American threat is greater than any other that faces them, including starvation. The vaunted Cuban nationalism to which regime apologists continually refer may dissolve before our eyes once wider options of association—both with the United States and with the Cuban-American community—are available.

THE DILEMMAS OF SUCCESS

It ought to be said straightforwardly that even the most expeditious and peaceful political transition will not resolve all of the Cuban policy dilemmas facing the United States. Quite the contrary: it will merely pose new ones. In the first place, the morning after we are almost certain to see a massive flight of Cubans from the island, particularly those who have relatives in the United States. Very early on, therefore, the United States will have to decide whether to discontinue its current policy of granting automatic political asylum to those who succeed in escaping; it will also have to devise methods of implementing that policy. If the U.S.-Mexican border (leaving aside the Haitian territorial waters) is any indication, that may prove extraordinarily difficult from a logistical point of view, quite apart from the obvious political controversy that such an event would provoke in Southern Florida and within the Cuban-American community.

Second, the United States will have to make a determination on when the regime has ended, and therefore when to begin normalization of relations. Current policy defines the transition by free elections open to international supervision, but in all probability a fresh leadership, a different discourse, and some moves toward opening up the system would be sufficient to reopen sub-ambassadorial missions and lift some trade and travel restrictions.

Third, the determination of when the transition has begun is bound to become a political and ideological question. Inevitably, Castro's overthrow or collapse will unleash vigorous debate among Cubans, between Cubans on the island and Cuban-Americans in the United States, and between both of them and the U.S. government over the shape of the new Cuba and its relations with the outside world. There is no way that this conflict can be contained within the boundaries of the island, because Cuba will re-enter the Western world in acute need of foreign assistance, the largest single source of which will surely be Miami. However, it is also true that those Cubans who have remained at home and paid the price for the Castro regime for nearly two generations will naturally feel that the future is theirs to determine, not those who have spent that period in (what to them will seem) more comfortable circumstances. The U.S. government may not succeed in mediating between the two sundered halves of the national community, but it will be forced to try, because even without the Miami factor, post-Castro Cuba will be ripe for civil conflict.

Fourth and finally, it is by no means assured that in the post-Castro era Cuba will be able to resume its historic relationship with the United States as first among Caribbean equals. Its old quota of sugar imports has been divided up among many other countries and cannot be immediately restored.[8] Competitive tourist infrastructures now exist in the Dominican Republic, Puerto Rico, Jamaica, and elsewhere; independent tribunals must settle several billion dollars' worth of confiscated American property; and many other Latin American and Caribbean countries will be competing for a special trade relationship with the United States based on geographical proximity, low labor costs, or comparative advantage.

To think seriously about a post-Castro Cuba is to contemplate, then, a series of new problems: a continuing flow of immigration, legal and illegal; political unrest, possibly aggravated by revanchist elements or contending parties based in Florida; heightened commercial competition between Cuba and its neighbors; and in the short term at least, the need for massive infusions of food, medicine, and other forms of assistance.

However, the United States faces this prospect somewhat better equipped than it would have been a decade or two ago. The Democracy Endowment now has experience in more than a dozen Latin American countries, and

Congress and the State Department have established tighter standards for human rights compliance. Other Latin American countries, particularly Venezuela, Mexico, and Colombia, seem better disposed to assist the United States than a generation ago, and the ideological climate is much cooler and more pragmatic.

In most ways, the changes that have occurred in the world over the last few years work in favor of a new and more constructive relationship with post-Castro Cuba. One, however, that does not is the vast demographic and cultural shift that has occurred on the island since 1959. Much of Cuba today is black rather than white, poor rather than rich, passive rather than active, pessimistic rather than hopeful, fearful of the future and nostalgic for a brief moment in the past when all things seemed possible through the catharsis of revolution. Except for nostalgia (but for 1958 and before, rather than 1959), the Cuban-American community represents precisely the opposite of all of these things. Cuba cannot enter the future without bringing the two halves together, a task that the United States cannot accomplish on its behalf. But it is also a task toward which, for reasons political, historical, and human, the United States cannot remain indifferent. The roots of our own history have been entangled with those of Cuba for 200 years. The prospect of Castro's demise emphasizes the point in a new and dramatic way. It also suggests that U.S. policy should concentrate less on how to oust Castro— an event that, to repeat, must happen sooner or later—than on how to deal with his doleful legacy once he is gone.

NOTES

1. Whether there were political motives behind the dismissal is unclear. There have been rumors that Castro Diaz Balart was in contact with dissidents, but also that he had personal problems and was living the high life. Hard evidence is not abundant.

2. Castro could even have it both ways by accepting the principle of normalization, while raising conditions that he would know in advance no American president could accept, at least not without protracted negotiations and Senate approval. One example would be withdrawal from the U.S. naval base at Guantanamo.

3. Arthur Schlesinger Jr., "Four Days with Fidel: A Havana Diary," *New York Review of Books*, Vol. 39, No. 6, March 26, 1992.

4. According to a recent poll conducted among Cuban-American adults in Dade County, Florida, 66 percent favor a policy of "confrontation" with the Castro regime; a mere 23 percent prefer "dialogue." *Miami Herald*, May 2, 1992.

5. It might be argued that since the United States continued to recognize right-wing military governments during the 1970s in countries like Argentina, Chile, and Guatemala, it would constitute no departure to normalize relations with Cuba. But in fact during that period the domestic opposition in such places—as well as the human rights community in the United States—always viewed U.S. diplomatic and trade relations (even trade slightly circumscribed by the lack of Overseas Private

Investment Corporation (OPIC) guarantees or Eximbank loans) as a virtual endorsement of undemocratic regimes. While such claims were undoubtedly exaggerated, it was also true that the elements of normality in bilateral relations introduced a note of ambivalence that was not always helpful—to say the least—in advancing the overall goals of U.S. policy. On this subject see Daniel Pipes and Adam Garfinkle, eds., *Friendly Tyrants: An American Dilemma* (New York: St. Martin's Press, 1991).

6. Cited in Note four.

7. This nicely avoids the possibility that for many inhabitants of the Caribbean (including present-day Cubans) the situation of Puerto Rico, with all its problems, might well be a source of envy.

8. A democratic Cuba would, of course, have a lobby in the United States conceivably stronger than any other sugar-producing area. And the current treatment of U.S. interests by the Philippines suggests that its current share (16 percent of the quota) might be ripe for reallocation.

10

In Search of a Modern Cuba Policy

Gillian Gunn

U.S. policy toward Cuba is caught in a time warp. Whereas policy regarding the rest of the Third World is breaking out of Cold War patterns, policy toward Cuba remains frozen in the anti-Communist mind-set of the 1960s, when it was conceived.

This would be simply a curious anomaly if it were not for the negative effect fossilized U.S. policy is having upon the transition process within Cuba itself. Even more worrying, that effect could contribute to developments in Cuba that significantly damage important U.S. interests. As one U.S. government employee colorfully put it, if Washington's policy contributes to a "Yugoslavia-type situation" on the island, the "splatter effect" in the southeastern United States, and in the Caribbean as a whole, would be formidable.

Current U.S. policy toward Cuba is virtually unchanged from the early 1960s. The embargo, imposed in February 1962, remains in place, and indeed was strengthened in October 1992 by the passage of the Cuban Democracy Act (also known as the Torricelli Law after its sponsor, Representative Robert Torricelli, a New Jersey Democrat). U.S. politicians' public rhetoric regarding Cuba, in both the Democratic and Republican parties, is still emotional and confrontational. In the 1992 election campaign, President Bush and Democratic candidate Bill Clinton vied to issue the most aggressively anti-Castro rhetoric as they competed for the critical Florida vote. The former's pledge to be the "first U.S. president to set foot in a free Cuba" and the latter's claim that the Bush administration had lost an opportunity "to put the hammer down on Fidel Castro" could just as easily have been issued in 1962 as in 1992.

THE ANGOLA OPPORTUNITY

This situation was not inevitable. As the Cold War began to thaw in the late 1980s, there was a key opportunity for U.S.-Cuban relations to shift course. U.S.-Cuban collaboration in the Angola/Namibia negotiations created ideal conditions for a policy reassessment. The fact that the opportunity was forfeited may come back to haunt American decision makers in the future.

Since Cuban troops entered the Angolan conflict in 1975, the Cuban presence in Africa had been a thorn in the side of U.S.-Cuban relations. U.S. leaders repeatedly stated that relations could not be normalized until Cuban troops were withdrawn from the continent. When President Reagan took office in 1981, he linked support for the independence of Namibia from South Africa to the withdrawal of Cuban troops from neighboring Angola.[1]

For years, negotiations on the withdrawal of Cuban troops stagnated. South Africa repeatedly invaded Angola, and Cuba claimed it could not depart until Angola's "sovereignty" was secure. In 1987, however, the dynamics changed. The Soviet Union under Gorbachev became less enthusiastic about pouring resources into a faraway war with no clear relevance to immediate Soviet security interests. The South African public became ambivalent about pursuing the war in Angola, especially after Cuban troops fought a South African invading force to a standstill at the famous battle of Cuito Cuanavale in January 1988.[2] Cuba, weary of its protracted involvement in an open-ended war and somewhat disillusioned with its Angolan ally, began to look for an honorable way out of the conflict.

Thus, in May 1988, Cuba joined U.S., South African and Angolan negotiators around the conference table, and all four parties began to negotiate seriously. In December of that year, as Ronald Reagan was about to leave office, two accords were signed. They provided for the withdrawal of Cuban troops from Angola over a twenty-seven-month period and the initiation of a Namibian independence process on April 1, 1989.[3]

In the course of the negotiations, Cuban and U.S. representatives were often closeted in the same room for hours, and interpersonal relations began to be characterized by mutual, if grudging, respect. An event shortly after the signing of the agreement helped consolidate this rapport. A Cuban ally, the South West African People's Organization (SWAPO), violated the agreement on April 1, 1989, and South Africa threatened to back out of its obligations as a result. The United States hoped Havana would bring its SWAPO ally into line. Cuba, equally disturbed that SWAPO might disrupt an accord that was permitting it to bring its troops home with honor, carried out the task with enthusiasm. The United States obtained South Africa's compliance with the accord, and for a brief period, Havana and Washington were actual allies. In part due to this collaboration, the Angola/Namibia accords are now regarded as among the most smoothly implemented international agreements in recent history.

In late 1988 and early 1989, as the negotiating process concluded and implementation of the accords began, Cuba made discreet overtures to Washington via U.S. officials Havana had come to trust in the course of the above diplomacy. Specifically, Cuba suggested that a similar negotiating approach be applied to outstanding bilateral problems. When the message was conveyed to the White House and the State Department, it was ignored and various message carriers were reprimanded. There are unconfirmed reports that the overture became known to conservative elements in the Cuban-American community, who applied pressure for it to be rejected. This incident had a chilling effect on other U.S. diplomats, who henceforth tended to discuss alternative Cuba policies only in private, and upon Cuban officials, who concluded that the United States was not interested in diplomatic solutions to bilateral problems.[4]

THE BUSH ADMINISTRATION

As the Bush administration took over from Reagan, the Cuban government still harbored some hopes that relations could improve. Havana viewed Bush as a moderate Republican, likely to be more pragmatic than his predecessor. These hopes were soon dashed. In fact, a year after Bush took office, a Cuban government official wryly commented to the author: "Who thought we would ever be nostalgic for the good old days under Reagan."

Several factors accounted for Bush's policy approach. First, he had close ties to the Cuban American National Foundation (CANF), and conservative elements of the Cuban-American community that make up the foundation's constituency. CANF Chairman Jorge Mas Canosa had supported Bush's candidacy early in the Republican primaries, well before it was clear Bush would be the nominee. This support, combined with generous financial donations from Cuban-American conservatives, meant that Bush would come to office with an ear already attuned to hard-line arguments.

Second, Bush's son, Jeb, had strong connections with conservative Miami Cubans. Jeb Bush made his home in Florida, spoke good Spanish, had a Mexican wife, and seemed interested in launching a political career based in part on a Hispanic constituency. Third, the collapse of the Berlin Wall in November 1989 and the subsequent implosion of the socialist world apparently caused Bush to conclude that Cuba would soon succumb to the fate of its eastern allies, and therefore there was no point in establishing dialogue with a near-defunct regime.

One of Bush's earliest moves was to harden terms for normalizing relations with Cuba, announcing that relations would not improve until Cuba had free elections, established a market economy and reduced the size of its military. This contrasted with the United States' previous conditions, which demanded an end to Cuban export of revolution, withdrawal of troops from Africa and reduction of military ties with the Soviet Union. Then, in January 1990, the U.S. Coast Guard fired artillery at the Cuban chartered freighter, the Hermann, in international waters when it failed to permit the Guard to carry out a drug inspection. Mexican authorities subsequently found the Cuban ship to be drug-free.[5]

Bush also moved ahead with Television Marti, a project long-cherished by the Cuban American National Foundation. The Reagan administration had officially supported the project but delayed implementation, perhaps because of concern about its legality under international law. In March 1990, Bush initiated the U.S. Information Agency broadcasts to Cuba from a balloon suspended high above the Florida Keys. Although the body responsible for settling international broadcasting disputes—the International Telecommunications Union—declared the transmissions illegal, and Cuban jamming prevented the Cuban population from viewing the programs, the broadcasts continued.

Rhetoric also stiffened. Secretary of State James Baker awkwardly refused to rule out an invasion of Cuba when questioned on this point in a February 1990 visit to the Soviet Union. In March 1990 Vice President Dan Quayle remarked that change in Cuba might only be brought about by establishing a resistance movement similar to the contras in Nicaragua.[6]

Two months later, in May 1990, the United States executed three simultaneous military maneuvers—"Global Shield," "Ocean Venture" and "Defex"—in the Caribbean. The exercises entailed, among other things, a simulated evacuation of personnel from Guantanamo and landings by U.S. assault troops at Viques Island in Puerto Rico, which many observers interpreted as a practice invasion of Cuba.[7] How much of the hard-line posture was motivated by Bush's own views and how much by Cuban-American lobbying is impossible to say. However, it is clear that the CANF developed a swift, informal communication channel with the Oval Office. A March 1991 incident illustrated the importance of this connection. The UN Commission on Human Rights was in the midst of its annual meeting in Switzerland, and the CANF became aware that a U.S.-sponsored resolution condemning Cuba probably would not pass due to Latin American abstentions and negative votes. Mas Canosa asked Jeb Bush to persuade his father to personally call Argentina's President Menem and request that Argentina change its vote. Jeb did so, his father was convinced, and Menem instructed his representative to alter her vote. She resigned in protest, but her replacement complied.[8]

Rumors circulating in Washington during the second half of 1991 and first half of 1992 increased tension still more. A few Pentagon officials suggested that the Bush administration draw up contingency plans for "humanitarian intervention" in Cuba should civil unrest break out on the island. Though those advocating the policy later said they intended it only as a last resort and not as a preemptive measure, the "humanitarian intervention" theme continued to crop up intermittently thereafter. The holding of another "Ocean Venture" exercise in May 1992, combined with the reinforcement of personnel at Guantanamo in connection with the housing of Haitian refugees there, made the "humanitarian intervention" rumors appear even more ominous to those predisposed to distrust U.S. intentions.[9]

THE 1992 U.S. ELECTIONS

The 1992 presidential elections then caused domestic U.S. politics to exert even greater influence over American policy. Since 1989, Senator Connie Mack of Florida had been trying to obtain passage of his "Mack Amendment," which prohibited U.S. subsidiaries abroad from trading with Cuba. This prohibition had existed earlier but was lifted in 1975 after Washington concluded that it disrupted relations with allies, who claimed that the prohibition violated their sovereignty through extraterritorial imposition of U.S. law.[10] The State Department initially opposed the Mack Amendment, arguing that it would re-create the same problems that existed prior to 1975, and that it would engender support for Cuba in the Third World. Testifying in Congress in April 1992, Deputy Assistant Secretary for Inter-American Affairs Robert Gelbard said that "had the embargo applied to U.S. companies in third countries, Cuba would likely have won the U.N. debate" condemning the embargo.[11] Bush refrained from contradicting the State Department's position.

In early 1992, Democratic Congressman Robert Torricelli, whose New Jersey constituency has some Cuban-Americans, used his new post as chairman of the House Western Hemisphere Subcommittee to formulate a bill titled "The Cuba Democracy Act" (CDA). The original motivation of the bill's drafters appears to have been to enhance communication between the American and Cuban people, focus the damage caused by the U.S. embargo on the Cuban government rather than on the Cuban people, provide some incentives to entice the Cuban government to reform, and simultaneously increase pressure on the Cuban regime.

As the bill made its way through Congress, however, the "carrots" grew smaller and the "sticks" more formidable. This was due, in large part, to effective lobbying by the Cuban American National Foundation and the disorganized opposition mounted by more moderate Cuban-American organizations. By the time the bill reached its final form, it contained not only the Mack Amendment language, but also a shipping prohibition.

Furthermore, the bill undermined low-key, confidence-building discussions under way between U.S. non-governmental organizations (NGOs) and the Cuban authorities on what had been considered apolitical technical issues. Representative Torricelli repeatedly referred to improved communications as a "weapon" with which to "subvert" Cuba. Havana, in response, hardened its terms to discussions with NGOs on phone and postal communications. It also shifted responsibility for the talks from technical authorities to the Ministry of Foreign Relations, symbolically making improved communications contingent on, rather than a step toward, improved bilateral relations.

The bill also restricted future U.S. policy flexibility by stating that the president has to certify, among other things, that Cuba is "moving towards establishing a free market economic system" before the bill's provisions can be waived. This raised questions about how a reformist, more democratic, but still socialist post-Castro government could be treated.

That said, a few liberal provisions did survive in the final bill. It appears that under the bill the president could, if he chose, encourage certain U.S. companies to enhance communication-related trade, neutralize the new shipping restrictions by instructing the Treasury Department to regularly issue shipping licenses, and facilitate additional travel to Cuba by U.S. citizens engaged in educational and religious activities.

Initially, the Bush administration took the same position on the CDA as it had on the Mack Amendment, pointing out that the subsidiary provision was viewed by many as an extraterritorial imposition of U.S. law, and would therefore damage U.S. relations with important allies.

Electoral politics then intervened. Although Democratic presidential aspirant Bill Clinton had been counseled by several Latin America advisers to oppose the bill, in late April 1992, when his campaign coffers were critically low, he traveled to Florida and publicly endorsed the CDA. "I think this administration has missed a big opportunity to put the hammer down on Fidel Castro and Cuba," Clinton told a crowd of Cuban-Americans. To many, it appeared no coincidence that Clinton raised $275,000 in South Florida shortly after his announcement.[12]

Anxious to retain the Cuban-American vote, Bush soon reversed his own position. The administration had been letting the bill die in committee, a strategy often used when a president thinks a measure unwise but does not want to publicly oppose it. Then Bush sought to preempt the bill by adopting, through executive order, two of its less-important aspects. Finally, aware that the polls showed Clinton gaining a significant share of the Cuban-American vote, on May 5, 1992, Bush reversed his stance and endorsed the full bill.[13]

On August 10, 1992, Deputy Assistant Secretary Gelbard returned to the Hill and metaphorically ate his words of just four months earlier, testifying that "although modifications to the bill would make it even stronger, we support it as it stands."[14] The CDA subsequently passed both houses of Congress, and on October 23, two weeks before the elections, Bush signed it into law at a gala ceremony in a Miami hotel, to which the CANF was invited and, ironically, the Democratic author of the bill, Torricelli, was excluded.[15]

One week later, however, the Democratic Party got its own moment in the limelight with the CANF when Bill Clinton had a much-publicized meeting with Mas Canosa. By this time, perhaps recognizing that Bush would not win and it was time to change horses, Mas had announced that while he would vote for the president, Cuban-Americans "need not fear a Bill Clinton Administration."[16]

Gelbard's April analysis of international opinion was then proven entirely correct. On November 24, 1992, the UN General Assembly voted overwhelmingly to support a non-binding Cuban resolution urging Washington to lift the embargo. The vote was 59 to 3, with only Israel and Romania joining the United States in opposition. Seventy-one delegations abstained.[17] Several important U.S. trade partners, including Britain and Canada, also passed blocking legislation, prohibiting U.S. subsidiaries in their countries from complying with the CDA.

The UN vote was not so much the result of worldwide sympathy for the Castro government, but rather an expression of resentment against the United States for seeking to impose its laws on other countries. The Cuban press, however, had a field day, trumpeting the vote as a sign of international solidarity, and arguing that it was Washington, not Havana, that faced international isolation.

Increased paramilitary action by Cuban-American exiles also exacerbated tension between the United States and Cuba. In December 1991, three members of the Miami-based exile organization Commandos L were captured shortly after landing in Cuba with explosives and firearms. One was executed and the other two sentenced to thirty-year jail terms. Ten months later, in October 1992, a Commandos L boat strafed the Spanish-Cuban five-star Hotel Melia in Varadero with machine-gun fire. The FBI investigated the case as a possible violation of the Neutrality Act, but at the time of this writing had made no arrests.[18]

THE ALDANA INCIDENT

Activities by the Central Intelligence Agency also may have increased Cuban apprehension about U.S. intentions and inadvertently strengthened the hand of hard-line elements within the Cuban government in late 1992. The information that follows is unconfirmed, and should be treated as speculation. However, there is enough metaphorical "smoke" surrounding the incident to suggest that further investigation is warranted.

In September 1992, Carlos Aldana Escalante, then considered the third most powerful man in Cuba after Fidel and Raul Castro, was abruptly removed from his post as head of the Central Committee Departments of Ideology and International Relations and subsequently expelled from the Communist Party. According to the official Politburo explanation, the move was motivated by "deficiencies in his work and serious mistakes of a personal nature in his performance of his duties."[19] It subsequently emerged that Aldana had overseen a trade transaction involving a Cuban intermediary named Eberto Lopez Morales, who claimed to represent a foreign electronic equipment supplier. The goods were never delivered, and Cuba ended up losing $17 million. Individuals close to the intelligence community in Washington believe that the "scam" was part of a CIA plan to "bleed Cuba" economically via false business deals, and that while not intentional, Aldana's downfall was considered an added "bonus."

Aldana was a leading figure in the Angola-Namibia negotiations, was responsible for convincing SWAPO to comply with the accords, and was an instigator of the Cuban overture to Washington in late 1988 and early 1989. There was much controversy in Western circles in the 1990–92 period over whether he was a genuine reformer or simply expounded reformist ideas to U.S. visitors as a public relations ploy.

Whatever the truth, in a November 1991 interview with the author, Aldana advocated several reformist initiatives, including a fairly open candidate-nominating procedure for Cuba's elections and the establishment of a commission to rectify violations of "civil and political" rights. According to Cuban academic sources, within days of Aldana's September 1992 removal, language in the draft electoral document circulating in the National Assembly was adjusted, removing the possibility of a more open nominating process. These academic sources believe that hard-line Cuban political figures had long been searching for a way to discredit Aldana, and the Lopez incident provided them with a perfect tool. If reports of a Lopez-CIA connection are correct, then Washington, either accidentally or intentionally, sabotaged the political career of a figure who had shown himself open to improving relations and advocated reforms that would have at least partially responded to U.S. criticism of Cuba's internal political system.

CLINTON'S CONFUSION

At the time of this writing in early 1993, U.S. policy toward Cuba is caught up in yet another controversy. At the behest of prominent African-Americans, most particularly Vernon Jordan, President Clinton indicated his intention to name black Cuban-American lawyer Mario Baeza as assistant secretary of state for Inter-American Affairs, apparently knowing little of Baeza's views regarding his homeland. Before the decision could be formally announced, however, conservative Cuban-Americans launched an intensive lobbying effort to get the nomination rescinded, complaining that Baeza was insufficiently tough on Cuba. Baeza had participated in a 1992 conference on business opportunities in Cuba sponsored by the European magazine *Euromoney*, and was said to oppose some provisions of the Torricelli Law. The conservative Cuban-American lobbying caused Baeza's nomination to be put on indefinite hold by the Clinton transition team.

The Baeza controversy illustrated a growing tension between U.S. business interests and U.S. policy. Many American corporations have become uneasy that European and Latin American firms are taking advantage of

Cuba's new openness to foreign investment and are rapidly occupying market niches. Once U.S.-Cuban relations improve enough to permit lifting of the embargo, some U.S. corporations fear that they will find rivals already exploiting the most lucrative opportunities. Due to this concern, many American corporations have instructed their lawyers to discreetly explore opportunities for current and future business in Cuba. While staying within the law, some of these corporations have let the U.S. government know that they would appreciate a relaxation of parts of the embargo so as to reduce their competitive handicap.

As a corporate lawyer representing clients with interests in Latin America, it is reasonable to assume that Baeza's presence at the *Euromoney* conference was related to this trend. His reported unease with the Torricelli Law, which further restricts U.S. business, is also logical for a lawyer representing such interests. The ferocity with which conservative Cuban-Americans have attacked Baeza, and the fact that at the time of this writing they were forcing Clinton to reconsider his nomination, illustrate the odd disjunction between U.S. economic interests and government policy, and suggests that Washington may be no nearer a modern Cuba policy under Clinton than it was under Bush.

In sum, U.S. policy was gradually shifting toward a more normal (though far from normalized) relationship with Cuba at the end of the Reagan administration, in large part due to U.S.-Cuban collaboration during the Angola negotiations. Throughout the Bush years, policy progressively hardened, first by reversing the warming trend initiated under Reagan, then by increasing rhetoric and symbolic military gestures, and finally by tightening the U.S. embargo via the Torricelli Law. President Clinton's initial actions suggest that he may be continuing along the same path. As the Cold War has thawed, U.S.-Cuban relations paradoxically have become more frigid than at any point since the early 1960s.

PROVISIONS OF THE CUBAN DEMOCRACY ACT

- Gives the president authority to deny aid to any country that provides assistance to Cuba.
- Permits donations of food and medicine to non-governmental organizations and individuals in Cuba. (This was already legal.)
- Authorizes exports of medicine and medical equipment, but with the proviso that the United States must be able to verify "by on-site inspection" or other means, the use of the exported item. (The latter was inserted at the behest of conservative Cuban-Americans after liberal congressmen introduced the authorization. As Castro is certain to forbid on-site verification, unless acceptable "other means" of verification can be found the condition will render the authorization meaningless.)
- Authorizes establishment of additional telecommunications services between Cuba and the United States, but says that such an agreement "shall not require"

withdrawal from any blocked account. (This actually impedes some negotiations on telecommunications improvement, since Cuba has linked release of the frozen account, containing Cuba's share of past payments for telephone calls between the two countries, to the establishment of new lines.)

- Instructs the U.S. Postal Service to provide direct mail to Cuba on charter planes in the absence of common carrier service. (Cuba has long held the position that it will establish direct mail with the United States only in the same manner that the United States has direct mail with other countries—on regularly scheduled aircraft. As Cuba will not accept direct mail on charter planes, the only current form of air communication, this provision has no effect on mail service.)
- Says the United States may assist NGOs in Cuba to promote nonviolent democratic change.
- Prohibits trade with Cuba by U.S. subsidiaries incorporated in third countries, though trade related to the establishment of telecommunications appears to be exempted. (This means that telecommunications subsidiaries abroad whose parent companies have not done business with Cuba before—and therefore do not have blocked accounts subject to the above-mentioned "shall not require" clause—could trade with Cuba regardless of the subsidiary restriction. However, this would still only be possible if Havana were willing to de-link the old blocked account issue from new business. U.S. NGOs have the impression that while Havana was willing to start afresh before the Torricelli Bill became law, it reacted to the bill's passage by reinstating the linkage.)
- Prohibits vessels from loading or unloading freight in the United States for 180 days after having carried goods or passengers to or from Cuba, unless they have special licenses. (This provision could be neutralized by the liberal issuance of licenses.)
- Defines the conditions under which the president may waive the law's restrictions. To do so he must determine and report to Congress that Cuba: has held "free and fair elections conducted under internationally recognized observers"; has permitted opposition parties to organize; is respecting human rights; "is moving towards establishing a free market economic system"; and "has committed itself to constitutional change that would ensure regular free and fair elections."
- Slightly expands the purposes for which U.S. residents can travel to Cuba, adding "educational," "religious" and "human rights" activities to the existing exemptions for news gathering and academic research. (The new categories of activities have to be "reasonably limited in frequency, duration and number of participants," however.)
- Adds "transmission" of "information and informational materials" to the previous embargo exemption for export and import of information. (This could be interpreted to permit U.S. television to run Cuban transmissions—for example, sports events.)
- Increases the penalties for violation of the embargo to a maximum of $50,000, in comparison with the previous $10,000 threshold.[20]

EFFECT ON THE CUBAN TRANSITION

There is one conclusion on which all observers, within and outside Cuba, pro- and anti-Castro, can agree: Cuba is about to embark on a transition of some sort. The key question therefore becomes: What kind of change, carried out in what manner? The most desirable scenario from the United States' perspective is that Cuba swiftly embark on democratic and market-oriented reforms in a peaceful manner free from civil conflict. Violent change has a number of risks. If bloodshed were to occur, many Cuban-Americans would feel morally bound to support the anti-Castro forces, at the least sending material supplies, and possibly contributing personnel themselves. Such a scenario, even if it did produce a democratic, market-oriented government, would cause Washington enormous headaches. The civil conflict would generate a massive migration outflow, making the Mariel exodus of 1980 appear a minor incident. Such migrants would not only overburden the social services of South Florida, but would also turn up on the shores of other countries in the region, most of which are far less able to cope with the responsibility.

Such civil conflict would also create strong pressures for the United States to intervene, particularly if significant numbers of Cuban-Americans were involved in the melee. Intervention by U.S. troops would create tensions between the United States and its Latin American allies, many of whom grudgingly admire Castro's willingness to stand up to Washington. It would lead to the loss of U.S. lives, for a sufficient number of well-armed Castro loyalists would continue to fight a guerrilla war even after the major population centers were subdued by superior U.S. military force. Intervention would also hamper the legitimation of any successor regime. Given the history of Cuban resentment of repeated U.S. intervention over the last century, any government that took office on the heels of a foreign military operation would find it difficult to establish its nationalistic credentials, a key to credibility in the Cuban political culture.

In sum, civil conflict in Cuba and the U.S. intervention that could well follow would have extremely negative implications for U.S. interests. The "splatter effect" could be costly in lives, money and political resources.

If a violent transition would negatively affect a whole variety of U.S. and regional interests, how is current policy influencing Cuba's transition? Is it making peaceful change more or less likely? Many, including this author, argue that current policy significantly increases the potential for violence.

For a variety of historical reasons, including class and racial divisions exacerbated by the long and bloody struggle for independence, Cuban political culture has a tendency to view conflicts in terms of absolutes. In both Havana and Miami, many Cuban political activists define all who disagree with them as "traitors," not worthy of respect, let alone tolerance. Over the last few years, however, the societies on both sides of the Florida Straits have begun to produce a small number of leaders who fear that the dogmatism of their colleagues could lead to a national tragedy. These leaders have started groping toward a new political style that includes tolerance for at least some diversity of opinion.

This new development was encapsulated in a meeting in May 1990, at which eight Cubans, including exiles and Cuban Communist Party members, met in a Miami restaurant for what one later described as "intense but friendly" dialogue, in which a "conscious effort" was made to "find common ground while never once giving in on issues of principle."[21]

It is these sorts of interchanges, between and within the Miami and Havana communities, that provide the best hope for a peaceful transition in Cuba. And it is precisely these initiatives that have been undermined by recent U.S. policy. U.S. actions and rhetoric have placed Cuban reformers—those most willing to consider dialogue with their opponents—on the defensive.

In late 1989 and most of 1990, there was a brief political opening in Cuba, related to the *llamamiento* or "call" for the Fourth Party Congress, eventually held in October 1991. For a few months, the Cuban leadership responded to the crisis in the socialist world by seeking to enhance its domestic support through a slight opening in the political system. Cubans were encouraged to speak out more openly so as to create genuine, rather than simulated unity. Huge red and black billboards proclaiming "Your Opinion Counts" sprouted throughout the countryside. The state-run magazine *Bohemia* remarked: "Our idiosyncracy was forged in the love of independence and the hatred of oppression. But it also left colonial intolerance of the narrow-minded Spanish."[22]

A remark by a young pro-Castro academic reflected the new mood. "Some of us feel," he said, "that . . . dissidents are not dangerous. . . . It would be much wiser to refute their ideas through public debate than inflate their apparent importance, and give the U.S. a propaganda tool, by imprisoning them."[23]

Roberto Robaina, leader of the Union of Young Communists, took a similar position when he responded to the call by dissident Gustavo Arcos for a dialogue among all Cubans, within and outside the island. Although the Arcos proposal was flatly rejected by the government, Robaina admitted at a press conference: "We have to find national solutions to national problems. Even the discontented and dissidents have space in this debate, but only those who are in Cuba. . . . We know that not everyone is with the Revolution."[24]

Robaina implicitly rejected Arcos' call for dialogue with the Miami exiles, but left the door open for conversations with opponents who remained within Cuba.

Discussions about the economy also became more open, with some participants advocating reforms that would lead to a mixed, rather than a purely socialist, system. Some of Cuba's younger political leaders also intimated, though they did not directly state, that a multiparty system might eventually better serve Cuba's needs than the current single-party structure. A few well-connected individuals privately ridiculed the idea that the United States sought to overthrow the Cuban revolution through violence, arguing that such claims were simply put forward by hard-line figures who wanted an excuse not to change.

The opening did not last long, however, and Castro set a new tone in September 1990. Using an epithet for counter-revolutionaries absent from official rhetoric since the 1980s, he declared: "Gusanos, a tus huecos" ("Worms, to your holes").[25]

A chilling article in the Cuban magazine *Trabajadores* (Workers) further reflected the retrenchment. *Gusanos*, it said, used to be transparently counter-revolutionary. Now, however, there is a more dangerous version that, under the guise of seeking to improve socialism through critical debate, actually "hears the siren song of capitalism. . . . He portrays himself . . . as a pragmatist . . . when actually he is easily frightened, a coward. . . . Like bull-fighters we must steer clear of them until we need to use the sword."[26] This language bore little resemblance to *Bohemia's* criticism of the Spanish legacy of intolerance published earlier in the year.

A high-ranking Cuban official expressed the new official line in an October 1990 interview:

The Cuban revolution is now under more external threat than ever before. . . . The changes . . . would involve opening up the political system. . . . But we have to be in a position to hit back hard against the threats facing us. When you hit with an open palm you are weak. [He pulled his fingers into a fist.] But when you hit back like this, you can really defend yourself. We have to unify, to be ready to resist the threat. We cannot afford the divisions these changes would permit.[27]

Many officials then backtracked from their previous positions. In an autumn 1990 interview, Robaina claimed that his earlier favorable remarks about Arcos had been misunderstood. Because the dissident movement permitted itself to be used by the United States to try to undermine the revolution, he argued, it was not entitled to participate in the debate. Academics also hedged their bets. One who had previously argued strongly for change, now commented, "We must not do anything which might make us appear to be giving in to outside pressure. Perhaps now, when the pressure from outside is so great, is not the best time to undertake major changes."

Since the re-restriction of political space after the brief 1989–90 opening, there has been a strange bifurcation in Cuban policy. Some of the economic reforms advocated during the *llamamiento* debates have been implemented, particularly those relating to the activities of foreign capitalists. But in the political field, the hard-line element has appeared to gain ever greater authority. Activities by human rights activists that used to produce no more than a metaphorical slap on the wrist now lead to arrests, trial, and long prison terms. Electoral reforms were watered down until they represented little real change from the previous system. While religious believers and

homosexuals were extended constitutional protection against discrimination
in the new 1992 constitution, the political mood in general became far more
polarized.

What impact did U.S. policy have on this evolution? It would be pre-
posterous to claim that the hard-line position adopted by the Bush administration was primarily responsible for the erosion of the position of those
reformers most likely to facilitate a peaceful transition. After all, the *llamamiento* debates got under way in the midst of hostile U.S. rhetoric in
early 1990. And many other factors clearly prompted the crackdown: Castro's
fear of losing control of the political process; the realization that economic
austerity was going to worsen far more quickly than previously anticipated;
and the desire of the older generation to hang on to power.

But U.S. policy certainly provided a convenient pretext for conservatives
to rein in reformist energies, for the hard-liners were able to argue that the
increasingly hostile U.S. position meant that a major political opening would
invite ill-intentioned meddling from the Colossus of the North. Military
maneuvers in the Caribbean that included rehearsals for an invasion of Cuba;
tightening of the embargo via the Torricelli Law; talk of "humanitarian intervention"; a U.S. political discourse in which presidential candidates vied
to deliver the most anti-Castro rhetoric; terrorist acts by U.S.-based exiles;
and evidence, albeit unconfirmed, of CIA mischief all created a context in
which the arguments of the hard-liners became more plausible. It no longer
seemed so ridiculous to claim that Cuba could not afford the political instability associated with reform because the United States would pounce on
any vulnerability to try to finish off its hated enemy.

In the course of interviews in September 1992, previously reformist academics, whom the author had expected to find profoundly disaffected,
actually defended the various crackdowns, arguing that the position of the
United States had eliminated all room for maneuver. Many reformers, who
were so dedicated to pluralist ideas that they had seemed on the verge of
becoming dissidents only two years before, now acquiesced to the very
policies they had criticized. (Of course, their new attitude may have been
related to fear of official reprisal as well.)

The United States had done Fidel Castro an enormous favor. It had provided an explanation for a refusal to reform that was plausible to the very
constituency most likely to effectively protest the political stagnation—the
well educated. The United States was not responsible for the hard-line shift.
Cuban domestic politics, Castro's character and other events in the international arena had done that. U.S. policy did, however, legitimate the shift
in the eyes of many Cubans.

The increased threat perception engendered by U.S. policy also created
a psychological context conducive to a nationalistic rallying of the population
behind Castro. Just as the American people united behind George Bush as
the perceived threat from Iraq became greater, so under similar circum-

stances did politically undecided Cubans tend to unite behind their national leader and question the patriotism of critics.

Finally, the close association of wealthy, largely white, Miami exiles with U.S. policy further assisted Castro. Many Cubans, and particularly those in the (disproportionately black) lower social classes, fear that a political transition could lead to the loss of the social safety net they have come to take for granted. Some who are not content under Castro's rule will nonetheless defend him if they are convinced that the alternative is a return to rule by "racists" who would "take orders from Washington" and remove their children's access to free health care and education. Recent U.S. policy has made it much easier for the Cuban leader to claim that this would be the logical result of his regime's demise.

Is it in the interest of Washington to sabotage the position of the very individuals who might be able to facilitate a "soft landing" when Cuba finally adjusts to the new international context? Is it wise to place potentially tolerant leaders from a highly nationalistic culture in the position of choosing between nationalism and reform? Is it good judgment to encourage the lower classes to believe that only Castro can protect them from exploitation by the wealthy exiles?

History has shown what can befall a society when the international context changes but, due to in-built or externally imposed rigidities, the society itself is slow to adapt. The result can be long-term surface tranquility followed by a social upheaval. To the extent that U.S. rigidity legitimates Cuban rigidity, American policy indirectly heightens the likelihood that Cuba's eventual transition will be bloody, with all the negative consequences for U.S. interests discussed above.

THE ALTERNATIVE

If a swift peaceful transition to a pluralist, market-oriented society is unlikely, and a violent transition might seriously damage U.S. interests, what are the alternatives? All are unpalatable, for they involve a gradualist approach and a willingness to accept Castro at the helm of Cuba for some interim period as the price for stability. Distasteful though these alternatives are, however, they are more realistic than the first scenario, and less damaging to U.S. interests than the second. Indeed, one Western diplomat interviewed in Havana recently went so far as to say: "It may turn out that the only way to avoid bloodshed in Cuba is to have a partial transition while Fidel remains in control, leaving full democratization until he passes from the scene." This, from an individual implacably opposed to Castro, is a remarkable statement. It is also probably true.

There are some policy initiatives that could create a context conducive to a partial transition, even while Castro remains head of the government. The following measures would reduce Cuba's threat perception, and make it more difficult for the hard-liners to avoid reform pressures in the name of nationalism. They would also make it more difficult for the regime to blame the island's economic problems on Washington. The United States could:

- Eliminate rehearsals of Cuban invasions in the Caribbean exercises, and invite Cuban military observers to participate in the maneuvers as a sign of good faith.
- Accept the judgment of the International Telecommunications Union and suspend Television Marti.
- Cease all aggressive rhetoric, especially that which entails violent metaphors. (President Clinton would have to end references to "bringing hammers down.")
- Implement the Torricelli Law in a manner that minimizes the harm done by its sticks and maximizes the small carrots it still contains. This could involve encouraging telecommunications trade by companies without blocked accounts and publicizing the fact that a broader range of Americans are now exempted from the travel restrictions. President Clinton could order liberal issuance of shipping licenses, subject the subsidiary provision to review by an international body whose judgment he pledges to accept, and declare that he has verified by "other means" that U.S. medicine shipments will not be used for nefarious purposes, thereby freeing up exports of such goods.
- Remove all restrictions on food exports to Cuba, including direct sales to the Cuban government.
- Initiate government-to-government talks with Havana on the ideologically neutral area of environmental protection as a confidence-building measure.
- Publicly state that despite the language in the Torricelli Law, Cuba does not have to adopt a market economy in order for the embargo to be lifted. President Clinton could indicate that while significant progress toward full democracy must proceed the lifting of the embargo, Washington will accept whatever form of social organization the Cuban people choose.
- Coordinate policies with allies in Latin America and Europe, many of whom are uncomfortable with present U.S. policy and favor a more flexible approach.
- Distance Cuba policy from the conservative Cuban-American community, thereby diminishing the impression that Washington wishes to install a puppet government of wealthy exiles.
- Cease pressure on other countries not to invest in Cuba, as exposure to Western business practices appears to be broadening the worldview of Cuba's economic managers.[28]

This collection of policies would not bring democracy to Cuba overnight, or even guarantee a democratic transition at any point in the future. And it would have short-term costs, for Castro would claim that he had won the battle with Washington, and issue self-satisfied rhetoric that would temporarily strengthen his regime. But over the long term, these policies would work against the growing polarization of Cuban politics and remove the government's justification for rigidity. Castro would not necessarily become more flexible of his own volition, but his anti-reform position would seem less legitimate to many. This would increase the vigor of the internal debate and strengthen the position of reformers. Cuba's more pragmatic leaders would not be able to convince Castro to institute a capitalist economy and carry out major democratic reforms, but they could well convince him to accept a series of small steps in that direction, including some of the measures that were proposed and rejected in the lead-up to the Fourth Congress. In a context of decreased threat perception, the political space available to Cuba's human rights activists might re-expand back to the level of 1988, when Cuba was far less repressive toward those groups than currently.

In such circumstances, the Cuban transition would be painfully slow and incremental, with only partial progress on the issues that the United States deems important. But the above policies would be far more conducive to a peaceful transition, and lay at least some of the groundwork for a smooth completion of the process once Castro passes from the scene. And if, despite these precautions, civil conflict nonetheless did erupt, at least these policies would make it harder for the international community to hold the United States responsible and less likely that Washington would be expected to foot the full bill for reconstruction.

Any president implementing such a policy would be vulnerable to accusations that he was rewarding a dictator. However, this could be refuted by pointing out that the bulk of the embargo remains in place. Washington could make it clear to Havana that the maximum prize, eradication of the embargo, could not occur until irreversible steps had been taken toward democracy.

If policy continues on its present course, Cuba could do to the Clinton presidency what it did to his governorship. Riots of imprisoned Mariel refugees at Fort Chaffee, and Clinton's difficulty in dealing with that explosion, partially contributed to his failure to win a consecutive second term as Arkansas governor. The "splatter effect" of a Cuban explosion could conceivably do the same to his aspirations for a second presidential term.

But far more important, continued U.S. rigidity could contribute to a major human tragedy on the island, which exacerbates hatreds and pushes back still further the day that it will be ruled by a government deemed both democratic and legitimate by its citizens.

NOTES

1. Gillian Gunn, "Keeping Namibian Independence on Track: The Cuba Factor," *CSIS Africa Notes*, No. 103, October 23, 1989.

2. Gillian Gunn, "A Guide to the Intricacies of the Angola-Namibia Negotiations," *CSIS Africa Notes*, No. 90, September 8, 1988.

3. Gunn, "Keeping Namibian Independence on Track."

4. Confidential interviews with U.S., Cuban and South African sources, 1989 and 1990.

5. Gillian Gunn, "Will Castro Fall?" *Foreign Policy*, No. 79, Summer 1990, pp. 148–49.

6. Ibid., p. 149.

7. Pascal Fletcher, "Cubans Encircle US Base in Nationwide Defense Alert," *The Washington Times*, May 4, 1990.

8. Mirta Ojito, "Bush Phone Call Changed UN Vote," *Miami Herald*, March 8, 1991.

9. "Ejercicio Ocean Venture 92–Inicia Estados Unidos Grandes Maniobras Militares en la Region," *Granma*, May 5, 1992. "Que Prepara Estados Unidos en Guantanamo?" *Granma*, May 5, 1992.

10. Donna Rich Kaplowitz and Michael Kaplowitz, *New Opportunities for US-Cuban Trade* (Baltimore: Johns Hopkins University, 1992), p. 60.

11. Statement by Robert S. Gelbard, principal deputy assistant secretary for Inter-American Affairs, before the Committee on Foreign Affairs, House of Representatives, April 9, 1992.

12. "Clinton Backs Torricelli Bill; 'I Like It,' He Tells Cuban Exiles," *Miami Herald*, April 24, 1992.

13. "Bush Gives Support to Cuba Bill," *Miami Herald*, May 6, 1992.

14. "The Cuban Democracy Act and US Policy Toward Cuba," Robert S. Gelbard, deputy assistant secretary for Inter-American Affairs, statement before the Subcommittee on Trade of the House Ways and Means Committee, Washington, D.C., August 10, 1992. *US Department of State Dispatch*, August 17, 1992, Vol. 3, No. 33, pp. 657–58.

15. "Bush to Sign Cuba Bill in Miami," *Miami Herald*, October 23, 1992.

16. "Clinton-Mas Meeting Shocks Cuban Miami," *Miami Herald*, October 29, 1992.

17. "UN Backs Cuba on US Embargo," *Washington Post*, November 25, 1992.

18. "Commandos L Strike Again," *CubaInfo*, October 27, 1992.

19. "Text of Politburo Note on Aldana Dismissal Noted," Havana Radio Rebelde Network, October 10, 1992.

20. Derived from the Cuban Democracy Act of 1992.

21. Sergio Lopez Miro, Op-Ed, *Miami Herald*, May 10, 1990.

22. Luis Sexto, "Saber Convivir," *Bohemia*, April 20, 1990.

23. Confidential interview with Cuban academic, Havana, 1990.

24. Ana Cerrud, "Arremeten en Cuba contra los Cubanos en el Exterior que Quieren Dialogar con Castro," *Diario las Americas*, June 27, 1990.

25. Speech of Fidel Castro at the Anniversary of the Committees for the Defense of the Revolution, September 28, 1990.

26. *Trabajadores*, October 6, 1990.

27. Interview with an official at the National Assembly of People's Power, October 1990.

28. For a more detailed examination of the impact of foreign investment on Cuban internal politics, see "The Sociological Impact of Rising Foreign Investment," *Georgetown University Cuba Briefing Paper Series*, January 1993.

11

The United States and Cuba: From a Strategy of Conflict to Constructive Engagement

Donald E. Schulz

There is a nagging sense that an important moment has come. Part of me thinks there is something we should be doing other than let it fall by its own weight. But I can't think what it is.

Susan Kaufman Purcell[1]

There is a moment in "I, Claudius" in which the Roman emperor looks back at all that had happened during his lifetime and before and decides that it is all rotten and has to be destroyed. Claudius says: "Let all the poisons that lurk in the mud hatch out."

In a very real sense, Claudius' curse sums up much of what has happened in Cuba during the last several years. All of the weaknesses and pathologies of the Castro regime, many of which had been hidden beneath the placid, monolithic facade, have come to the surface. The revolution has soured. The situation has grown so bad that most political observers today assume that the regime is in its final hour. Cuba is "collapsing," and the only real questions are when and how Castro will go and what will replace him.[2]

While Castro must leave sooner or later, reports of his impending demise have been much exaggerated. A *golpe de estado* (coup d'état) is possible, but not probable. Neither is it likely, under current circumstances, that the Cuban masses will rise up and overthrow the dictatorship. And although Castro could become a casualty of assassination, suicide, or natural death, this is not the kind of thing that is readily subject to prediction or that would necessarily lead to the collapse of the regime. For a variety of reasons, Castro's "final hour" seems likely to last for several years, perhaps longer. Indeed, rather than speaking of termination, it may be more appropriate to think in terms of a new stage in the revolution that could persist for the foreseeable future.

Within this context, it is time to reconsider the strategy to which the United States has been wed for over three decades. There are both reason and evidence to suggest that existing policy is not only ineffective, but counterproductive. Put simply, it is actually helping to prop up the regime. Beyond this, it must be recognized that the national interest of the United States rests not simply in getting rid of Castro, but in promoting a transition that will be relatively painless for all concerned. In these respects, the policy into which we have been locked (primarily for ideological, psychological, and domestic political reasons) has been neither effective nor constructive. Not only is it likely to contribute to Castro's survival in the short run, but it could very well build up tension within Cuba to the point where a peaceful transition becomes impossible in the longer run.

BACK TO THE FUTURE: THE CUBAN SOCIOECONOMIC CRISIS

In March 1990, Castro announced the coming of a "Special Period in Time of Peace"—in effect, an economic state of emergency. In August, drastic measures were imposed to ration petroleum. Daily gas and fuel deliveries were to be reduced by 50 percent in the state sector and 30 percent in the private. Household electrical consumption would be cut. Cement and construction plants would reduce their hours of operation. The Punta Gorda nickel plant would be closed. The new oil refinery in Cienfuegos, built with Soviet aid, would not open. To ease the anticipated crisis in transportation, hundreds of thousands of bicycles and two bicycle manufacturing plants would be purchased from the People's Republic of China. A nationwide project would be instituted to replace tractors and combines with oxen. Cuba, it seemed, was entering an era of spiraling underdevelopment. If it was not exactly going back into the Stone Age, it was at least experiencing substantial deindustrialization.

While the immediate precipitator of these measures was a huge shortfall in Soviet oil deliveries, the larger cause of the crisis was the accelerating collapse of Communism in the Soviet Union and Eastern Europe. During the latter half of 1989, Cuba had begun to experience serious trade disruptions due to *perestroika*. By then, Soviet firms had acquired the right to trade directly on foreign markets. Cuba had to deal with individual Soviet enterprises, which preferred customers who could pay in hard currency to those who could not. As a consequence, deliveries from the Soviet Union had become increasingly unreliable.

At the same time, the Eastern European Communist regimes were falling like dominoes, and the impact on Cuba was dramatic. Between the first half of 1989 and the first half of 1990, sugar exports to the island's primary buyers in the region fell by 56 percent.[3] The decline in these markets and the erosion of the Soviet sugar subsidy[4] underscored the risks of a development strategy that had put most of Cuba's "eggs in one basket." In spite of a worldwide oversupply of sugar and generally low world prices, the Castro government had continued to invest heavily in that industry on the assumption that Cuba's Council on Mutual Economic Assistance (henceforth COMECON) market was secure and that high prices were guaranteed.

By the turn of the decade, Cuba was even more dependent on sugar than it had been before the revolution. Now, however, its Eastern European trade partners were fleeing, and its relations with the Soviet Union were increasingly uncertain. To make matters worse, all of this was occurring at a time of disastrously low world market prices, when most traditional buyers were becoming largely self-sufficient (due to sugar beet production), and changing consumer tastes (diet colas, light beer) and a revolution in technology (laboratory-produced sugar) were threatening to "devastate the few remaining economies still heavily dependent on sugar."[5]

At the January 1990 meeting of COMECON, moreover, the Soviets proposed that trade between member countries be conducted on the basis of market prices and hard currency beginning the following year. In tense meetings in Moscow and Havana, they informed the Cubans of their intention to drastically cut economic aid in virtually every category, from barter trade to subsidized prices for Cuban goods and low-interest debt financing. No longer would the Castro government be allowed to resell excess petroleum deliveries abroad for hard currency.

The Soviets did try to let the Cubans down as easily as possible. Even in 1991, they continued to purchase Cuban sugar at more than twice the world market price. At the same time, they sold the island oil at half the market price.[6] But they made it clear that there would be no more long-term concessionary agreements. The Soviet subsidy, estimated at just under $4 billion in 1990, slid to $2.5 billion. However, there were signs that the trade pact for 1991 was not being fully implemented and that the real subsidy might be as low as $1.5 billion.[7] And there was worse to come. In the words of a Soviet Embassy spokesman in Havana: "On 27 December it will be all over. Of course, we will be pleased to conduct trade with Cuba afterwards, but at world market prices. And in addition, the question of debts must be settled."[8]

By fall 1991, Cuba's trade with Eastern Europe was virtually paralyzed; its ability to buy goods from the Soviet Union had been reduced by billions of dollars. Overall, the island was importing 50 percent fewer foreign goods than it had two years earlier.[9] On top of everything else, the disintegration of the Soviet Union meant that the Cubans now had to negotiate with the authorities in the various union republics, as well as with the 20,000-odd firms still interested in the island's exports. Reports from Moscow, moreover, suggested that the economic disruption in that country might soon become so severe that the Soviets, once the world's leading producer of petroleum, might have to import the product themselves.[10] The implications for future deliveries to Cuba were obvious.

The island was now mired in the most serious socioeconomic crisis since at least the Great Depression. Castro himself proclaimed it the most difficult period in Cuban history.[11] The question was whether and when the economy would bottom out and begin to recover or whether it had entered a process of terminal decline.

The new year brought no relief. In July 1992, after more than three decades as Cuba's main petroleum supplier, the Russian pipeline finally ran dry. During the first half of the year, the two countries had agreed to exchange a million tons of raw sugar for 1.8 million tons of oil.[12] But talks to extend these arrangements were cancelled, and by mid-year the last shipments of petroleum and sugar had reached their destinations. Although some trading of Cuban sugar for equipment and spare parts continued, the amount involved was minuscule compared with the past. Neither did the prospects for the future look promising. Since 1988, Russian oil production had fallen by almost 35 percent. Domestic needs and standing commitments to Ukraine and Belarus were expected to absorb almost all of the available supply. At the same time, soaring prices for basic goods had led most Russians to cut back on sugar consumption, even as private firms were beginning to look to Western Europe for that product. Increasingly, the Cubans found themselves out in the cold.[13] While they had agreements to supply sugar to China, Kazakhstan, Lithuania, and a few other countries, they had to scramble on the spot market to survive.

The impact of the oil cutoff was immediate. Even with greatly scaled-back consumption, Cuban domestic petroleum production could supply only a third of the island's electrical needs. By late July, blackouts had become an almost daily occurrence in Havana. The price of candles on the black market soared to ten pesos, almost a tenth of the monthly salary of the lowest-paid workers. Even so, they rapidly disappeared. By October, the state-controlled press was providing Cubans with instructions on making their own candles.

By autumn, trade relations with the former Soviet Union, including Russia, were at a "nadir."[14] The drastic reduction of fuel had turned the political management of the country into "an agony."[15] Only in November, with the signing of a new one-year trade pact, did Cuba's prospects improve a bit. The agreement called for the exchange of one million tons of sugar for 1.6 million tons of crude. A separate protocol and an "option" clause, however, held out the possibility that, if everything went well, Russia might sell as much as 3.3 million tons of crude and refined products to Cuba in 1993.[16]

Still, in the short run at least, there was no way out. While Cuban officials had for some time been planning for the day when they would have to acquire new trade partners overnight (the "zero option," as they called it), the Castro regime lacked the hard currency that was a prerequisite for establishing such extensive new commercial relations. Even the favorable terms of the San Jose Pact, under which Mexico and Venezuela sold oil to Central American and Caribbean countries at preferential rates, seemed beyond Havana's reach, since the latter had no way of meeting the agreement's requirement that 80 percent of every purchase be paid in cash.

Neither did the government's attempts to attract foreign capital through joint ventures and production-sharing arrangements seem likely to do much more than make a dent in the problem. Even if the regime's most optimistic predictions were realized (which seemed improbable), tourism would not produce net annual earnings of more than a few hundred million dollars within the near future. Nickel production also held some promise, but even a doubling of exports seemed unlikely to bring in more than an additional $400 million.[17] The government's much-ballyhooed biotechnology program had mixed success at best. A few of these products were on the technological cutting-edge. Now that the COMECON market was no longer available, however, the prospects for this sector looked much less promising. Cuba faced the problem of breaking into a world market dominated by large multinational corporations, a formidable task considering its lack of testing, marketing, packaging, and financing skills.[18]

The one wild card in the deck was oil. Cuba has been encouraging France, Canada, and other countries to explore the potential for offshore development. A major strike could still turn the island's economic equation on its head. However, this is a fairly long shot. There is oil out there, but it is mostly high-density crude. While Cuba may be able to use limited amounts of this in its own industries, it will be of little interest to potential foreign customers. To date, no significant amounts of light crude have been found and no revenue produced. Without such discoveries, the various other components of the Cuban strategy seem unlikely to bring in more than a billion dollars in new revenue annually in the years immediately ahead.[19] This is not very much when one takes into account what has been lost. In his traditional 26th of July speech, which was delayed until early September, Castro revealed that Cuba had suffered a direct loss of $4.7 billion a year due to the lower prices that it was now receiving for its sugar, rising import costs, loss of credits, and other factors. Another billion dollars in indirect losses was attributed to the destabilization of supplies, problems in export production, and unspecified financial problems. Thus, altogether, Cuba would lose an estimated $5.7 billion in 1992, in comparison with 1989.[20]

Neither was this all. Castro now announced that work on Cuba's largest industrial project, the Juragua nuclear power plant, would have to be discontinued. The Russians were demanding $200 million in cash to continue work on it. They were also insisting that Cuba meet a $300,000 monthly payroll for technicians and that another $200 million in financing be obtained from third countries.[21] These were impossible demands. Bowing to the inevitable, Fidel declared that work would be suspended until economic conditions permitted a resumption. (However, he also raised the possibility that the stoppage might be permanent.)

It is difficult to overstate the shock effect of this development. For many Cubans, the nuclear facility had been a symbol of the long-hoped-for future, the one bright spot in an otherwise bleak economic horizon. Over the years, more than $1.1 billion had been poured into the project. Now, it seemed, that enormous investment would be lost. Moreover, few could miss the suspension's implications for the island's economic recovery. Official predictions that Cuba would be out of the woods by 1995 were based on the assumption that at least part of the Juragua plant would be on line. The stoppage meant that there was no hope of solving the energy crisis in the foreseeable future.

Toward the end of 1992, the government's leading economic planner, Carlos Lage, gave a comprehensive accounting of Cuba's decline: Since 1989, he disclosed, net import capacity had fallen from $8.1 billion to $2.2 billion.[22] Seventy-three percent of the island's import resources and over three-fourths of its markets had been lost. Two-way trade with the countries making up the former socialist bloc (the Soviet Union and Eastern Europe) was only 7 percent ($830 million) of what it had been. Oil imports had fallen from over 13 million tons to 6.1 million tons. Because of sharp declines in fertilizer, herbicide, chemical, and animal feed imports, the government's food program had failed to meet the needs of the population. Milk production, for instance, was down by 45 percent. Cuba, moreover, was getting few breaks from the international market: The price of its wheat and milk imports had risen, while that of its nickel and sugar exports had declined. So desperate was the government to sell its sugar that it was dumping it on the world market at *below* the going rate of 6 cents to 8 cents a pound.[23] Neither was there any relief in sight. The 1993 sugar crop, he predicted, would be smaller than even the modest 1992 harvest. Cubans would have to prepare themselves for another hard year, "as difficult . . . or even more so" than 1992.[24]

All in all, between 1989 and 1992, the Cuban gross domestic product seems to have declined by between 34 percent and 51 percent.[25] This was enough to discourage even the eternally optimistic Castro: "I will be a sigh in history," he mused.[26] Increasingly, the old dictator seemed depressed and out of touch. No doubt the thought of ultimate defeat, of the destruction of all that he had worked so long to build, weighed heavily on his mind.

And not only his. By now, it had become evident that as long as Castro remained in power, Cuba would be a miserable place to live. As the economic noose tightened, social pain intensified. In response to the crisis, the government imposed a series of drastic austerity measures, including a major expansion of rationing. Basic food items, as well as such "conveniences" as soap, shampoo, tobacco and toilet paper, were tightly rationed. Public transportation was cut sharply; factories were closed and workers laid off. Hospitals began to run out of medical supplies; eight-hour blackouts became commonplace. In Havana, dumpsters full of rotting produce and other refuse lined the streets because there was not enough gasoline for garbage trucks to make frequent pickups. Meanwhile, office workers were rotated through rural cooperatives in a desperate attempt to achieve agricultural self-sufficiency. Housewives spent endless hours waiting in line for meager rations of milk, eggs, and bread. For most, meat and fresh fish had disappeared long ago.[27] Increasingly, the question that seemed to be on people's minds was: "How long can Fidel keep going?" In this atmosphere of intensifying stress and repression, the prospects of a social explosion or military coup never seemed better.

CAN CASTRO SURVIVE? THE PROSPECTS FOR A REVOLUTION FROM BELOW

But appearances can be deceiving. Socioeconomic hardship alone is not enough to create a revolutionary situation. In recent years, the security apparatus has been purged and strengthened, and the regime has not hesitated to aggressively use it to suppress dissent and prevent the formation of an organized opposition. This absence of any autonomous agency of change is likely to be the crucial missing variable in any revolutionary scenario. As long as the security apparatus can effectively penetrate and neutralize society and the political-military institutions of the state, the likelihood of a successful coup or popular uprising is fairly remote.

A mass uprising is improbable for a number of reasons. The first, and most obvious, is the extraordinary system of controls that has been developed and perfected over the years. The history of revolutions suggests that "a minimum degree of freedom of expression, communication, and association are needed for the masses to be able to spearhead a revolution." Otherwise, the "spontaneous convergence" of thousands of unorganized, desperate individuals into a unified opposition strong enough to overthrow a totalitarian regime is not something that occurs easily.[28]

Part of the problem is overcoming the fear of repression. Beyond that, however, there is the need to communicate and plan political activities. The regime's strategy puts a premium on mobilization. Even before the current crisis, Cuba was one of the most militarized societies in the world. Now, almost every month brings an announcement of some new "defense brigade" or security measure to heighten control and vigilance even further. There have been mobilizations to send city dwellers to the countryside to help with agricultural production, to combat black marketeering, and to repress political malcontents. Most visible in the capital, thousands of workers have been mobilized to expand a huge network of "people's tunnels" beneath the streets of Havana—concrete shelters in which weapons and ammunition can be stored and people protected in the event of the U.S. attack that Castro keeps warning about.[29] The net effect as Sergio Roca said, is to "keep people busy, to keep them moving from side to side."[30] As long as their activities are closely supervised, they are unlikely to have the time, energy, opportunity, or courage to engage in anti-regime behavior.

Beyond this, surveillance has been so extensive and intensive as to effectively deter major organized opposition. To engage in such activity requires considerable trust among the participants. In Cuba, however, the security apparatus has so penetrated society and state that trust has become a scarce commodity. Most people have grown accustomed to wearing "masks," hiding their true feelings behind a facade of conformity and support for the regime, in order to avoid the sanctions that are the bane of anyone considered suspect. Recent reports that the president and two other members of the Cuban Democratic Coalition, a dissident group linked to the Cuban American National Foundation, were collaborating with the security police highlight the problem: If true, they suggest that no one can be trusted. The police have so infiltrated the dissident movement that people can never be sure to whom they are talking. However, such reports could also be disinformation designed to heighten distrust within and split the dissident movement. Either way, the effect is to weaken the movement, dissuading outsiders from joining and inducing insiders to drop out.

For those who are not deterred by such obstacles, there are other risks and costs: harassment, physical abuse, imprisonment, and the loss of employment, food rations, or housing. Dissident leaders are increasingly being put on trial, and the penalties are often draconian: Omar del Pozo of the National Civic Union has been sentenced to fifteen years on charges of treason; Yndamiro Restano, leader of the Harmony Movement, received ten years for producing pamphlets calling for a multiparty system; Sebastian Arcos was given four years and eight months for spreading "enemy propaganda." At the same time, new instruments have been created to supplement the already extensive network of military, paramilitary, and police institutions. Rapid Response Detachments have mobilized civilian volunteers to enable the authorities to more quickly suppress public expressions of discontent. A Single Vigilance and Protection System has been formed to coordinate the activities of frontier troops, police, and neighborhood vigilance groups. Increasingly, the regime seems to be acquiring the capability to detect acts of defiance before they occur. On a number of recent occasions, security police and government supporters have lain in wait at the site of public protests. When the demonstrators revealed themselves, they were quickly subjected to attack and arrest. Through such prompt and effective measures, the momentum of the dissident movement has been contained.

This points to one of the fundamental weaknesses of the opposition: the absence of institutional sanctuaries in which to masquerade and develop political activity. In Cuba, there is no church comparable to the Roman Catholic Church in Poland, no independent labor union like Solidarity that can mobilize the masses against the government. Neither is there any organization of dissident intellectuals like Charter 77 in Czechoslovakia. As Enrique Baloyra has observed, this institutional vacuum has "made the atomization that characterizes Stalinism more effective in preventing the development of horizontal solidarities that normally precede the crystallization of organized forms of public protest." In the absence of this form of protest, the government has had no need of engaging in massive physical violence. "The water cannon, the baton, the cattle prods, the gas canisters and gas masks are all ready to be utilized, but they have been unnecessary thus far."[31]

Absent, too, are dissident leaders of the stature of a Lech Walesa or a Vaclav Havel, who might galvanize the masses to rebel through their example. In the one instance where a nationally known figure with charismatic qualities appeared to have that potential, he was killed. The trial and execution of Division General Arnaldo Ochoa, "Hero of the Republic" and former commander of the Cuban expeditionary forces in Angola and Ethiopia, sent a forceful message to would-be dissidents both within and without the regime: No opposition will be tolerated. No one is safe. If this could be done to Ochoa, it could be done to anyone. Dissidents know that their lives will be spared only as long as they do not pose a serious threat to the government. Castro can afford to let them survive precisely because they do not constitute a major danger. Current levels of repression are sufficient to maintain control and keep the small dissident organizations fragmented and in disarray.

Given this lack of personal and institutional leadership, it should not be surprising that the dissident movement has no mass following. These groups are composed almost entirely of intellectuals; few workers or students have joined. Most Cubans see no viable alternative to Castro. They fear the unknown, and the regime skillfully plays on these insecurities to promote passivity where it cannot generate active support. The slogan "Socialism or Death" sums up the bleak options as they are presented to the populace. Few opportunities are missed to inform Cubans of their likely fate should a capitalist restoration occur. Stories of economic chaos, hardship, political disintegration, and ethnic strife in Eastern Europe and the former Soviet Union serve as potent warnings for those who might be tempted to opt for a free market and democracy. Other stories compare Cuba favorably with the poverty and insecurity that suffuse daily life in most other Latin American countries. Commentators pointedly note Washington's failure to "keep its promises" to needy friends like Nicaragua, Panama, and Russia. The message is obvious: Even if Cuba were to go capitalist, it could expect little help from the United States.

Considerable effort also is being made to reassure Cubans that their government will not abandon them. In contrast to the economic "shock therapy" being applied in the former Communist countries and Latin America, the Castro regime makes a point of emphasizing that no one will be allowed to starve. Many Cubans still believe that the current system spares them from the worst aspects of capitalism: hunger, homelessness, soaring medical costs, and so on. The system may be in utter decay, but it shields them from competition, provides them with security, and avoids the crushing poverty and enormous gaps between rich and poor that are found in most other Latin American countries.

In short, life with Castro may be hard, but it is all that most Cubans know. Constant surveillance and mobilization, fear of repression, the perception that there are no alternatives (or at least no desirable ones), and the energy-sapping, time-consuming requisites of daily survival (which, among other things, entail long waits in seemingly endless lines for basic necessities) all militate against a revolution from below. People are isolated, suspicious, and fearful. Rather than openly resist authority, they adapt, remain passive, or seek refuge in escapism. Most would rather hide or run than fight: Thus, the significance of the growing number of Cubans who are willing to "take their chances at sea." (About 2,500 a year succeed in making it to the United States; many more die in the attempt.) The regime well understands the importance of such escape mechanisms. Both openly and covertly, it seeks to use them to contain or siphon off social tension. At the same time, it has been careful not to engage in the kind of gratuitous bloodshed that might spark a spontaneous uprising or massive demonstration. Without such government violence to dramatize the moral issues and break through people's natural defense mechanisms, it is unlikely that the kind of emotional catharsis can occur that might produce large-scale anti-regime actions.

For all these reasons, plus several others that will be discussed below, a revolution from below does not seem to be in the cards, at least, not at this time. After an initial wave of hope among anti-Castro forces during the collapse of Eastern European and Soviet Communism, inertia has set in. People are demoralized and tired; there is a pervasive sense of powerlessness. Most have become resigned to having Castro around for some time to come.

CAN CASTRO SURVIVE? THE PROSPECTS FOR A REVOLUTION FROM ABOVE

Neither do the prospects of a *golpe de estado* look particularly good. Castro is nothing if not a master politician. ("I am a slave to power," he has remarked.)[32] The Ochoa affair dramatically underscored the risks for disgruntled members of the political-military apparatus who might also be tempted to remove their "masks."[33] At the time, there was evidence of considerable discontent within the armed forces and Ministry of Interior (MININT). Some officers may even have begun to develop a program for a National Salvation Front that might have served as the nucleus of a political opposition.[34] Fidel's brother, Raul, had openly fulminated against those who criticized and "congregate[d] against the figure of our command-in-chief."[35] Subsequently, Raul Castro used the occasion to purge the MININT of hundreds of security personnel. The institution was effectively decapitated, with all key officials being removed from office and remanded for trial on charges of corruption, dereliction of duty, and the illegal use of government funds. In their place were assigned officers from the Ministry of the Revolutionary Armed Forces (MINFAR), under the direction of General Abelardo Colome Ibarra, a long-time *raulista*, who as the new minister of the interior became arguably the third most powerful man in Cuba.

At first glance, the MININT purge seemed little more than an effort to cleanse an institution that had been corrupted by drug trafficking and other illicit activities. Below the surface, however, these developments reflected a long and bitter rivalry between the MINFAR and the MININT, and especially between Raul Castro, the minister of defense, and General Jose Abrantes, the minister of interior. Raul Castro's victory over Abrantes was also a victory of the MINFAR over its traditional institutional enemy. The MININT now became an appendage of the military. Subsequently, counterintelligence operations were broadened within both ministries and a centralized control system was activated to monitor the location of high-level officers twenty-four hours a day.[36]

These events had a chilling effect on the kind of internal dissent that was beginning to emerge prior to the Ochoa affair. No doubt that alienation has persisted—indeed, it has almost certainly spread and intensified—but the conditions no longer exist in which it can be transformed into organized opposition. As in the case of Cuban society at large, atomization and distrust pervade elite circles.

Notwithstanding the above, it would be a serious mistake to assume that Castro no longer enjoys any elite or mass support or that the support that he does have is entirely coerced. Unlike the Communist revolutions in Eastern Europe, which were mostly imposed from above by the Soviet Army, the Cuban revolution had indigenous roots. Castro came to power independently, and he was never a Soviet puppet. To many Cubans, he remains a charismatic figure—part hero, part father, and always larger than life. He is the personification of the revolution and, to some, the living symbol of the nation, sources of legitimacy that should not be underestimated even in these troubled times. The Cuban elite, in particular, is still largely composed of first-generation revolutionaries, whose personal devotion to their *lider maximo* (and, to a lesser extent, their ideological commitment) probably remains fairly high in spite of all that has happened. Over the years, these people have benefited enormously from Castro's rule, and most probably still do.[37]

Such sources of loyalty often produce unquestioning obedience. Intellectual dependence and submission have been carefully cultivated in Cuba at both elite and mass levels. Witness, for instance, the response of Jesus

Montane, one of the participants in the legendary attack on Moncada Barracks, when asked what recent advice he had given Castro. His reply: "I do not advise him. He does not need it because he has full use of his mental faculties. I support his decisions, especially those dealing with the country's economic development."[38]

Not everyone, of course, is a docile as Jesus Montane. One who was not was Carlos Aldana. As a Politburo member with wide-ranging responsibilities for foreign policy, ideology, culture, education, science, and sports, Aldana was Cuba's premier bureaucrat. He was also something of a reformer.[39] He had initially been an admirer of Mikhail Gorbachev's economic restructuring program, once even telling an interviewer that a lack of flexibility had doomed the Eastern European Communist regimes. From time to time, he had been identified with such liberal attitudes as a willingness to tolerate dissent (even going so far as to suggest that dissidents be able to participate in parliamentary elections) and permit greater freedom for Cubans to travel abroad.[40] In December 1991, however, he abruptly shifted gears, delivering a vitriolic attack on dissidents before the National Assembly of People's Power.[41] Since part of this speech rang with self-criticism for his past sympathy for *perestroika*—Castro had been so good as to correct him on this matter—one could not escape the impression that his embrace of the hardliners' position constituted a rectification for previous errors. But it was too late; his reversal did not save him. By June, rumors were circulating that Aldana was in trouble. And in September he was removed from office, ostensibly for "deficiencies in the exercise of his post and serious mistakes in his personal behavior."[42]

While Cuban authorities were quick to reject any suggestion that Aldana had been a dissident or that his ouster had been for political reasons, skeptics noted that the kind of charges leveled against him were not ordinarily sufficient to result in a dismissal from high office. They seemed more of a pretext than anything else. Moreover, they came at a time when a number of other lower-level officials—some of whom had been identified with reform—had been replaced. In combination, these developments suggested that Castro was sending a warning to those who might be tempted to pursue a more independent agenda. Aldana may not have been Arnaldo Ochoa, but his removal was likely to reinforce paralysis among the elite. If even this "moderate" could be disgraced, no one was safe.

Meanwhile, Castro was further centralizing and expanding his powers. The constitution has been revised, giving him tighter control over the military. Castro is now head of a newly created National Defense Council, whose mission is to direct the country in conditions of war or during a general mobilization or state of emergency. He now has the legal framework he needs to declare a state of siege should economic conditions continue to deteriorate or political turmoil break out. Many dissidents expect him to do just that sometime in 1994.

Finally, and perhaps most important, under present circumstances the Cuban elite has no collective interest in Castro's ouster. Indeed, quite the opposite is true: The continuation of the existing system is its sole guarantee of survival. If Castro goes and the regime collapses, members of the elite lose their power, privileges, and, perhaps, their lives. Even alienated members of the elite are unlikely to seek Castro's overthrow, since many are "convinced that U.S. policies ... are geared to bring down the entire apparatus without distinction and not just the diehard Stalinists. They read those policies as intending to destroy everyone ever associated with the regime."[43] Unless that perception changes, the vast majority of the elite will continue to either actively support Castro[44] or remain passive, regardless of the dolorous implications for the country's future.

THE STRATEGY OF CONFLICT AND THE POLITICS OF COUNTER-PRODUCTIVITY

This brings us to yet another source of regime stability: U.S. policy and behavior. Many years ago, Jean-Paul Sartre remarked that if the United States did not exist, the Cuban revolution would have to invent it. The specter of an external threat—whether in the form of a U.S. invasion, sabotage, embargo, or a revanchist Cuban exile community poised to return to the island to wreak vengeance and recover lost properties—has long been one of the keys to Castro's survival. By manipulating the fears that these images invoke, Castro has been able to wrap himself in the cloak of Cuban nationalism and pose as the defender of the Cuban people and the revolution. This has enabled him to mobilize both the elite and masses behind his leadership and policies to a degree that would not otherwise have been possible.

This is not an easy issue to come to terms with. For many Americans, current U.S. policy remains not only the most obvious and appropriate response to Cuban hostility but the one with the most innate emotional appeal. There is a personal quality to this three-and-a-half decade conflict that has rarely been noted, but that nevertheless remains very much at the heart of the relationship. To many, Castro is not merely an adversary, but an enemy—an embodiment of evil who must be punished for his defiance of the United States as well as for numerous other reprehensible deeds. In this sense, U.S. policy has sought more than a simple isolation or containment of Cuba. There is a desire to hurt the enemy that is mirrored in the malevolence that Castro has exhibited toward us. If Castro suffers from a "nemesis complex," so most assuredly do we.[45]

The problems with such an approach to the Cuban dilemma are several. On the one hand, there are the issues of morality and effectiveness so clearly posed by the Cuban Democracy Act (popularly known as the Torricelli Law), which seeks to tighten the U.S. embargo on the island. After having recently had so much unsuccessful experience with economic sanctions, one would have thought that the United States would have learned that such measures rarely have the effect intended. Sanctions did not punish Manuel Noriega, Saddam Hussein or General Cedras nearly as much as they did the Panamanian, Iraqi, and Haitian people. The masses, rather than the elites, have to bear the brunt of the hardship. This was why these measures failed in those cases and why they are unlikely to succeed in Cuba, where the vast majority of the trade in question is in food and medicine.[46] For all his rhetoric, Castro does not really care that much about the Cuban people. (If he did, he would have retired some time ago.) What matters most to him are personal power and grandeur. He thinks of himself as a world historical actor. For over three decades, Cubans have been a vehicle for an enormous ego trip, and they will continue to be used for that purpose as long as he remains in power. Regardless of any sanctions that the United States might levy, Castro will continue to fight to the last drop of his people's blood for the principles he professes to believe in.

But apart from questions of morality and effectiveness, there is the issue of counter-productivity. All too often, we have behaved in ways that have had precisely the opposite effect from what was intended and required by U.S. interests. Put bluntly, we have strengthened the regime and made a peaceful transition to democracy even more difficult.

Castro is a master at manipulating American fears and anger. He knows how to push all the right buttons in order to generate the foreign "threat" that he so desperately needs. Unfortunately, we have a tendency to react instinctively to his provocations, thus playing his game and falling into his traps. In so doing, we have encouraged the passivity of those Cubans who are alienated from the regime and have energized Castro's supporters.[47]

The U.S. dilemma, of course, is complicated substantially by the fact that there is a large, politically influential and viscerally anti-Castro Cuban-American community in (primarily) southern Florida. It would be going too far to say that our Cuban policy has been "made in Miami." Nevertheless, Cuban-American influence, primarily through the Cuban American National Foundation (CANF), has been palpable and has strengthened the hard-line inclinations already dominant in U.S. foreign policy circles. This influence has been all the more potent because there is no political constituency for a "softer" or more flexible line toward Cuba. There are no domestic political gains to be made by changing current policy, while the political costs are obvious. The result is that the Cuban-American community has been able to exercise a virtual veto over U.S. policy.

And that is a problem. Emotions as intense as those that many Cuban-Americans feel toward Castro can often cloud sound judgment. The Cuban Democracy Act, in which CANF played a major role, is a prime example. The law has provided Castro with a superb target, and he has taken full advantage of it by launching one of the largest propaganda campaigns in years.[48] The government has organized street protests and workplace demonstrations, lambasted the measure in front-page editorials, and reported virtually anything negative that anyone has said about it anywhere in the world. The impression is being cultivated that the United States intends to starve the Cuban people into submission. The effect has been to intensify the siege mentality that already existed, fanning nationalistic fervor, deflecting public anger away from the regime and onto the "Colossus of the North," and providing a pretext for stepped-up repression. In the process, the government's supporters have been mobilized and its foes further demoralized and isolated.

This demoralization, of course, is not restricted to those actively engaged in political dissent; it also afflicts the populace at large. To the extent that the Torricelli Law is effective and life becomes even harder, demoralization and docility may be expected to increase. As Tocqueville pointed out many years ago, these are not conditions that are likely to give rise to active resistance.[49] Revolutions rarely occur when conditions are so bleak that people can see no way out; rather they happen when things are improving, or, at least, when there is a perception that change and improvement are possible. Rising hopes and expectations are critical missing ingredients for a new Cuban revolution. And the Torricelli Law does nothing to foster them.

Beyond this, moreover, we have effectively isolated ourselves on the issue. With the exception of Israel, even our closest allies do not support us. (In November, only two countries joined the United States in voting against Cuba's U.N. General Assembly resolution urging repeal of the U.S. embargo.) There is widespread resentment of Torricelli's sanctions against foreign ships and U.S. subsidiaries that do business with Cuba. Many countries view these measures as violations of their sovereignty, as well as international law. Some also cannot but feel a certain sympathy for the Cubans. The United States has come away from the affair looking like an arrogant bully.

But more important than the Torricelli Law and its ramifications, there is the much larger issue of the "Miamian." There is a widespread fear in Cuba that Castro's fall will be followed by the return of a conquering horde of exiles who will reclaim their confiscated properties and wreak vengeance on all who have collaborated with the regime. These fears are not simply the product of Castro's propaganda. In August 1990, the University of Miami's Research Institute for Cuban Studies and a former Dade County commissioner began gathering data for a register of properties expropriated by the Cuban government. Exiles were invited to record their claims, with the expectation that the list would be used to recover properties after Castro's ouster. Within a week after the story appeared in the *Miami Herald*, more than a thousand inquiries were made. Predictably, the Cuban media had a field day. The story "sent chills up the spines of millions of Cubans who were living in properties once owned by exiles."[50]

By 1991, exile groups were publicly fighting over how to dispose of the confiscated properties once they had been recovered by a post-Castro government. The CANF unveiled a Cuban reconstruction program that called for the sending of 10,000 Cuban-American professionals to teach the islanders how to adapt to a free-market economy. A draft constitution was drawn up. Some even called for the formation of a provisional government-in-exile and suggested that exile seniority should be the criterion for leadership. Meanwhile, war fever was spreading fast. Increasingly, militant right-wing exiles were conducting training exercises and engaging in commando assaults on the island. In rally after rally, anti-Castro crowds took up the chant "War! War! War!"

All this played into Castro's hands wonderfully. The regime had long sought to foster the specter of an exile threat as a means of manipulating domestic opinion. (At least one of these organizations, Alpha 66, had apparently even been given Cuban government funds to launch attacks on the island.)[51] Such behavior reinforced the image of the "neocolonial Miamian," bent on reconquering Cuba and returning it to the status of a U.S. protectorate; it inflamed nationalistic, class, and racial passions, making it all the more difficult for those who were disenchanted with Castro to engage in active opposition. Among other things, Cuba now has a predominantly non-white population, while the Miami exile leadership is overwhelmingly white. No matter how alienated from Castro Cuban blacks and mulattoes might be, it was hard to imagine them rushing to embrace an exile restoration. Many might well fight to prevent a restoration of the old order.[52]

Let us be clear. What is being criticized here is not the Cuban-American community per se, or even the Cuban American National Foundation. The anti-Castro sentiments of the vast majority of exiles are entirely understandable, and this writer, for one, has a deep empathy for them. Similarly, the CANF has done much admirable work—for instance, in helping Cubans to escape from the island and adjust to their new lives in the United States. But the dominant elements in the Cuban-American elite have their roots in the pre-Castro era; they long ago lost touch with the hopes and fears of Cuban Cubans. Moreover, their primary leader, Jorge Mas Canosa, is a man of enormous ambition, who has made no secret of his desire to become the next Cuban president. In many respects, Mas is a capitalist mirror image of Fidel Castro: demagogic, intolerant, dictatorial, with an enormous ego and a propensity for delivering "thundering speeches" of "hatred and intransigence."[53] He has often played to the worst instincts of Cuban-Americans, encouraging (intentionally or unintentionally) violence-prone elements to attack or harass not only Castro's Cuba but anyone (the *Miami Herald* comes quickly to mind) who expresses views on the subject that are different from his own. This is not a democratic alternative to Fidel Castro, and those islanders familiar with Mas are not anxious to trade their leftist dictator for one from the opposite extreme.[54]

Unfortunately, Mas Canosa and his followers have had a powerful influence on U.S. policy. In part, this has been the product of domestic politics. No president or presidential candidate since Jimmy Carter has been willing to risk losing Florida's large bloc of electoral votes by appearing to be "soft" on Castro. (Bill Clinton had rushed to embrace the Torricelli Bill even before George Bush; the latter's State Department was leery of those provisions that risked undermining U.S. relations with the international community.) The Reagan and Bush administrations, moreover, were especially sympathetic to the right-wing exiles, whose anti-Communist, pro-capitalist beliefs so closely mirrored their own. For their part, the exiles were useful allies in promoting some of the Reagan administration's pet projects: They played a key role in the efforts to organize and wage the contra war; and had helped win U.S. military aid for the UNITA rebels in Angola. Over the years, President Bush's son, Jeb, became an informal liaison between the White House and the Miami Cuban leadership. In this capacity, he spared no effort to attract leading Republican fund-raisers—including his father and President Reagan's daughter, Maureen—to speak at local events where they invariably played to the anti-Castro emotions of their audience. The result of this *abrazo* (embrace), by the turn of the decade, was that the United States had become locked into a policy straitjacket at precisely the moment that flexibility was most needed.

THE UNITED STATES, CUBA AND THE FUTURE: FROM A STRATEGY OF CONFLICT TO CONSTRUCTIVE ENGAGEMENT

Cuba is stuck at a crossroads, and so is U.S. policy. Rather than facilitating change, the United States has helped shore up the status quo. Castro plays the confrontation game extremely well. Over the years, he has been highly successful in manipulating the specter of the Yankee threat to mobilize his countrymen behind his leadership and policies. In effect, successive U.S. administrations, both Republican and Democratic, have repeatedly played into his hands by enabling him to wrap himself in the cloak of besieged nationalism. In the process, it has been the Cuban people, especially political dissidents, who have suffered. It is no accident that passage of the Torricelli Law was followed by a new crackdown on the internal opposition, including the vicious beating of Cuba's leading dissident, Elizardo Sanchez Santa Cruz. Once again, the United States had provided Castro with a pretext for repression.

One is reminded of the metaphor used by Radio Marti's J. Richard Planas: We have failed to notice that the wall, which is indeed falling, is leaning in our direction. Consequently, by pushing rather than pulling, we have actually helped prop up the regime. Castro survives by fostering political passivity among the masses and by solidifying his support among those who have supported him in the past. Within this context, predictions about the dictator's imminent fall—whether by U.S. political leaders or the Miami exile elite—send the wrong message to the Cuban people. News that the exiles are making military preparations and are drawing up constitutions and economic recovery programs for a post-Castro Cuba suggests that the solution to the Cuban problem will come from abroad, and that there will be little role for those Cubans still in Cuba. Not only do these predictions mislead the masses about the probable course of future events, but they relieve them of the responsibility for dealing with their own problems. If Castro is going to be toppled by external forces, there is no incentive for Cubans to take the initiative and risk their lives. By the same token, the message simply energizes and helps Castro mobilize his supporters, who fear for their homes, privileges, careers, and even their lives.[55]

In short, threats, isolation, and punishment are not the way to promote change in Cuba. They are not likely to bring Castro down in the short run. They will, however, aggravate the current crisis and prolong Cuba's agony, and this could well make a peaceful transition, democracy, and economic recovery even more difficult to achieve. Make no mistake about it, there is an enormous amount of repressed tension in Cuba today. By seeking to heighten and bottle up that stress, U.S. policy could well contribute to a bloody social explosion in the longer run.

What is the alternative? If, as has been argued, we have been playing to Castro's strengths, then the logical thing to do would be to change the nature of the game so as to better exploit his weaknesses. A policy of constructive engagement, designed to lower tensions and open up Cuba to U.S. influence, would pose major problems for the regime. Among other things, it would undermine the rationale for the garrison state and make political and social control much more difficult. Such a strategy would seek to dissolve the siege mentality that justifies the regime's repression; it would flood the island with ideas and information and expose Cubans to alternative political and social values and lifestyles. There is nothing more potentially subversive to such regimes than the exposure to democratic ideas and materialistic temptations. The more contact Cubans have with Western values, the more their appetites would be whetted and the more difficult it will be for Castro to convince people of the desirability of maintaining the status quo. If, in addition, this can be done in a way that does not threaten the Cuban elite with extinction, it may just be possible to facilitate a peaceful transition to a more open society.

A TACTICAL AGENDA

What specifically should be done? Here one must differentiate between measures that can be taken immediately, without waiting for favorable actions from Cuba, and those that should await negotiation and should come as a result of positive (perhaps reciprocal) moves from Havana.[56]

The first aim is to try to lower the level of U.S.-Cuban hostility and tension through a campaign of threat reduction. Our rhetoric must be toned down. Cubans need to be reassured that the United States is not planning to invade or otherwise engage in unprovoked attacks on the island. This is already the officially declared U.S. policy, but it needs to be emphasized early by President Clinton and reiterated from time to time by other high-level officials. This is needed to help counteract the fears that are being so skillfully manipulated by Castro.

Along these same lines, the new administration should distance itself from Jorge Mas Canosa and the Cuban American National Foundation. There are other, more moderate elements in the Cuban-American community who should be consulted in the making of our Cuban policy. (Carlos Alberto Montaner's Cuban Democratic Platform, Eloy Gutierrez Menoyo's Cuban Change, Enrique Baloyra's Cuban Social Democratic Coordination, and the newly formed Cuban Committee for Democracy come to mind.) This does not mean that the CANF should be ignored; it is far too important for that. But as Elliott Abrams has observed,

It is a mistake for Washington to appear closer to any one of these groups in what everyone agrees is going to be a power struggle. . . . Some distancing is now needed to avoid verifying Castro's propaganda that Cuban-American millionaires and Washington are in collusion.[57]

One way of doing this is to depoliticize Radio Marti. Even at its best, the station's favorable, detailed coverage of Mas Canosa and CANF always gave the impression that the latter's projects and leaders represented U.S. policy. In recent months, the radio has fallen under the sway of the Miami community's hard right. Its originally dispassionate presentations have increasingly been replaced by demogogic rhetoric. (Another concern is CANF's cozy oversight relationship to the station. Mas Canosa heads the Presidential Advisory Board on Broadcasting to Cuba.) This needs to be changed. Radio Marti plays an important role in informing the Cuban people about current events that are ignored or distorted by the official media. To ensure its objectivity and credibility, it should be placed under the direction of nonpolitical leadership, less susceptible to pressure by clientele groups. At the same time, another CANF project, TV Marti, should be closed. The station operates in violation of international conventions signed by the United States, which prohibit the use of another country's assigned television channel. Its broadcasts, moreover, are easily jammed. It is an unnecessary irritant, ineffective for purposes of communicating the news, and has simply provoked Castro into retaliating by interfering with U.S. radio broadcasts.

It may also be useful to use Radio Marti to publicize positive aspects of the economic reforms in Eastern Europe and China, and to assure Cubans on the island that their homes will not be taken away without providing them with comparable or better housing. Assuring bureaucrats and military officers not involved in crimes that they have nothing to fear from a political opening and market reforms would also be helpful, as would a greater willingness to criticize such actions as the Miami "real estate registry."[58]

In addition, the Clinton administration should strongly disassociate itself from exile paramilitary operations against Cuba. Such attacks are militarily useless and only play into Castro's hands by "proving" his claims of a foreign threat. The attorney general should publicly reiterate the government's determination to enforce the Neutrality Act and adopt a more visible and aggressive posture, in cooperation with local authorities, to prevent violent assaults from being launched from U.S. territory.

At the same time, it may be possible, even at this early stage, to begin taking some confidence-building measures in the military arena. At minimum, we should give the Cuban government advance notice of any U.S. military exercises in the region. We should also avoid any operations that might give the impression of being a dress rehearsal for an invasion of Cuba. Havana might even be invited to send observers. Granted, under the current climate of hostility and suspicion, Castro would probably not accept this overture. But there is no reason that we should not begin preparing the ground for such contacts. Eventually, it may even be possible to invite Cuban participation in the Inter-American Defense College.

In an ideal world, too, the Torricelli Law would be repealed. Unfortunately, such a move will be politically difficult. (Among other things, it would represent a reversal of President Clinton's previous support for the measure.) Nevertheless, messages need to be sent both to the Cubans and to our foreign friends and trading partners. To the former, we need to give assurances that we are not trying to starve them into submission. U.S. policy is not—or, at least, should not be—malicious. To the latter, we need to indicate that we respect their sovereignty and will abide by our international commitments. We must not allow Cuba to become a divisive factor in our relations with other countries. Should the president decide that the political costs of repeal are too great, Torricelli should simply remain unenforced.

The current crisis also provides us with an excellent opportunity to demonstrate that we can set aside old grudges when humanitarian issues are at stake. A modest humanitarian aid package for Cuba, composed of sorely needed medical supplies and food, should be proposed by the administration and passed by Congress.[59] Those few remaining obstacles to the provision of such items by private charitable groups and Cuban-Americans should be removed. Cuba's agony gives us an opportunity to show that we care about the Cuban people by directly helping to alleviate their suffering. Such measures would send a powerful message both to the islanders and to the international community. They would speak eloquently about what we as a nation stand for, as opposed merely to what we are against. At the same time, they might well serve as a step toward substantive negotiations. We could let it be known that, if the Cuban government were willing to respond constructively to some of our concerns, we would be willing to partially lift the embargo, so that food and medicine could be sold to Cuba directly, rather than indirectly through foreign subsidiaries.

A second group of proposals would seek to go beyond a mere lowering of tensions and begin the more ambitious and difficult process of building a positive relationship and fostering constructive change. What is involved here are the basic elements of what Gillian Gunn has called a "communications strategy."[60] This would emphasize the promotion of person-to-person contacts between U.S. and Cuban citizens through mail, telephone, and transportation services, tourism, scientific and cultural exchanges, the establishment of press bureaus, and so on. One of the weaknesses in our current policy of isolation and economic strangulation is that it has not taken advantage of important opportunities to promote a freer flow of ideas and information. Washington believes that to allow U.S. citizens, especially tourists, to travel to the island in large numbers would benefit the Cuban economy. Thus, we severely restrict the number of U.S. visitors and limit the amount of money they can spend.

This is a mistake. One of the factors fortifying the Castro regime is Cuba's insularity. The fact that it is an island makes the task of isolating the populace from potentially corrupting outside influences much easier than was the case in Eastern Europe. Means must be found to break through this insularity. The more contact we have with the Cuban people, the better. If this enables Castro to earn a bit more foreign exchange, then so be it. The amount would be minor compared to what has been lost in recent years—certainly not nearly enough to salvage the regime. Indeed, increased U.S. cultural penetration could be expected to exacerbate Castro's problems of control by exposing Cubans to North American lifestyles and political ideas, demonstrating that capitalism does work (and that even the Cuban government recognizes this), and highlighting the inequalities in the government's policy of "tourism apartheid." This last has already created much resentment among ordinary Cubans, who are not allowed to patronize many of the restaurants and recreational facilities that tourists frequent. While the regime will continue to try to isolate the populace from the subversive effects of foreign contact, it is doubtful whether it can succeed. Tourists will want to see Havana and Santiago, as well as Varadero Beach. In such large urban settings, it will be extremely difficult, if not impossible, to prevent interaction between Cubans and North American visitors.

By the same token, telephone communications between the two countries should be upgraded. Existing facilities could be vastly improved, but so far such measures have foundered on the embargo. The law prohibits funds from being transferred to the Cuban government; consequently, Havana's share of past earnings remains frozen. This is a relatively small amount of money and ought not to be allowed to stand in the way of measures that would greatly facilitate contacts between U.S. and Cuban nationals. (Cuban-Americans would especially benefit from such changes.) Accordingly, AT&T should be allowed to upgrade its services, and the Cuban government should be given its "full and fair" share of past and future revenue.[61]

The embargo should also be modified to allow the export of computer-related hardware, software and other telecommunications and printing devices (fax and photocopying machines, desk-top publishing equipment, hand-held camcorders, and so on). Such technology played an important role in opening up societies and bringing down regimes in the Soviet Union and Eastern Europe. While conditions in Cuba are significantly different—the absence of strong and independent social organizations or a leadership willing to accept substantive reforms are crucial variables—in the long run, the information revolution should help foster the emergence of a civil society.[62] Even in the shorter run, such communication would increase the flow of ideas and information into, out of, and within Cuba, making it easier for dissident elements to communicate and fostering an increasing fragmentation and alienation of the elite.

Along these same lines, we should lift prohibitions on the direct marketing of books, periodicals, newspapers, records, compact disks, VCRs, video-tapes, and other communications items. Direct mail service should be established. U.S. press offices should be set up in Havana and Santiago. (In return, Prensa Latina should be allowed to open bureaus in the United States.) The U.S. government, both on its own and by encouraging private institutions, should seek to promote scientific, educational, and cultural exchanges. It should also stop pressuring foreign corporations from investing in Cuba, since exposure to Western business practices may be expected to broaden the worldview of Cuba's economic managers.[63] The object of all these measures would be to increase Western contacts with all levels of Cuban society—with elites as well as masses. It should be our aim to flood Cuba with foreign students, business managers, teachers, tourists, research-ers, journalists, artists and other carriers of the liberal democratic, materi-alistic virus. To facilitate these efforts, a civil aviation agreement should be reached to allow regularly scheduled air flights between the United States and Cuba.

A third category of measures relates to government-to-government co-operation on matters that are in the interest of both countries. Such items would include counter-narcotics operations (the sharing of intelligence, joint interdiction); an agreement to regularize Cuban migration to the United States and provide for the return of illegal entrants who have committed serious crimes; the forecasting of hurricanes and other weather-related dis-asters; joint efforts in environmental protection and reclamation; and a new anti-hijacking agreement. This last is badly needed to deter airline and boat seizures, which are becoming increasingly commonplace. Such cooperation might well lead to other reforms, such as the reciprocal inspection of nuclear power plants. (This issue will be of major interest to residents of south Florida if Cuba's Juragua plant ever becomes operational.)

ON THE PITFALLS AND PROSPECTS OF THE FUTURE

The above measures can be taken at minimum cost (and, indeed, some net gain) for the United States. They will neither save Castro nor restore Cuba to prosperity. Neither do they "give away the store" by surrendering our bargaining chips before more substantive negotiations have begun. We are speaking here of an adjustment, rather than a repeal, of the U.S. embargo. Most trade restrictions would be retained; U.S. investment in Cuba would continue to be prohibited. This is only prudent. To permit investment under current conditions would be reckless. Castro has made a career out of "hitting the Yankees." He nationalized U.S. properties once; and, given the right circumstances, he might do so again. Moreover, one can only speculate what his successors will do. CANF leaders, for instance, have said that, if they come to power, they will confiscate the businesses of the regime's foreign "collaborators."

In short, the most difficult issues—including a transition to democracy, the full lifting of the embargo, and the return of Guantanamo—will not be soon or easily resolved. Castro remains, always, a master manipulator. He will almost certainly resist any changes that would undermine his power or his ideological vision of what Cuba ought to be. As far back as 1987, he correctly diagnosed the dangers inherent in *glasnost* and *perestroika*, warning of the disintegrative effect that they would have on the Soviet bloc. More recently, at the Fourth Party Congress, he rejected any substantive political or economic reforms as too risky under current conditions.

However, I would argue that, due to the current crisis, constructive engagement now has a better chance of working than ever before. Previous proposals to "soften" U.S. policy have always suffered from the fact that Castro had an attractive alternative to coming to terms with the United States. Rigidity and defiance cost him little, since the Soviets were willing to subsidize his economic blunders and foreign adventures. That is no longer the case, however. Cuba has lost its economic lifeline; it stands alone and vulnerable. Under these circumstances (the "double blockade," as Castro calls it), the incentive or temptation to come to terms will be much greater than in the past. Cuba needs us now, whereas it did not before. That gives us a source of bargaining leverage that can and should be exploited. No doubt Castro will try to counteract and contain the erosion of his personal power, as well as that of his regime. But it is by no means clear whether or to what extent this can be done. The opening of Cuba to U.S. influence would mean that both sides would be sailing into uncharted waters, and the results cannot confidently be predicted.

One should state right up front that this strategy is not without a certain

amount of risk. Among other things, it might contribute to the destabilization
of Cuba. One need only recall the impact of the massive return of Cuban-
Americans to the island during the Carter administration: It produced a
social explosion that led to the emigration of some 129,000 Cubans via the
Mariel express. Conditions are much worse now than they were in 1980,
and the impulse to flee will be much greater, should the opportunity arise.

This being said, another massive exodus on the scale of or larger than
Mariel seems improbable. Mariel was possible only because the Carter
administration made the mistake of allowing Cuban-Americans to provide
the boats by which the vast majority of refugees fled. It is unlikely in the
extreme that President Clinton would make the same error (witness his
turnaround on the Haitian refugee issue). Without external sources of transportation, Cubans would probably be limited to those crafts that they could
build or commandeer. As the United States has demonstrated in the Haitian
crisis, it has the ability to stem this kind of exodus. A more massive and
unmanageable outpouring could occur only with the complicity of Cuban
authorities—for instance, by using the government's merchant marine fleet
to provide the necessary transportation. Such a move would constitute an
act of war and would probably be treated as such.[64] For precisely this reason,
it seems unlikely to occur.

There is, of course, a possibility that an opening up of Cuba might lead
to such turmoil that the government would lose control. A reduction (and
elimination, if possible) of the "Yankee threat" would deprive Castro of much
of his rationale for repression. It would erode his capacity for control and
make it much more difficult to mobilize the masses behind his leadership
through the use of jingoistic appeals. It would also make it more difficult for
him to escape responsibility for Cuba's economic woes by blaming the Americans. Beyond this, an opening of Cuba to outside influences, especially if
it were to be accompanied by political and economic reforms and an improvement in socioeconomic conditions, might foster hopes, expectations
and demands that the regime would be unable to handle. Again, it is when
people see that there is a possibility of change that they will be most likely
to revolt.

This could be a slippery slope. The most dangerous moment for a bad
government is when it tries to reform.[65] A misstep—say, police overreaction
to a spontaneous disturbance—could escalate into something much larger.
By the same token, exposing the Cuban elite to U.S. influences (including
elite-to-elite contacts) might accelerate the former's abandonment of the
regime. A coup, rebellion, or assassination is not beyond the realm of possibility, especially if changes in U.S. policy are able to reduce the threat
perception of the elite. (As matters now stand, would-be rebels within the
regime do not know whether we would greet them as heroes or hang them.)

The irony of constructive engagement, then, is that it might well prove
to be a more effective way of undermining the dictatorship than the hard-

line policies of the Castrophobes. At this stage, however, arguments as to its stabilizing or destabilizing effects are purely speculative. Castro is not without resources to defend himself. Most likely, he will be around for some time regardless of what we do.

The bottom line is that getting rid of Castro is much less important than preserving Cuba's stability. It is not in the United States' interests to promote a violent solution to the crisis. The results could be very bloody, and we could easily be drawn into a civil war. The pressure to intervene in order to prevent a bloodbath would be considerable. In a desperate situation, Castro might resort to desperate measures (an attack on Florida's Turkey Point nuclear power facility, for example). Cubans have a long and glorious tradition of heroic martyrdom. Castro might prefer to go out in a blaze of glory rather than surrender to his nemesis.

Our primary goal should be to minimize the possibility of such a cataclysmic ending. Beyond that, we should try to create an atmosphere that would allow a reduction of repression and the introduction of real reforms. A lessening of tensions between Cuba and the United States is a prerequisite for such a liberalization. Castro himself might be willing to begin this process. Although one may be skeptical as to how far he would be willing to take it, a beginning is better than nothing at all.

While we are at it, we should take the opportunity to explore Castro's recent hints that he might be willing to step down in return for an end to the embargo and a normalization of relations. "If I were the obstacle," he said, "I would be willing to give up not only my positions and responsibilities, but even my life."[66] Although he was quick to qualify this offer (it would not be a "personal" decision; he would have to consult his colleagues), it may be useful to push him on the issue. The possibility of a gradual transition, culminating in an "honorable" withdrawal, may seem like a long shot. But it is not beyond the bounds of possibility, especially if his health fails. At worst, if Castro proves recalcitrant and progress on other matters stalls, we could have Radio Marti repeatedly rebroadcast the remark to remind Cubans who the real "obstacle" is.

In any event, Castro will not be here forever. We must think in terms of the long run. A political transition that would span the last years of the dictatorship and the initial post-Castro era may offer the best chance for peaceful change. Accordingly, it may be time to begin cultivating very discretely those elements in the elite who are receptive to reforms, with a view to facilitating more profound transformations once Castro has gone. This will admittedly be a touchy proposition. If it is done in a ham-handed manner, it could undermine the very people we are trying to help. Thus, the need is crucial for careful thought and planning. If this cannot be done in a way that will not jeopardize potential friends and allies, it is better not to do it at all.

The United States will be in a stronger position than ever before to use its influence to encourage such developments. Cuba's desperate socioeconomic plight and its lack of viable alternatives give us an opportunity to use our bargaining leverage effectively for the first time in over three decades. By employing a combination of positive and negative incentives (rather than all sticks and no carrots, as we have usually done), we may well be able to coax Cuba in the direction of greater political, social, and economic freedom. In the past, Castro has always had a vested interest in hostility with the United States. The trick will be to give him sufficient political and economic incentives to change.

In short, we should continue to press our concerns about human rights and democracy and encourage the regime to undertake substantive reforms. But we must be ready to reward positive behavior. At the same time, we should seek to involve other democratic governments in Latin America and Europe in a common approach to the Cuban problem. It is better to stand together with our friends and allies than to try to impose a solution unilaterally.

It might be objected, of course, that, however desirable this strategy may be in the abstract, it is irrelevant, since domestic political considerations make it unlikely to be adopted. This is a serious problem. The veto of Mario Baeza by the Miamians demonstrates the continuing influence of hard-line elements in the Cuban-American community.[67] Still, the struggle over Cuba policy is just beginning. There is a new and more liberal administration in office, one that owes little to the Miamians. In spite of his strong, early support for the Torricelli Law, candidate Clinton won only about 20 percent of the Cuban-American vote.[68] The campaign is now over. If he has the will, the new president should be able to take some initiatives relatively free from the pressures and constraints of electoral politics. A window of opportunity is opening on the Cuba issue. If this administration can initiate policies, rather than merely react to crises (as did its predecessor), there is a possibility that the dialectic of hostility that has so long dominated U.S.-Cuban relations can be tempered and perhaps broken.

In the end, it may be that Castro is "so entrenched in a bunker mentality"[69] that he would reject our attempts to reconstitute the nature of the U.S.-Cuban game. But if so, then at least the onus of responsibility would be on Castro, where it belongs. It is a gamble worth taking.

NOTES

1. Quoted in Andrew Rosenthal, "Soviet Pledge on Cuba Leaves U.S. Paralyzed," *New York Times*, September 13, 1991.

2. See Susan Kaufman Purcell, "Collapsing Cuba," *Foreign Affairs*, Vol. 71, No. 1, 1992, pp. 130–45; Andres Oppenheimer, *Castro's Final Hour: The Secret Story Behind the Coming Downfall of Communist Cuba* (New York: Simon and Schuster,

1992); and Eleana Cardoso and Ann Helwege, *Cuba After Communism* (Cambridge, Mass.: MIT Press, 1992).

3. For details, see Jorge F. Perez-Lopez, "Swimming Against the Tide: Implications for Cuba of Soviet and Eastern European Reforms in Foreign Economic Relations," *Journal of Interamerican Studies and World Affairs*, Vol. 33, No. 2, Summer 1991, p. 107.

4. Between 1984 and 1989, the price paid by the Soviet Union for Cuban sugar fell from almost 915 rubles per ton to about 749 rubles per ton.

5. Howard J. Wiarda, "Is Cuba Next? Crises of the Castro Regime," *Problems of Communism*, Vol. 40, Nos. 1–2, January-April 1991, p. 89.

6. Foreign Broadcast Information Service (FBIS), *Daily Report: Latin America*, October 8, 1991.

7. Gerald F. Seib, "Soviets Scale Back Presence in Cuba, but Intend to Keep a Listening Post 90 Miles Off U.S. Coast," *Wall Street Journal*, October 9, 1991.

8. FBIS, *Daily Report: Latin America*, October 8, 1991. As of 1990, Cuba owed the Soviet Union at least 15 billion rubles, or more than $24 billion at the official exchange rate. Beginning in 1995, that debt will be payable in dollars at a rate that has yet to be determined. Interestingly enough, however, the Cubans themselves estimated that the Soviet figure was at least 2 billion rubles too low. Howard W. French, "Cuban Defector Tells of Soviet Cuts," *New York Times*, September 13, 1990.

9. FBIS, *Daily Report: Latin America*, October 16, 1991.

10. FBIS, *Daily Report: Latin America*, October 10, 1991.

11. FBIS, *Daily Report: Latin America*, January 2, 1992.

12. In December 1991, the Soviet Union had ceased to exist. Russia became an independent country, part of the Commonwealth of Independent States.

13. Ken Gluck, "Cuba Receives Last Shipment of Russian Oil," *Miami Herald*, July 20, 1992.

14. In the words of First Deputy Foreign Minister Fernando Ramirez. FBIS, *Daily Report: Latin America*, August 31, 1992.

15. According to Politburo member Osmani Cienfuegos, in FBIS, *Daily Report: Latin America*, September 1, 1992.

16. Juan O. Tamayo, "Russia-Cuba Oil Deal Signals Warming Ties," *Miami Herald*, November 16, 1992.

17. This is assuming a world market price of $8,000 a ton. Unfortunately for Cuba, the price of nickel has recently fallen to about $5,800 per ton. Moreover, nickel production for 1992 was about 25 percent less than expected.

18. Andrew Zimbalist, "Teetering on the Brink: Cuba's Post-CMEA Economic and Political Crisis." Paper delivered at the SSI roundtable on "Cuba and the Future," U.S. Army War College, Carlisle, Pa., January 16, 1992, pp. 11–13.

19. And this is an optimistic estimate. In addition to tourism, nickel, and biotechnology, some additional revenues may be gained from citrus, fish, tobacco, and a few other products. But this revenue is not significant. Moreover, even if light crude is found, it normally takes five to seven years to bring a discovery into production.

20. FBIS, *Daily Report: Latin America*, September 9, 1992.

21. To make matters worse, they also informed Cuba that they would be unable

to supply an automated control system, considered a crucial safety feature ever since Chernobyl.

22. Actually, Cuba's purchasing power was probably closer to $3.5 billion. Lage, apparently, was only including the state-sector purchasing power. Some Cuban companies and joint enterprises with foreign partners operate independently of state central planning. See Mimi Whitefield, "Cuban Foreign Trade Down 75 percent Since '89," *Miami Herald*, November 16, 1992; see also the figures of Leonel Soto, in FBIS, *Daily Report: Latin America*, December 4, 1992.

23. Most of the world's sugar is sold in national and regional markets at highly subsidized prices (around 40 cents a pound). Most of the remainder goes to various national or supra-national markets, such as the United States and the EC. (At this writing, the European Community buys sugar at 25.7 cents a pound, and the United States at 21.6 cents a pound.) The remainder—making up less than 2 percent of all sugar sales—is the "world market."

24. FBIS, *Daily Report: Latin America*, November 12 and 16, 1992.

25. See, for example, Andrew Zimbalist, "Treading Water: Cuba's Economic and Political Crisis," in *Cuba and the Future*, Donald E. Schulz, ed. (Westport, Conn.: Greenwood Press, forthcoming).

26. FBIS, *Daily Report: Latin America*, September 8, 1992.

27. In place of normal food, the state-controlled media promoted such exotic delicacies as the "grapefruit steak." (Remove the rind, season, cover with bread crumbs and fry.) There were, it seemed, a thousand and one ways to prepare potatoes and tomatoes.

28. J. Richard Planas, "Why Does Castro Survive?" Paper delivered at the SSI roundtable on "Cuba and the Future," U.S. Army War College, Carlisle, Pa., January 16, 1992, p. 3.

29. See Lee Hockstader, "Castro's Tenacious Art of Survival," *The Washington Post*, May 9, 1992.

30. Quoted in Howard W. French, "Castro Steels a Suffering Nation for Confrontation," *New York Times*, October 12, 1992.

31. Enrique Baloyra, "Where Does Cuba Stand?" Paper delivered at the SSI roundtable on "Cuba and the Future," U.S. Army War College, Carlisle, Pa., January 16, 1992, pp. 7–8.

32. FBIS, *Daily Report: Latin America*, September 27, 1991.

33. Ochoa had apparently been trying to build a power base of his own within the Western Army. He was courting other officers with gifts and engaging in "populist" appeals. At the same time, he was trying to expand the powers of that command (which he had been scheduled to assume prior to his arrest) to include the air, naval, and anti-aircraft defense forces in the region. The portrait presented in Raul Castro's speech to the Western Army and his report to the military tribunal that heard the case was that of a man who was increasingly alienated and disrespectful of Fidel Castro and who had criticized the latter's handling of the Angolan campaign and other policies as well. For details of the Ochoa case, see *Narcotrafico: Crimen Sin Fronteras* (La Habana: Editorial Jose Marti, 1989); also Oppenheimer, *Castro's Final Hour*, pp. 17–129.

34. According to such defectors as General Rafael Del Pino and Major Florintino Azpillaga. See Radio Marti Program, U.S. Information Agency, *Cuba Annual Report*

1987 (New Brunswick, N.J.: Transaction Publishers, 1991), pp. 12, 242–47, 411–15, 435. Some Cubanologists have expressed skepticism about such reports.

35. See Raul Castro's speech to the Western Army, in FBIS, *Daily Report: Latin America,* June 20, 1989.

36. Planas, "Why Does Castro Survive?", p. 9.

37. Members of the elite do not suffer the same kind of deprivation as ordinary Cubans. They still have access to all kinds of privileges (hard-currency stores, good food, luxury items, quality medical care, and so on). No doubt they have been inconvenienced by the current crisis, but this is not the same as most folks are experiencing.

38. FBIS, *Daily Report: Latin America,* January 9, 1992.

39. Although whether he was a real reformer or merely an opportunist remains a subject of debate among Cubanologists.

40. See Mimi Whitefield and Andres Oppenheimer, "No. 3 Man in Cuba Is Booted," *Miami Herald,* September 24, 1992.

41. FBIS, *Daily Report: Latin America,* January 6, 1992.

42. FBIS, *Daily Report: Latin America,* October 23, 1992.

43. Baloyra, "Where Does Cuba Stand?", p. 8.

44. The need to preserve Castro's leadership is so great that some sectors of the elite give the appearance of trying to bolster his morale by telling him what he no doubt desperately wants to hear: that Cubans still overwhelmingly support him and the single-party system and are determined to save the fatherland and the revolution. See Andres Oppenheimer on the dubious science of public opinion polling in Cuba: "Increasingly, Castro Loses Touch with Cuba," *Miami Herald,* July 28, 1992.

45. On Castro's "hubris-nemesis complex," see Edward Gonzalez and David Ronfeldt, *Castro, Cuba, and the World* (Rand Corp., R–3420, June 1986).

46. Almost 90 percent of Cuban imports from U.S. subsidiaries in foreign countries is in food and medicine. There is some question, however, as to the effectiveness of these sanctions. If they can't buy goods from U.S. firms, the Cubans will probably take their business to companies that are entirely foreign-owned. For a comprehensive critique of the Torricelli Law, see the testimony of Wayne S. Smith before the Subcommittee on Trade, House Ways and Means Committee, August 10, 1992.

47. This argument, it should be noted, is very different from the old claim that the United States "pushed Castro into the arms of the Soviets." Conservative Washington and revolutionary Havana were about as compatible as oil and water. Through both their actions and their inactions, they drove each other away. For a detailed treatment of this theme, see Donald E. Schulz, "The Cuban Revolution and the Soviet Union" (Ph.D. dissertation, Ohio State University, 1977), Vol. 2.

48. It is surely no accident that Cuban intelligence agents, who had taken over the leadership of one of the "dissident" groups on the island (the Cuban Democratic Coalition), had publicly supported the Torricelli Law.

49. See Alexis de Tocqueville, *The Old Regime and the French Revolution* (Garden City, N.J.: Doubleday, 1955), p. 176.

50. Oppenheimer, *Castro's Final Hour,* p. 323.

51. See the testimony of Francisco Avila Azcuy, Alpha 66's senior military commander, in *New York Times,* November 11, 1992.

52. This is probably true of many who have benefited from the revolution over the years. It is hard to say how much popular support Castro retains, but he clearly

has some. He appears to have the backing of many rural Cubans. Beyond this and the black and mulatto element, the regime also has roots among the older sector of the population. See Oppenheimer, *Castro's Final Hour*, pp. 304–37; and Howard W. French, "Rural Cuba Speaks Out for Castro," *New York Times*, July 12, 1992.

53. Oppenheimer, *Castro's Final Hour*, p. 328.

54. On Mas Canosa, see especially Lee Hockstader and William Booth, "Cuban Exiles Split on Life after Castro," *Washington Post*, March 10, 1992; Larry Rohter, "When a City Newspaper is the Enemy" and "A Rising Cuban-American Leader: Statesman to Some, Bully to Others," in *New York Times*, March 19, and October 29, 1992, respectively; and Carla Anne Robbins, "Dateline Washington: Cuban American Clout," *Foreign Policy*, Vol. 88, Fall 1992, pp. 170–82.

55. Comments of J. Richard Planas at the SSI roundtable on "Cuba and the Future," U.S. Army War College, Carlisle, Pa., January 16, 1992.

56. Similar, though by no means identical, proposals have been offered by the Inter-American Dialogue, in *Cuba in the Americas: Reciprocal Challenges* (Washington, D.C., Inter-American Dialogue, October 1992), pp. 6–8; and Gillian Gunn, "In Search of a Modern Cuba Policy," in *Cuba and the Future*, Donald E. Schulz, ed. (Westport, Conn.: Greenwood Press, forthcoming).

57. In Linda Robinson, "After Castro Moves Out," *US News and World Report*, May 4, 1992, p. 42.

58. I am indebted to Carmelo Mesa-Lago for these suggestions.

59. Distribution might be supervised at the Cuban end by international observers, such as the United Nations or the Red Cross, to ensure that these materials are not diverted to the *nomenklatura* or other unintended purposes.

60. Gillian Gunn, "Will Castro Fall?" *Foreign Policy*, Vol. 79, Summer 1990; see also Edward Gonzalez and David Ronfeldt, *Cuba Adrift in a Postcommunist World* (Santa Monica, Calif.: Rand Corp., 1992), pp. 71–77.

61. Inter-American Dialogue, *Cuba in the Americas*, p. 6.

62. Gonzalez and Ronfeldt, *Cuba Adrift*, pp. 73–74.

63. Gunn, "In Search of a Modern Cuba Policy"; see also *Latin American Weekly Report*, March 11, 1993.

64. I have been told by more than one knowledgeable U.S. government source that the Cubans have been informed in no uncertain terms that we will not permit another refugee crisis.

65. See Tocqueville, *The Old Regime*, p. 176.

66. *Miami Herald*, March 5, 1993; see also FBIS, *Daily Report: Latin America*, February 26, 1993.

67. Baeza was to be nominated as assistant secretary of state for inter-American affairs until the Miamians got wind of it.

68. Mirta Ojito and Alfonso Chardy, "Mas, Foundation May Face Competition in Shaping Cuba Policy," *Miami Herald*, November 5, 1992.

69. Wayne S. Smith, "Castro: To Fall or Not to Fall?" *SAIS Review*, Vol. 12, No. 2, Summer 1992, p. 110.

Postscript: The Cuban Crisis in the Summer of 1993—An Opportunity for the United States?

Donald E. Schulz

Since the preceding chapters were completed, a number of developments have occurred which have implications for the authors' analyses, as well as for their conclusions and recommendations. One is the accelerating deterioration of the Cuban socioeconomic situation. In March 1993, Cuba was hit by a devastating storm, which flooded Havana, crippling the island's power grid, causing extensive harm to its crops, and leaving some 150,000 people homeless. Official estimates placed the damage at around $1 billion which, if true, amounted to nearly a tenth of the economy, or the equivalent of almost half of Cuba's imports for the previous year. Not long thereafter, reports of a mysterious epidemic began to circulate, sowing panic throughout the populace. Tens of thousands of Cubans, it seemed, were in danger of going blind, apparently due (at least in part) to Vitamin B deficiencies.[1]

By now, most Cubans had been largely without meat or dairy products for two years. Milk was available mainly for children under the age of seven. Adults were receiving one egg a month from government-controlled stores. There was no beef, pork, or chicken (except on the black market, if you could afford it). There were no fruits or vegetables, except for black beans, rice, and lettuce. In desperation, some Cubans had taken to eating their pets. Indeed, Guantanamo reported a heavy infestation of banana rats, fleeing for their lives into that American-held naval base.

The passing months brought no relief. In late May, the government disclosed that the sugar harvest had fallen to around 4.28 million tons, down from 7 million tons the previous year. This was the sharpest drop in output in the country's history. Moreover, a few days later the island was hit by another torrential storm. Subsequently, officials announced that Cuba would be unable to fulfill its sugar commitments to foreign clients. With little to celebrate and anxious to avoid gathering large numbers of people together, the government announced the cancellation of the traditional 26th of July rally marking the beginning of the revolution. Instead, Castro held a "simple, quiet . . . solemn but austere" meeting of party loyalists in Santiago's Heredia Theater, where he revealed the latest grim news about the state of the economy. (Among other things, he estimated that Cuba would be able to import only $1.7 billion worth of goods in 1993, down from $2.2 billion the previous year and $8.1 billion in 1989.)[2]

All this had predictable social consequences. As oil and electricity became increasingly scarce, more factories and offices closed and even more people were thrown out of work. Juvenile delinquency and crime rose. Power outages stretched from 12 to 16 hours a day in the capital, reaching up to 20 hours a day in the provinces. By August, Havana was sweltering under a heat wave that left hard-to-find food spoiling in warm refrigerators and drove thousands to sleep on their rooftops in search of cool breezes. Increasingly, people took advantage of the dark of night to stage an unprecedented rash of small rebellions. Demonstrators smashed and looted state stores, hurled rocks at police cars, sprayed anti-Castro graffiti on walls, and occasionally even clanged pots and pans in a traditional symbol of protest.

In turn, the regime intensified the repression. In one incident, several would-be refugees were shot by the Cuban coast guard, sparking a spontaneous popular protest in Cojimar. In September, the Communist Party newspaper *Granma* warned that robbery, vandalism, and anti-government behavior had reached "unacceptable" levels and that "delinquents and other anti-social elements" who tried to create disorder would receive a "crushing reply from the people."[3] Shortly thereafter, it was announced that vandalism of state property—including the breaking of windows—would henceforth be considered sabotage and would be punished by eight years in jail.

THE POLITICAL IMPLICATIONS OF ECONOMIC REFORM

Cubans were still descending into the depths. No one appeared able to say with confidence when the economy would finally bottom out. What did seem clear, however, was that misery would be the norm for the foreseeable future; moreover, that social tensions were building, perhaps to some kind of climax.

It was within this context that the government announced a daring series of reforms designed to stop the downward slide of the economy. In his annual 26th of July speech, Castro declared that from now on Cubans could legally possess and spend hard currency (essentially dollars). Beyond this, more exiles would be allowed to visit the island. These "concessions," he said, were made because of Cuba's "pressing and vital need" to stave off economic collapse.[4]

This was a courageous move, but it was also a desperate one. Economists estimated that, as a result of "dollarization," Cuban exiles might send several hundred million dollars more a year to their relatives on the island. This would certainly help, but it was hardly enough to turn the economy around. More important, the unintended side effects were potentially explosive. Among other things, they could turn the Cuban class structure on its head. Those most likely to benefit from these measures were often among the least loyal elements in the population, while regime supporters would find themselves at a severe disadvantage. Few Blacks, after all, had rich relatives in Miami. Soon, many party members and military officers might find themselves worse off than counterrevolutionary taxi drivers and plumbers. How would Castro manage the inevitable resentments that would arise?

The reforms hit at the core of the revolution's institutional and social power base. More broadly, they also raised questions about the regime's ability to control the society at large. As the country's sole employer, the government had always been able to coerce reluctant Cubans to do its will. Now, however, it seemed probable that large numbers of workers, who were making the equivalent of only $3 a month in their state jobs, would simply quit and join the informal economy, where their opportunities for profit were infinitely greater. All this had political, as well as economic, implications. Could the regime still make dollar-holders do "voluntary" work and attend political rallies? If the number of exiles allowed to visit the island were to be tripled (and, as of this writing, it is still unclear how many will actually be admitted), could political and social contamination be avoided? The visitors would hardly be sympathetic to the revolution. They would bring with them ideas, values, and information that could potentially be very destabilizing. Again, one could not but recall the explosive consequences of a similar influx in the late 1970s.

The immediate effect of "dollarization" was to drive up the value of U.S. currency. In an effort to check an onslaught of "dollar fever," the government increased the price of goods sold at hard-currency stores by 50 percent. At the same time, the value of the peso on the black market fell from 60 to the dollar to over 100 to the dollar. For decades, Cubans had been able to accumulate considerable savings, the result of a combination of decent salaries and a paucity of consumer goods. Now, almost overnight, those nest eggs began to disappear.

In September, moreover, the government further compounded its social and political problems when it decreed that 117 categories of workers—from barbers and mechanics to cheese makers and computer programmers—could now engage in private business. The problem was that self-employment was not extended to managers of state enterprises or, indeed, to anyone with a university degree. This meant that many professionals—including many of the regime's supporters—would not be able to take advantage of the opportunities that were opening up.

This announcement was almost immediately followed by the revelation that cooperative farms would be given more autonomy and that private citizens would be allowed to work small, unused plots of state land. Though these measures were very limited (farmers would still have to sell their crops to the state, presumably at prices determined by the latter), they represented yet another step away from a centrally controlled economy and another concession to private initiative. Inevitably, some of this produce would escape the government's hands and end up on the black market.

Toward the end of the month, the dangers inherent in the regime's new course were brought home dramatically by the separate defections of two air force pilots. In subsequent interviews, both men complained that the "dollarization" of the economy had turned Cuban soldiers into second-class citizens and created enormous discontent within the armed forces. (Military officers, who had long been under orders to break all ties with their relatives abroad, made the equivalent of about $5 a month. In contrast, other Cubans with relatives in Miami could now legally receive up to $100 a month). At the same time, there was growing resentment among the lower ranks against the generals, who were the only officers who had ready access to dollars. The question, increasingly, was whether soldiers would be willing to fire on civilians if mass disturbances broke out. Increasingly, it seemed that the answer might well be "no."

THE PROSPECTS FOR STABILITY REVISITED: THE SHIFTING EQUILIBRIUM

Clearly, the Cuban political equation was changing in important, and potentially destabilizing, ways. The economic reforms were rapidly undermining Castro's bases of support in both the mass public and the critical institutions of the party-state. A new privileged class was being formed, composed in large part of elements which had little sympathy for the regime. At the same time, stalwarts in the Communist Party, the Revolutionary Armed Forces, and the mass organizations were in effect being penalized for their loyalty and sacrifice. The resulting disillusionment and bitterness could not but raise doubt as to the Castro brothers' continuing ability to control the apparatus of repression. As of October, the prospects of a mass uprising or coup seemed much greater than they had been even a few weeks earlier.

Nor in the short run were things likely to get much better. While some of the reforms might alleviate hardships and buy some popular support, the latter would in all likelihood be very limited. Either the measures did not go far enough and thus might actually increase public frustration (the agricultural reforms, and the opening of certain occupations to private enterprise) or those who benefitted were already so alienated from the regime that they were not likely to feel much gratitude ("dollarization"). Beyond this, a process had been set in motion. As the months passed and traditional beneficiaries of the revolution were increasingly bypassed by the new privileged socioeconomic elite, resentment within Castro's core constituency could be expected to grow, even further undermining the regime's legitimacy.

Now, moreover, there were signs that a real civil society (that is, one that is independent of government control) might be emerging. In September, the Catholic Church took a dramatic step in the direction of opposition by issuing a strongly worded pastoral letter calling on the government to surrender its monopoly on political power and begin a national dialogue to save Cuba from social and economic collapse. The bishops were immediately denounced in the official press, but within a matter of days thousands of copies of the document had been bought up by ordinary citizens. All this strengthened the church's prestige considerably and suggested that it might become a political force to be reckoned with.

Yet, for all the decay that was occurring, the Cuban state was still intact. The highest political and military leaders were still privileged and still, apparently, loyal. Within the armed forces, opposition continued to be diffuse, while the omnipresent counterintelligence apparatus effectively deterred organized resistance.

Moreover, civil society was still very weak. The church had never been much of a political factor, and it was by no means clear that it could become the center of an opposition movement, even if its leaders were willing to go that route (which they were probably not). And while the number of human rights and dissident organizations was mushrooming, the movement as a whole remained deeply divided. Most of these groups were very small and were closely watched. As always, the authorities seemed intent on preempting opposition before it could become active or effective. (In September, for instance, they launched predawn raids in Cienfuegos province, arresting dozens of people with a "high social risk index." Others with "flawed behavior" were merely given a warning.) The upshot was that, although dissident activity was sharply on the rise, the society as a whole was still largely atomized, demoralized, and passive.

Under these circumstances, the regime might survive for some time. Summer was now over, the heat was subsiding, and demands on electricity and petroleum were declining. The Russians had agreed to guarantee fuel, fertilizers, and spare parts for the coming harvest and to import at least 2 million tons of sugar. (In addition, they pledged to provide $350 million in credits for Cuban oil, nuclear energy, and nickel-mining projects that the former Soviet Union had supported.) It seemed unlikely that the island would soon be hit by more storms of the severity of those with which it had been plagued during the past year. (Cuba's luck had to change sometime.) There was therefore some reason to believe that the economy had at last bottomed out.

But if Castro might yet outlast the crisis, it seemed equally likely that, sooner or later, he would go down in flames. As of October, one could only wait in anticipation of the long, hot summer of 1994.

ON NEGOTIATING WITH CASTRO

In the face of Cuba's spiralling disintegration, U.S. policy was rapidly being overtaken by events. To be fair, the Clinton administration had shown a willingness to change some of the most obviously counterproductive aspects of that policy. Some of the recommendations set forth in the preceding chapters had been adopted; others were being considered. Official rhetoric had been lowered. The Commerce Department had approved a number of large, one-time shipments of medical supplies and other goods by private U.S. groups. Some travel restrictions had been eased. American doctors had visited the island to advise their Cuban counterparts on the epidemic. On a couple of occasions, Havana had been notified in advance of U.S. military maneuvers in the region. The two sides had begun to cooperate on such matters as counternarcotics, airplane hijackings, and the repatriation of Cuban-born prisoners being held in U.S. jails for crimes committed since the 1980 Mariel boatlift. With Washington's blessing, Sprint, MCI, and AT&T had gone to Havana to negotiate increased telephone services. Warnings had been issued that anyone attempting to launch armed attacks against Cuba would be subject to legal penalties. A few arrests had even been made.

These were substantial changes, but they were simply not enough. Cuba's socioeconomic and political crises were deepening so fast that the Clinton administration had to run ever more rapidly just to stay even. Increasingly, this was a losing race. Part of the problem was that the United States, having altered its tactics, had not yet developed a coherent policy. What it had, rather, was a policy that was being torn asunder by conflicting factions. On the one hand, there were those who wanted to soften the traditional approach, the better to open up the island to outside influences. On the other, there were those who were determined to continue isolating and pressuring the regime in the hope that at some point it would crack and shatter. The upshot was a contradictory policy that further weakened Castro without allowing him a way out of the crisis in which he, as well as his countrymen, were trapped. The end result was likely to be either more repression and hardship or a further loss of control that could plunge the island into chaos and perhaps civil war.

The trick, for both the Cubans and the United States, was to find a way of making a peaceful transition possible. Clearly, the political and socioeconomic dimensions of the problem were inextricably related. The formula was very simple: (1) As long as the United States was unwilling to normalize relations, Cuba would not be able to gain the resources (from the U.S. government; the Miamians; private companies, banks, and investors; international lending agencies) to repair its shattered economy and society. (2) As long as the Castros remained in power, that change in American policy would not occur. If the Castrophobes could no longer dictate U.S. policy in its entirety, they could still exercise veto power over its core components.

(3) Therefore, Fidel and Raul had to go. This was the minimal requirement for the deadlock to be broken.

But how was that possible? After all, power and grandeur have always been the central motivating forces in Castroism.[5] Would Fidel ever give up power voluntarily?

Perhaps. One must understand that this is a man who has no good options. His purgatory is to witness the destruction of everything that he has created in his 35 years in power. He is an historical anachronism, and he knows it. He is also old, sick, tired, and probably quite depressed, if one can judge by his own words. ("I will be a sigh in history.")[6] For the first time, we may have an opportunity to exploit a split that may be occurring within Castro's own psyche between the compulsion for power and the compulsion for grandeur. Put simply, if Fidel clings to power, his aspirations for historical greatness will go down the drain as Cuba continues to disintegrate and he has to accept the lion's share of the blame. Given this stark reality, if he were to be made the right offer—one that would enable him to salvage his place in history—he might very well take it.

In short, the time has come to take up Castro on his proposal to step down in return for a lifting of the U.S. embargo on Cuba. Toward that end, exploratory talks should be initiated. They should be held in strict secrecy, with a view toward providing an honorable exit for both Fidel and his brother, Raul.

The principle of an "honorable exit" is crucial. As John Kennedy understood so well during the Missile Crisis, one should not back a foe into a corner unless one really wants to fight. Castro must be given a way of escaping from the trap in which he is ensnared. We must remember that this is a man who sees everything through the prism of his own ego. He undoubtedly continues to believe, in spite of all evidence to the contrary, that the Cuban people need him in this time of grave national crisis. As matters now stand, he cannot leave without seeming to "desert" them. Thus, the trick will be to give him a way to redefine his options so as to enable him to perform "one final service for Cuba." If this is done right, we may be able to offer him a last chance to play his favorite role as "savior of the nation" by magnanimously sacrificing himself for the good of his people. Given his obsession with his place in history and his current lack of viable alternatives, he just might buy the idea.

Such a solution would, of course, require the Clinton administration to haul itself out of the bind in which it presently finds itself and take the initiative. This may not be easy. There will be those who will not want to give Castro even a fig leaf, and the policy set forth in these pages would give him much more. In effect, he would become a collaborator in and beneficiary of this strategy. One should simply ask whether the alternatives— continuing repression and/or massive bloodshed, with the possible flight of hundreds of thousands of refugees to southern Florida—would be preferable.

The details of such a settlement have only just begun to be seriously explored. A suitable place of exile would have to be found for the Castro brothers. Plans would have to be made for a political and economic transition. In this process, Washington must resist the temptation to be heavy handed. Cuba is a sovereign country, and a solution cannot be unilaterally imposed. While a settlement will have to involve several parties, both in Cuba and the United States, the role of the Cuban Cubans must be central. One cannot expect the current elite to negotiate its own destruction. Nor can we expect it to allow the "Miamians" to return to the island as conquering heroes. If we want a peaceful transition, we must be ready to work with many of Cuba's present leaders to promote a change to political democracy and a more open (though not necessarily a full-scale free-market) economy. Though we can certainly help—and here the role of the Cuban American community will be crucial—in the final analysis it must be the islanders themselves who determine the fate of Cuba.

Finally—and this is the bottom line—we must be generous. Cuba will need massive economic aid and investment. While the bulk of this will have to come from private sources (especially in Miami) and international lending agencies like the IMF, the World Bank, and the Interamerican Development Bank, some will also have to come from the U.S. government. (Among other things, Cuban Americans will have to be at least partially compensated for the loss of properties nationalized by Castro, and a post-Castro government will simply not have the resources to do that.) What is needed is a Marshall Plan for Cuba, internationally organized and funded, with a direct U.S. contribution on the order of $1 billion a year for at least 5 years.

Again, there will be those who will resist that kind of a commitment. Times are tough, and foreign aid unpopular. Nevertheless, one must operate in the world of reality. Cuba is a time bomb, and unless it is defused it is likely to sooner or later explode. Under such circumstances, it would be incredibly short-sided to be niggardly. There may now be a possibility of getting rid of Castro and effecting a peaceful transition to a democratic and prosperous Cuba. But how long that opening will exist, no one can say. We must seize the moment.

NOTES

1. By September, the illness seemed to have subsided after having impaired the vision and damaged the nerves of nearly 51,000 people. The cause was still unknown. The most likely explanation was probably a combination of a nutritional deficiency and some other unknown factor, most likely toxic.

2. Foreign Broadcast Information Service (FBIS), *Daily Report: Latin America*, July 27, 1993.

3. Mimi Whitefield, "Cuba Promises 'Crushing Reply' to Disorder," *Miami Herald*, September 9, 1993.

4. FBIS, *Daily Report: Latin America*, July 27, 1993.

5. This is not to deny the importance of ideology in Castroism, but ideology has been primarily a dependent, rather than independent, variable in the equation. It is the vehicle through which power and grandeur have been expressed. For a detailed analysis see Donald E. Schulz, "The Cuban Revolution and the Soviet Union," Ph.D. dissertation, Ohio State University, 1977, vol. 1.

6. FBIS, *Daily Report: Latin America*, September 8, 1992. A number of recent observers have commented on his chalky complexion and tired appearance. There have been rumors of a heart condition and cancer, but no hard information has emerged. On the advice of his doctor, he has given up smoking cigars.

Bibliography

Baloyra, Enrique, and James A. Morris, eds. *Conflict and Change in Cuba.* Albuquerque, N.M.: University of New Mexico, 1993.

Basdeo, Sahadeo. "Cuba in Transition: Socialist Order Under Seige." *Caribbean Affairs*, Vol. 71, No. 1, 1992: 130–45.

Cardoso, Eliana, and Ann Helwege. *Cuba After Communism.* Cambridge, Mass.: MIT Press, 1992.

Centro de Estudios Sobre America. *The Cuban Revolution into the 1990s.* Boulder, Colo.: Westview Press, 1992.

"Cuba: Facing Change." *NACLA Report on the Americas*, Vol. 24, No. 2, August 1990: 12–48.

Dominguez, Jorge I. "Secrets of Castro's Staying Power." *Foreign Affairs*, Vol. 72, No. 2, Spring 1993: 97–107.

———. *To Make a World Safe for Revolution.* Cambridge, Mass.: Harvard University Press, 1989.

"Enemy of Convenience: The United States vs. Cuba." *NACLA Report on the Americas*, Vol. 24, No. 3, November 1990: 12–39.

Erisman, H. Michael, and John M. Kirk, eds. *Cuban Foreign Policy Confronts a New International Order.* Boulder, Colo.: Lynne Rienner Publishers, 1991.

Farber, Samuel. "Castro Under Siege." *World Policy Journal*, Vol. 9, No. 2, Spring 1992: 329–48.

Fermoselle, Rafael. *Cuban Leadership After Castro: Biographies of Cuba's Top Commanders.* Miami: University of Miami, 1992.

Fitzgerald, Frank T. *Managing Socialism: From Old Cadres to New Professionals in Revolutionary Cuba.* New York: Praeger, 1990.

Freedom House, ed. *Cuba in the Nineties.* Washington, D.C.: Freedom House, 1991.

Gonzalez, Edward, and David Ronfeldt. *Castro, Cuba and the World.* Santa Monica, Calif.: Rand, 1986.

———. *Cuba Adrift in a Postcommunist World.* Santa Monica, Calif.: Rand, 1992.

Gunn, Gillian. "Will Castro Fall?" *Foreign Policy*, No. 79, Summer 1990: 132–50.

Halebsky, Sandor, and John M. Kirk, eds. *Cuba in Transition*. Boulder, Colo.: Westview Press, 1992.

Horowitz, Irving L. *Cuban Communism*, 7th, rev. ed. New Brunswick, N.J.: Transaction Publishers, 1992.

Inter-American Dialogue. *Cuba in the Americas*. Washington, D.C.: A Report of the Inter-American Dialogue Task Force on Cuba, October 1992.

Jorge, Antonio, Jaime Suchlicki, and Adolfo Leyva de Varona. *Cuba in a Changing World*. Miami: University of Miami, 1991.

Kline, Michael. "Castro and 'New Thinking' in Latin America." *Journal of Interamerican Studies and World Affairs*, Vol. 32, No. 1, Spring 1990: 83–117.

Mazaar, Michael J. "Prospects for Revolution in Post-Castro Cuba." *Journal of Interamerican Studies and World Affairs*, Vol. 31, No. 4, Winter 1989: 61–90.

Mesa-Lago, Carmelo, ed. *Cuba After the Cold War*. Pittsburgh, Pa.: University of Pittsburgh Press, 1993.

Morris, James A. "The Ochoa Affair: Micro-faccion in the FAR?" Washington, D.C.: Radio Marti, 1989.

Oppenheimer, Andres. *Castro's Final Hour*. New York: Simon and Schuster, 1992.

Perez-Lopez, Jorge F. "Bringing the Cuban Economy into Focus: Conceptual and Empirical Challenges." *Latin American Research Review*, Vol. 26, No. 3, 1991: 7–53.

———. "Swimming Against the Tide: Implications for Cuba of Soviet and Eastern European Reforms in Foreign Economic Relations." *Journal of Interamerican Studies and World Affairs*, Vol. 33, No. 2, Summer 1991: 81–127.

Perez-Stable, Marifeli. "Charismatic Authority, Vanguard Party Politics, and Popular Mobilizations: Revolution and Socialism in Cuba." *Cuban Studies*, Vol. 22, 1992: 3–26.

Preston, Julia. "The Trial that Shook Cuba." *The New York Review of Books*, Vol. 37, No. 19, December 7, 1989: 24–31.

Purcell, Susan Kaufman. "Collapsing Cuba." *Foreign Affairs*, Vol. 71, No. 1, 1992: 130–45.

———. "Cuba's Cloudy Future." *Foreign Affairs*, Vol. 69, No. 3, Summer 1990: 113–30.

Robbins, Carla Anne. "Dateline Washington: Cuban American Clout." *Foreign Policy*, No. 88, Fall 1992: 170–82.

Schlesinger, Arthur. "Four Days with Fidel: A Havana Diary." *The New York Review of Books*, Vol. 39, No. 6, March 26, 1992: 22–29.

Schulz, Donald E. "Cuba and the Future." Carlisle, Pa.: SSI Special Report, January 1992.

Smith, Wayne S. "Castro: To Fall or Not to Fall?" *SAIS Review*, Vol. 12, No. 2, Summer 1992: 97–110.

Suchlicki, Jaime, ed. *The Cuban Military Under Castro*. Miami: University of Miami, 1989.

Wiarda, Howard J. "Is Cuba Next? Crises of the Castro Regime." *Problems of Communism*, Vol. 40, Nos. 1–2, January-April 1991: 84–93.

Index

About the Contributors

ENRIQUE A. BALOYRA is a professor of political science and former dean of the Graduate School at the University of Miami. He has published widely on Central America and the Caribbean Basin. His best-known works are *El Salvador in Transition* and (with John Martz) *Political Attitudes in Venezuela: Societal Cleavages and Public Opinion.* He is co-editor (with James A. Morris) of a forthcoming book on *Conflict and Change in Cuba.*

STEPHEN BLANK is a national security affairs research professor at the Strategic Studies Institute, U.S. Army War College. He has published numerous articles on the Soviet military and on Soviet policy in the Third World in journals such as *Orbis, Conflict, Comparative Strategy* and *Asian Survey.* He is the author of a forthcoming book on *Stalin's Soviet Commissariat of Nationalities* and editor of *The Soviet Military and the Future.*

MARK FALCOFF is a professor at the American Enterprise Institute. Among his books on Latin America are *Modern Chile: A Critical History* and the volumes he has edited with Robert Royal, *Crisis and Opportunity: U.S. Policy in Central America and the Caribbean* and *The Continuing Crisis;* and with Howard Wiarda, *The Communist Challenge in the Caribbean and Central America.*

DAMIAN J. FERNANDEZ is an associate professor of international relations and director of the Graduate Program in International Studies at Florida International University. He is the editor of a recent book, *Cuban Studies Since the Revolution.*

GILLIAN GUNN is a professor of political science at Georgetown University and formerly a senior fellow at the Carnegie Endowment for International Peace. She has conducted extensive field research in Cuba and interviewed many policy makers, including Fidel Castro. She has published articles on the Cuban crisis in *Current History*, on U.S.-Cuban relations in *Foreign Policy*, and on the Cubans in Angola in George Fauriol and Eva Loser, eds., *Cuba: The International Dimension*.

J. RICHARD PLANAS is a senior research analyst at Radio Marti. His specialties are Cuban-Soviet relations and Cuban domestic politics.

DONALD E. SCHULZ is an associate research professor at the Strategic Studies Institute of the U.S. Army War College. He is the main editor of *Revolution and Counterrevolution in Central America and the Caribbean* and *Political Participation in Communist Systems* and author of *The United States, Honduras and the Crisis in Central America* (forthcoming). His articles on Cuba and Central America have appeared in *Foreign Policy*, *Orbis*, *Journal of Interamerican Studies and World Affairs*, *Small Wars and Insurgencies*, *Newsweek*, *The Washington Post*, and other publications.

PHYLLIS GREENE WALKER is a doctoral candidate in political science at Georgetown University. She is currently completing her dissertation on the Cuban military and has published articles in *Cuba, A Country Study* and Irving Horowitz's *Cuban Communism*.

ANDREW ZIMBALIST is a professor of economics at Smith College. He is the author and editor of a number of books on Latin America, such as *The Cuban Economy*, *Cuban Political Economy: Controversies in Cubanology*, and *Cuba's Socialist Economy*. He is perhaps the foremost critic of the CIA's economic analyses of Cuba.